Dangerous Liaisons

The Clash between Islamism and Zionism

Rumy Hasan

Published by New Generation Publishing in 2013

Copyright © Rumy Hasan 2013

First Edition

The author asserts the moral right under the Copyright, Designs and Patents Act 1988 to be identified as the author of this work.

All Rights reserved. No part of this publication may be reproduced, stored in a retrieval system or transmitted, in any form or by any means without the prior consent of the author, nor be otherwise circulated in any form of binding or cover other than that which it is published and without a similar condition being imposed on the subsequent purchaser.

www.newgeneration-publishing.com

 New Generation **Publishing**

Contents

Acknowledgements 5

Preface 7

PART I   BACKROUND

Chapter 1   Zionism and Islamism: Key Precepts   15

- Zionism
- Islamism

PART II   ISLAMISM AND ZIONISM IN THE MIDDLE EAST

Chapter 2   Israel/Palestine: the Epicentre   33

- Background
- Israel and Hamas: from collaboration to confrontation

Chapter 3   Israel and the Shia Islamists of Iran and Hezbollah   65

- Israel and Iran: from discreet collaboration to confrontation
- Israel and Hezbollah: from confrontation to fragile peace

Chapter 4   Israel and Sunni Islamists   91

- Introductory remarks
- Israel and the jihadist terrorists of Al Qaeda
- Muslim Brotherhood
- Israel and the Islamists in the Arab Spring

PART III ISLAMISM AND ZIONISM IN THE WEST

Chapter 5 The Clash in the US   117

- Centrality of the Israel/Palestine conflict
- The context of 9/11
- The 'Ground Zero mosque' Controversy, New York
- The House Committee on Radicalisation of Muslim Americans
- Christian Zionism

Chapter 6 The Clash in Europe   150

- Britain
- The Netherlands
- France

Chapter 7 Conclusion   189

- Mutually reinforcing ideologies
- Defusing the clash

Bibliography   208

Index   229

Acknowledgements

I owe warm thanks to several people. Lisa Taraki provided some relevant sources for chapter 2; Geoffrey Toy read the early part of the manuscript and provided many helpful insights; and Fatih Kariem kindly translated some articles from Arabic into English. Daniel Cooke, Kate Foreman and the rest of the team at New Generation Publishing were most supportive and efficient. As ever, I owe an enormous thanks to Paola – who carefully read the whole manuscript and provided many helpful comments – for her unstinting encouragement and support.

Preface

Samuel Huntington's book *The Clash of Civilizations* aroused a storm of interest when it was published in 1996[1]. Its basic thesis was that in the aftermath of the Cold War, the fundamental antagonism among nations would be on the basis of 'civilisation' – taken to mean culture that encompasses language, history and religion – rather than ideology or economics. He posited eight major contemporary civilisations and suggested that conflict would likely arise at the intersection of these: Sinic [Chinese], Japanese, Hindu, Islamic, Orthodox, Western, Latin American, and African (Huntington, 1997 [1996], pp. 45-47). The thesis was heavily criticised on the grounds that it was much too generalised and simplistic and so limited in its relevance and applicability. Despite its grave limitations, the notion of 'clash' was, nonetheless, appealing, including to those who vehemently disagreed with the thrust of Huntington's argument. For example, Tariq Ali's *The Clash of Fundamentalisms* and Gilbert Achcar's *The Clash of Barbarisms* were clearly inspired by and, to some extent, responses to Huntington's work.[2]

Since September 11 2001, however, and the 'war on terror' the notion of the existence of a clash between two of Huntington's civilisations – the Western and the Islamic worlds – gained traction. A common refrain was that the war on terror was really a war on Islam waged by the US/West; but this was an assertion without any basis in reality. Nevertheless, a clash arose between certain ideological forces within each geopolitical tectonic plate, specifically, between Islamism and Zionism (including Christian Zionism). That these two ideologies are in firm opposition is not in doubt; in that Zionism

---

[1] This followed an exploratory article in *Foreign Affairs* in 1993.

[2] Another work which directly utilises Huntington's phraseology is Jonathan Cook's *Israel and the Clash of Civilisations: Iraq, Iran and the Plan to Remake the Middle East.*

is a European/Western ideology and the country whose constitution is based on it, Israel, is located in a Muslim-majority region, their clash manifests itself naturally in the Islamic world and has done so acutely since 1948. However, given that millions of Muslims have settled in Western countries, increasing numbers of whom have espoused Islamism, this clash has in recent years also arisen and with seemingly greater intensity in the Western world. The aim of this book is to signpost this reality which has been insufficiently acknowledged or explored.

The root cause of this particular clash is a tract of land – Palestine – and its colonisation by Zionist settlers from the late nineteenth century, which ultimately led to the creation of the Jewish state and expulsion from it of the majority of the indigenous, mainly Muslim, population. This conflict is a running sore that has shown no signs of resolution and has naturally received much attention. But, in the modern era, particularly in the 21st century, this clash is also about *identities* and, more specifically, *dual identities*. Millions of Jews not living in Israel strongly identify with the Jewish state – indeed, for many, being Jewish is tantamount to being Zionist, that is, to show allegiance to the state of Israel. This is not necessarily related to the fact that all Jews have automatic right to Israeli citizenship. Hence, an American Jew, British Jew, or French Jew has loyalty to his/her country of residence and citizenship but also to Israel – so that there is a dual identity. Given their close alliance, conflicts between these three countries and Israel are largely non-existent; hence conflicts between the national identities are also immaterial, that is to say, the dual identity retains its cohesiveness.

The situation of Muslims in the West is analogous but also significantly different. Millions have settled and taken up citizenship of their adopted countries. Unlike Jews, however, they are not indigenous but migrants or (more recently) asylum seekers. As is the norm for migrants, the first generation retains strong links and affinity with its origins in terms of country, region, ethnicity, language, religion, and culture. Interestingly – and counter-intuitively – such strong links and affinities have been passed on to a significant extent to subsequent generations by some (though not all) groups. In Britain, for example, second and even third generation Asians have shown this trait. By so doing, they espouse strong dual identities to the extent that, for some, the identity attached to the 'motherland' takes precedence over that of the country and society of residence and citizenship. My contention is that this has become a prevalent phenomenon among large numbers of Muslims in the West, that is to say, their most important indicator of identity is to their religion – and by extension – to Muslim countries and lands; in sum, to the global *umma*. It follows that any actual or perceived harm done to the faith and to Muslim lands is felt with great intensity and, as a natural corollary, equally great animosity is shown towards the perpetrators of such harm. At its most extreme, such animosity translates into Islamism and a profound Islamic identity. As we have witnessed since September 11, this can, *in extremis,* engender violent opposition, that is, jihadist behaviour.

My further contention is that dual identities engendered in Islamism and Zionism are of a deeper magnitude than the widespread phenomenon of the 'hyphenated identity' that has long been present as a marker of ethnic, racial, or geographical origins. Thus, in the US, there is the well-established phenomenon of the 'hyphenated American' (such as African–American, Asian–American, Irish–American, Italian–American etc). There is likely to be some affinity to the country or continent in the first part of the hyphenation but – admittedly in the absence of robust empirical evidence – the presumption is that this is not likely to be as intense as that residing in Islamism or Zionism and so not give rise to anything like the same level of political campaigning and support. An exception can, however, be made with regard to Cuban-Americans, large numbers of whom do appear to be characterised by a strong campaigning zeal relating to the Cuban (and anti-Castro) part of their identity. The obverse is likely to be the case for African-Americans, perhaps the overwhelming majority of whom – we can hypothesise – have little or no emotional or physical affinity to the African continent or to any African country; as such, this is predominantly an ethnic marker, interchangeable with 'black–American'.

There are, of course, substantive reasons as to why certain identities are stronger than others.[3] At its core, in the case of Zionism, this emanates from the aftermath of the Nazi holocaust so that Israel is thought of as a safe haven for world Jewry. In the case of Islamism, part of its appeal emanates from solidarity with fellow Muslims – the Palestinians (leaving aside that some are Christians) – who were expelled from their homeland. This is compounded by the perception that Western powers were ultimately responsible for the creation of the Jewish state[4] that led to this *nakba* and have, moreover, provided unstinting support to Israel despite this historic and continuing injustice. A further contributing determinant of a strong Islamist identity is the belief, noted above, that there is a war on Islam – the apotheosis of which is the US-led 'war on terror'.

So there has arisen a clash between these two ideologies and political movements: most acutely so in the Middle East but increasingly so in many Western countries. In the former, the war in Lebanon in the summer of 2006 can be thought of as the first war between Zionism (Israel) and an avowedly Islamist movement (the Hezbollah). There have also been severe tensions between Israel and the Islamic Republic of Iran. A war has not (yet) broken out between these two countries but, given Iran's strong support for Hezbollah, the 2006 war in Lebanon can be viewed as a proxy. The sheer antipathy between these ideologies suggests that another conflagration cannot be ruled out which, next time, would also involve Iran in direct military action. Indeed, senior Israeli figures are now actively contemplating attacking Iran's nuclear facilities, with incalculable consequences.

---

[3] The issue of ethnic identity is fruitfully discussed in Verkuyten (2006).

[4] It is important to note, however, that the role of the Soviet Union in support of the partition of Palestine was decisive in 1947; a fact that is invariably neglected (see Rucker, 2007).

Lesser explored and more recent is the 'softer' clash between Islamism and Zionism in many Western countries. Though nowhere near as serious as that obtaining in the Middle East it is, nonetheless, of importance and ought not to be proverbially brushed under the carpet: if the clash in the Middle East has often taken the form of wars, the clash in the West is akin to Orwell's 'war minus the shooting'.[5] Throughout Western Europe in particular and to a lesser extent also in North America, there have, in the post 9/11 era, arisen the desire on the parts of many of the governments of these countries to increase the integration of Muslims into mainstream society and to improve social cohesion. These laudable objectives and policy aims have gained focus because of widespread concerns regarding the situation of Muslim migrants, notwithstanding the fact that a key motivating factor has been to wean young Muslim males away from jihadi-inspired acts of terrorism. I have explored this issue in a previous book and located failings in the misconceived doctrine of multiculturalism and its successor 'multifaithism' (see Hasan, 2010). Here, I wish to argue that the antagonism between Islamism and Zionism in the West is a significant threat to integration and social cohesion; my aim is to draw attention to this *explicitly in terms of a clash.* This has been an important lacuna that needs to be highlighted, one which has rarely been acknowledged as such.

Some might argue that examining these societal issues through the prism of an ethno-religious political clash is much too pessimistic an approach: rather, what is being played out in Western countries is nothing more than a typical rivalry in democratic, pluralistic, societies where passionate support and campaigning zeal for causes, with attendant argument and debate, is a healthy sign. My response to such a criticism is that it is, of course, true that millions of people are extremely emotionally involved with myriad of causes and activities – perhaps none more so than support for sports teams. But the kind of chasm that is evident between Islamists and Zionists is,

---

[5] This was, of course, how Orwell famously described sport.

I would argue, of a different order. It means that members of the two groups tend to view each other through the mono-dimensional prism of identity on which a very fixed judgement has already been made. The consequence is necessarily an acute prejudice whereby suspicion abounds to the extent that normal human interaction is severely curtailed. This is certainly an issue deserving of in-depth research and substantive policy proposals and my hope is that this book will in some small measure help in this endeavour.

The book is set out as follows. Part 1 provides a background chapter on the key precepts of Zionism and Islamism. Part II examines the clash between the two ideologies and movements in various parts of the Middle East: chapter 2 focuses on the 'epicentre' of the clash – the Israel-Palestine conflict; chapter 3 discusses Israel and the Shia Islamists of Iran and Hezbollah and chapter 4 does the same for Israel and Sunni Islamists. Part III focuses on the clash in the West: chapter 5 explores the clash in the US whilst chapter 6 does the same for Europe, focusing on the three countries in which it is most acute, that is, Britain, the Netherlands, and France. Chapter 7 is the concluding chapter.

PART I

BACKGROUND

Chapter 1

Key Precepts of Zionism and Islamism

Zionism

'Zionism' derives from *Zion* the Hebrew word for the citadel of Jerusalem and which also refers to the Kingdom of Heaven. Though the epithet was coined by Nathan Birnbaum in 1890 (Sand, 2009, p. 257) the founding father of the ideology and political movement of Zionism was the Hungarian Jew and journalist-playwright Theodore Herzl who, in 1896, published the seminal pamphlet *The Jewish State* (*Der Judenstaat*). In this tract, Herzl passionately advocates a homeland for the Jews in the context of rising anti-Semitism in Western Europe[6] and pogroms in Russia and Eastern Europe. This was a high point of chauvinistic nationalism in Europe whence there developed a pernicious hostility to those not considered an autochthonous part of the nation: Jews in Europe were seen by many as its obverse, an allochthonous people. Herzl described anti-Semitism as a 'vulgar sport, of common trade jealousy, of inherited prejudice, of religious intolerance, and also of pretended self-defence' (Herzl, 1993 [1896], p. 15). In his diaries of 1895, he writes:

> I understand what anti-Semitism is about. We Jews have maintained ourselves, even if through no fault of our own, as a foreign body among the various nations. In the ghetto we have taken on a number of anti-social qualities. Our character has been corrupted by oppression, and it must be restored through some

---

[6] In the foreword, Israel Cohen states that the work was 'prompted and inspired by the emotions and reflections aroused in him by the Dreyfus trial [in France]' (*op. cit.*, p. 3). However, Tony Greenstein (2010, p. 101) points out that Herzl's 'journalistic writings at the time betrayed no concern with the Dreyfus trial' and nor does he refer to Dreyfus in *The Jewish State*.

kind of pressure (Herzl, 1960, vol. I, p.6).

His conclusion is profoundly defeatist: '[o]ppression naturally creates hostility against oppressors, and our hostility aggravates the pressure. It is impossible to escape from this eternal round' (Herzl, 1993 [1896], p. 26). Herzl thus assumes the impossibility of Jews properly assimilating/integrating with non-Jews (gentiles) because of the latter's ingrained anti-Semitism and expressed this in fatalistic terms: '... I achieved a freer attitude toward anti-Semitism which I now begin to understand historically and make allowances for. Above all, I recognised the emptiness and futility of efforts to "combat anti-Semitism"' (Herzl, 1960 vol. I, p. 6). An early Zionist, Leo Pinsker, had enunciated a similar explanation: 'Judeo-phobia is a psychic aberration. As a psychic aberration it is hereditary, and as a disease transmitted for two thousand years it is incurable' (cited in Weinstock, 1989 [1969], p. 44). Accordingly, for Zionists, the optimal solution for both Jew and gentile is the creation of a Jewish homeland and state. This neatly coincides with the wishes of anti-Semites who think of Jews as unwanted intruders – and for whom their destination is of no concern.

Following publication of his pamphlet, Herzl convened the World Zionist Conference in Basle, Switzerland, in 1897 – the Zionist bandwagon had started to roll in earnest. For Herzl, the destination of Jews was of great concern: he offered Palestine and Argentina as possibilities but asserted that 'Palestine is our ever-memorable historic home' (Herzl, 1993 [1896], p. 30). Indeed, the British Colonial Secretary Joseph Chamberlain also supported a Jewish homeland, but in East Africa; specifically, the Mau plateau of Kenya and Uganda was the suggested location in the British Uganda Programme of 1903. However, an exploratory mission for the Zionist Congress came away disappointed – one British Zionist, who was in Kenya at the time, summed up the difficulties in graphic terms: 'what with elephants by day and lions by night, together with an encounter with Masai warriors in full war regalia, they decided that Kenya was no place for Russian Jewry' (cited in Keay, 2003, p. 22). Thereafter, the focus was always on emigration to, and

Key Precepts of Zionism and Islamism

colonisation of, Palestine by European Jews.

Thus, Zionism as an ideology dates back to the late nineteenth century. It is peculiar in that it is a *political* and *national* movement based on *religious* myths and narratives. The religious claim – famously described by David Ben-Gurion, Israel's first Prime Minister, as 'the Bible is our mandate'[7] – is that Jews were exiled from their homeland in 70 CE with the destruction of their second temple under Roman rule. Since then, Jews have desired to return to their 'promised land' of Palestine, or 'land of Israel'. This key belief provides, in their eyes, the moral and legal justification for the settlement and colonisation of Palestine. It assumes implicitly that those who settled on the land after Jews were forced into exile are de facto squatters, lacking legitimacy to their claim on the land. The Bible provides support for this view: biblical Palestine (or Eretz Israel) was promised to the 'chosen people', the Jews.

No matter one's view of the reasoning behind such a narrative, the reality has been that for the bulk of the past 2,000 years Jews, in their overwhelming majority, have not 'returned' to their promised land, nor sought to do so. That is why the numbers of Jews in historic Palestine before the 20th century have been small both in absolute numbers and as a percentage of the total Jewish population – most have resided in Europe. This helps explain why Zionism as an ideology did not arise for some 1800 years after the destruction of the second temple, so that if there were indeed a desire or longing for the return, it certainly was not of sufficient strength to warrant attempts to enact it. Accordingly, prior to the growth of Zionism, there was no significant ideology which advocated mass emigration of Jews to Palestine. Indeed, Herzl was candid about the colonial

---

[7] This was told by Ben-Gurion (1970, p. 109) to the British Royal Commission of 1936. In *Recollections*, he admits to being secular and 'not religious [as] were the majority of the early builders of modern Israel' (op. cit. pp. 120, 121). His attempt at explaining this paradox is, unsurprisingly, unconvincing. See Masalha (2007) for a comprehensive critique of Zionism's claims based on the Bible.

nature of Zionism, as is evidenced, for example, in a letter he wrote to Cecil Rhodes in January 1902: '[h]ow, then, do I happen to turn to you, since this is an out-of-the-way matter for you? Because it is something colonial and because it presupposes understanding of a development which will take twenty or thirty years' (Herzl, 1960, vol. III, p.1194).

Curiously however, the Labour Zionists of Paole Zion assumed that the indigenous population of Palestine (hence, in their thinking, it was not an empty land) would integrate into Zionist society implying not only that Palestinians would offer no objection to their land being settled and colonised by Europeans, but also that the problem of integration – or lack of – was a peculiarity of Jews. Moreover, this further assumed that Zionist settlers would want or desire Palestinians to integrate with their society.

History has shown that all these explicit and implicit assumptions to be demonstrably false. In fact, the early Zionists did not have (clearly this remains the case for many present day Zionists) much respect or empathy for Arabs and Muslims so the possibility of a genuine amalgamation of the Jewish settlers and the indigenous population was always remote. Put bluntly, Arabs were viewed as little more that desert savages. David Ben-Gurion summed up this sentiment starkly by proclaiming that 'we live in the twentieth century while they [Arabs/Muslims] – in the fifteenth ... We live in a proper society ... amid the world of the Middle Ages' (cited in Shlaim, 2000, p. 96). In the same vein, writing during the 1948 Arab-Israeli war during which the Israeli army conquered Arab territories with ease, Ben-Gurion remarked that 'until then, he had believed that the Israelis' "secret weapon" was their spirit. But, in fact, it "was the Arabs; they are such incompetents, it is difficult to imagine"' (cited in Morris, 2008, p. 289). In fact, a similarly brusquely honest judgement has been made by Robert Fisk, perhaps the foremost commentator and journalist on the Middle East. In his monumental *The Great War for Civilisation,* he provides the following summary remarks regarding the 'crushing' of Palestinians and their complete dispossession:

The 1956 war, the 1967 Six Day War – and Nasser's blind folly in taking on the might of the Israeli army – the 1973 Middle East conflict and the 1982 invasion of Lebanon all further crushed the Palestinians, indirectly, and usually, directly. In 1967 the West Bank and Gaza fell under Israeli occupation, so that Israel at last had the entire former British mandate of Palestine under its control, the 'Palestine' in which Balfour had promised support for a 'national home' for the Jews ... The Arab 'friends' of Palestine turned out to be as woeful in their military as they were in their political ambitions. Fighting with numerically overwhelming odds on their side, the Arab armies were repeatedly mauled by the superior firepower, ruthless tactics and morale of the Israelis ... (Fisk, 2006, p. 463).

In a work purportedly intended to understand and empathise with the Arab world, *The Arab Mind*, Raphael Patai attempts to provide the cause for modern Arab incompetence as being rooted in Islam:

> The fact remains that under traditional Islam, efforts at human improvement have rarely transcended ineffectuality. In general the Arab mind, dominated by Islam, has been bent more on preserving than innovating, on maintaining than improving, on continuing than initiating. In this atmosphere, whatever spirit of research and inquiry existed in the great age of medieval Arab culture became gradually stifled; by the fifteenth century, Arab intellectual curiosity was fast asleep (Patai, 1976, pp. 154-155).[8]

Indiscreetly, Ben-Gurion (and to some extent Patai) betrays a feeling that is a hallmark of Zionists, that is, to assert their strong sense of identity and belonging with the European, Western world. He had made this clear in 1936: '[a]lthough we were an Oriental people, we had been Europeanized, and we wanted to return to Palestine in the geographical sense only. We intended to establish a European culture here, and we were linked to the greatest cultural force in the world ...' (Ben-Gurion, 1973 [1967], p. 50). Of course, what does not resonate

---

[8] Patai's book is, apparently, widely used by the US military as a 'cultural instruction' manual (Salaita, 2006, p. 208).

is the odd juxtaposition of this feeling and identity with the desire to settle in a non-European land supposedly long stuck in the Middle Ages. Similarly, if Arabs are deemed hopelessly backward because they are infused with the mind-set of a religion of a 7th century desert society, why use recourse to precepts of a religion that is far older as the basis for laying claim to a land? Such a seeming paradox never occurred to theorists of Zionism: in *The Jewish State* (ch. V), Herzl wrote effusively of the transformatory power of Jewish science, technology, finance, and organisation – importantly, in stark contrast with classical colonialism, without the desire for indigenous Palestinian labour; a view that was faithfully echoed by his Zionist successors.

In sum, therefore, the 'dream' and goal of Zionists from Herzl onwards was the creation of a homeland for Jewish people in Palestine. Ideally, this implied that there should be no non-Jews within the Jewish state but given that the desired land was already populated, the sub-optimal solution was – and remains – for the percentage of the non-Jewish (particularly Palestinian) population to be as small as possible whilst the land mass for Israel in Palestine should be as great as possible. The politics flow naturally from these guiding principles of Zionism: on the one hand the continuous removal or ethnic cleansing of Palestinians and, on the other, the systematic colonisation of ever greater amounts of the land by Jewish settlers. Jacqueline Rose makes the interesting observation that:

> Zionism and psychoanalysis are companions of the spirit, their journey coterminous even if radically divergent as to their ends. Precisely because Zionism had to make itself out of nothing – create a unity, a language, a homeland where there was none before – it knows itself as a child of the psyche, a dream, figment of the brain'. Citing Talmon's remark '[Zionists] were unwittingly offering a rationale to that of racial, exclusive nationalism, which Hess [a Zionist] so abhorred among the Germans, and indeed to anti-Semitism, in both its racial and social versions', Rose comments 'Israel inscribes at its heart the very version of nationhood from which the Jewish people had had to flee (Rose, 2005, pp. 67, 83).

Key Precepts of Zionism and Islamism

What this version of nationhood has meant to the Palestinian Arabs remaining in Israel is vividly described by David Shipler, writing some 40 years after its creation:

> Today, one out of every six Israelis is an Arab, but the Arab is not Israeli in the full sense. His citizenship is shallow. It taints his self-identity with complication. He exists at the edge of a society that can never, by its nature, accept him as a complete member in disregard of the religious and ethnic identities that set him apart. He is an alien in his own land, an object of suspicion in his own home, torn between his country and his people ... Just being an Arab in appearance is to wear a badge that commands the attention of the security services. Showing the official ID card with "Arab" written on the space labelled "Nationality" is to announce, " Suspect me. Watch me. Check me. Search me. Question me" (Shipler, 1987, pp. 428, 429).

Much of the world, including the West in its entirety, has had no qualms about such an outcome, being satisfied in describing Israel as a 'Jewish state' even though non-Jewish Palestinians are now one-fifth of the population. Given that such acute disregard for a large minority would simply be outlawed in the West, the extraordinary indulgence afforded to Israel is striking.

After the creation of the State of Israel in 1948, the Law of Return was enacted. This embodies Zionist thinking by its assumption that since 70 CE, Jews have been in exile scattered all over the earth and can finally return to their homeland, the land of Israel. Constitutionally and legally, this law provides any Jew the right of abode and full citizenship of Israel. This is a unique phenomenon in that a state is constructed on the presumption that a people was forced into exile and, 2000 years later, their descendants have the right to 'return' to this same tract of land that was promised to them in the Bible; in the process removing the indigenous population who had lived there for generations. It naturally follows that in this homeland for Jews, those not of world Jewry are necessarily accorded lesser rights and status – whilst those expelled from their land and homes since 1948 have no right of return. This, in essence, has been the demographic dynamic of Israel, rooted in Zionist logic, since its inception. What is clear is that another people wishing to set up a homeland/state on similar beliefs and principles would be in breach of the Universal Declaration of Human Rights, myriad laws, treaties, and conventions. That is to say, it would be illegitimate and illegal for a state to be defined in terms of the religion-ethnicity of its people (or at least a proportion of them).

Zionism's emphasis on exile and return assumes that all Jews have their origins in Palestine. This claim now seems untenable given that evidence suggests that European, Ashkenazi, Jews rather than hailing from Palestine, have their origins in the Caucusus, the Volga steppes, the Black Sea and the Slav countries – the location of the Jewish Khazar Kingdom between the 8th and 13th centuries (see Sand, 2009, pp. 210-249). If recourse to the supposed dislocation of a people in antiquity does not provide legitimacy for the later removal and colonisation of the land of another people, then this is compounded when it transpires that the bulk of those making claims to the land have no material connection with it.

But, might not the fact that a people (taken to mean of a particular 'race', ethnicity, or religion) who have long been subjected to oppression and persecution be accorded the right to a homeland and state? This, of course, is the justification for the Jewish state, that is, anti-Jewish hostility has frequently been so pernicious as to warrant a safe haven for the protection and survival of the Jewish people. In principle, such a right can be conferred to a persecuted people but with very careful caveats. There is a long history of individuals and groups of people fleeing violence, repression, threat of death to the point of genocide, or natural disasters, being granted asylum in other countries and lands. But there should be no right of asylum seekers to set up their own state in another people's land. Should a persecuted people, however, settle on empty land ('a land without a people') then the problem of contested terrain naturally does not arise. Thus, in such a scenario, the settlers can configure the polity in the manner of their choosing. In the modern world, this is a largely hypothetical scenario as long gone have been the days in which the world had empty, inhabitable, lands for an aspirant people to settle and mould to their will. Such settlement can, nonetheless, still be achieved

Key Precepts of Zionism and Islamism

but only through colonisation backed up by superior force. The reaction to this will be inevitable: opposition and resistance.

Given that the land coveted and subsequently colonised and occupied by Zionists had long had a majority Muslim population, there would inevitably be a clash with those whose ideology and politics were infused with Islamic thinking and doctrines; one aspect of which is that Islam too has claims to the 'holy land'. As we shall see in the following chapters, precisely such a clash has been nurtured and intensified as Islamism has become a major force not only in the holy land of Palestine, but throughout the Middle East, in many other Muslim majority countries, and also, of late, increasingly in the Western world. Indubitably, as will duly be highlighted, one crucial reason for the rise of Islamism has been the realisation of the Zionist project.

We now turn to the core tenets of Islamism before examining its clashes with Zionism in different contexts.

Islamism

In Islam, the world is divided into binary opposites of *Dar al Islam* (House of peace) and *Dar al harb* (House of war). It follows, therefore, that for Islamists[9], the ultimate objective is the Islamisation of society under Sharia law so as to achieve *Dar al Islam*. Potentially, then, any land that has not come under Islamic rule is deemed to be *Dar al harb* and so an area of holy war or *jihad* for Islamists. However, since the collapse of the Ottoman Empire, Muslim-majority countries have, as a rule, not waged holy wars – nor sought to do so – on non-Muslim lands; rather and almost in their entirety they came under colonial rule. Therefore, the desired goal of Islamists has been to remove the colonial powers from their lands usually as part of anti-colonial movements that were invariably dominated by non-Islamist leaders and organisations.

---

[9] Note that 'Islamic fundamentalist' and 'Islamicist' also have the same meaning.

In that Islam affects all aspects of life, Islamists view it as necessarily a political belief system, expressed as *Islam din wa dawla* ('Islam is religion and state') so that the faith and politics are entwined and inseparable – this is the essence of 'political Islam' which also encompasses an evangelical strain. Hassan al Banna, who in 1928 founded the most important early Islamist organisation, the Muslim Brotherhood, expressed the thinking unequivocally: 'the Quran is our constitution'; 'no other constitution but the Quran'; the Quran is our law and Muhammad is our model' (Carré, 1995, p. 197). Though al Banna's view of Islam as a comprehensive system of life and polity can certainly be justified through recourse to the Koran, *Hadith, Sunna,* and early Islamic history, nonetheless there has long existed a non-political version of Islam which we can aver is adhered to by the great majority of Muslims, in contradistinction to rulers and leaders of Muslim-majority countries. For this majority, Islam is a set of beliefs and rituals which centrally inform their values, folkways, and culture but does not lead to – at least to any significant extent – an overt form of politics. Perhaps the typology of 'hard/radical Islamists' and 'soft/moderate Islamists' to differentiate the two might be accurate but in recent years it has become common place to simply describe the former as Islamists and the latter as 'devout Muslims'.

Since the nineteenth century, Islamists have increasingly been prominent in the interface between the Western colonial powers and the Muslim world – a relationship that has necessarily always been political. Britain and later the US understood clearly that the Islamists were not principled anti-colonialists and anti-imperialists and so could be useful vehicles for their divide and rule politics. Indeed, this led Britain to support Islamists as de facto fifth columnists against nationalist movements in the colonial era. Precisely the same rationale was applied by the US against Arab nationalism and left organisations since World War 2 in the context of Cold War rivalry with the former Soviet Union. True, the Islamists ideally wanted the foreigners and infidels to leave their lands but, knowing full well that they did not possess the military might to effect this, they generally proceeded to collaborate with colonial rulers and willingly accepted their largesse – a fundamental motif of this 'unholy alliance' was that both the colonial powers and the Islamists preferred each other to the non-religious nationalists who tended to be much more principled anti-colonialists and anti-imperialists.

This alliance continued into the post-colonial era and continues to the present post September 11 era. This astonishing and insufficiently remarked history has been the subject of in-depth studies by Mark Curtis in *Secret Affairs: Britain's Collusion with Radical Islam* (focusing on Britain's long history of collusion with Islamists) and Robert Dreyfuss in *The Devil's Game: How the United States Helped Unleash Fundamentalist Islam* (focusing on the US and its nurturing of Islamist movements especially since World War 2)[10]. So Britain, the US, and the Islamists have played a double game: whilst rejecting each others' ideologies and *weltanschauung*[11] they have, without much compunction, worked as partners. Islamists profoundly reject Western ideas and morality including democracy (in that the Sharia prevails over all 'man-made' laws and constitutions) and secularism. As such, they rail against Muslims predisposed to non-Islamic cultural and ideological influences, whom they argue cannot be trusted. At the same time, they show little compunction in availing themselves of Western science, technology, and goods; a contradiction that does not trouble them in the least. The fact that non-religious nationalist movements and post-colonial rulers in Muslim-majority countries have invariably been corrupt and dictatorial has, over time, greatly boosted the Islamist cause and popularity.

From the 1980s onwards, there has been rising Islamic

---

[10] The Swiss journalist Richard Labévière's *Dollars for Terror: The United States and Islam* (1999) is another work that traces US support for Islamism in the pre-9/11 era but is not so well researched and sourced.

[11] For example, for Winston Churchill 'no stronger retrograde force exists in the world [as Islam]' and that 'Mohammedanisn is a militant and proselytising faith' (cited in Curtis, 2010, p. 2).

activism since when Islamist forces have coalesced and gathered strength. The key catalysts for this were the Iranian revolution of 1979 and, in December of the same year, the invasion of Afghanistan by the former Soviet Union. In the former, a Western-backed anti-clerical, autocratic, ruler was overthrown by a Shia uprising and replaced by an Islamist theocracy; in the latter, a Muslim land was invaded by 'Godless communists' which, during the 1980s, became a *cause célèbre* for jihadists from around the globe, in particular from the Arab world – with ample US support. Thus, from the beginning of the 1980s, political Islam became prominent on the radar screen of global politics. Though neither Afghanistan nor Iran had a Zionist element – leaving aside the fact that the Shah of Iran had forged close links with Israel – in due course, the struggle with Zionism would increasingly feature in both. Thus, on the one hand the Iranian regime under Ayatollah Khomeini founded the annual 'International al-Quds Day' (beginning in August 1979) on the last Friday of Ramadan in solidarity with the Palestinians and in opposition to Israel and its Western supporters; whilst post 9/11 Osama bin Laden would regularly invoke the Palestine cause in his tirades against the US, Israel, and the West.

In stark contrast, the Wahabbi, extreme fundamentalist, House of Saud has remained a firm ally of its Western protectors despite some tensions and disagreements. In retrospect, it seemed out of character when Saudi Arabia ratcheted up oil prices in the aftermath of the October (Yom Kippur) War of 1973, when the US intervened strongly on Israel's behalf. Since then, however, the Saudi regime has refrained from such "disloyal" acts and, in return, has had a free rein to rule over its subjects in a tyrannical manner without so much as a hint of criticism from the West. Though of far less importance, the Muslim Brotherhood has retained links with the Western powers – especially Britain – despite the invasions of Afghanistan and Iraq and their unstinting support for Israel (Curtis, *op. cit.*, p. 307 ff.). However, since 9/11, this historic and ongoing unholy alliance has become, for many Islamist groups and individuals, intolerable and, for the first time, they have actively begun to oppose Western policies – including,

Key Precepts of Zionism and Islamism

crucially, within the Western heartlands. This has inevitably seen conflicts between Islamists and Zionists.

With respect to Zionism, Islamists have been adamant that the creation of Israel was a humiliating defeat for Islam given the importance of Palestine in general (considered an Islamic *waqf* or endowment) and Jerusalem – the third most important city after Mecca and Medina – in particular. The humiliation was compounded by the Six Day War in 1967 when all of Palestine and large tracts of other Arab land came under Israeli occupation. This marked the beginning of the decline of Arab nationalism whilst concurrently giving traction to Islamism as a viable alternative. In line with the doctrine of *Dar al harb* the objective should have been to recover the lost land under Islam's banner, necessitating a political struggle with Zionism and its defenders. The reality, however, has been rather different. As we shall see in the next chapter, Islamists paid little heed to *Dar al harb* and were consistent in adhering to the principle of unholy alliance as they willingly collaborated with the Israeli authorities: the main enemy was, as ever, non-religious nationalists. It was the first intifada in late 1987 that shook the Islamists away from this stance.

There are/have been several Islamist groups with various shades of differences – though most are Sunni. The most important ones are the Salafists, the Muslim Brotherhood of Egypt (*Ikhwan al-Muslimin*) founded by Hassan al Banna in 1928 – the ideas of its leading member of the 1950s and 1960s Sayyid Qutub have particularly influenced Al Qaeda; the Pakistani Jamaat e Islami of Maulana Abdul Ala Maududi, the Darul Uloom Deoband (Deaobandi Movement) of India (which opposes acts of terrorism), and the Shia movement of Ayatollah Ruhollah Khomeini. The differences between them are particularly acute in Islamic countries but less discernible in the non-Muslim world. The broad thrust of each is to promote an ever greater role for Islam in all aspects of life, including the polity. Hence, where they are in a minority, Islamist groups tend to argue for special provisions and exemptions to the law in order to accommodate Islamic beliefs and practices. In Muslim-majority countries, the objective is for the constitution and for laws to be based on the Sharia or to ensure laws do not transgress Islamic doctrines. In other words, Islamists demand maximum tolerance and special rights in non-Muslim majority countries but – it can be generalised with much justification – offer minimal tolerance and rights to non-Muslims in Muslim-majority countries.

After World War 2, many Muslims migrated to Western countries, especially from former colonies. Gradually, the population of Muslims – as well as other religious-ethnic minorities – increased as they tended to congregate in certain parts of towns and cities (see Hasan, 2010, part I). It would be a fair generalisation to aver that prior to the 1990s, Muslims in the West were of a quietist, non-political disposition – which is not to suggest they were uninterested in the world around them. Certainly major events such as the Iranian revolution, the Russian invasion of Afghanistan, Israel's attack on Lebanon in 1982, the Iran-Iraq war of the 1980s, the first intifada of 1987, the issue of Kashmir, were doubtless of considerable interest to many Muslims in the West – but these did not arouse much overt Islamic activism.

Matters changed, however, during the US-led war against Iraq in February 1991. Despite the fact that many Arab countries either joined in the attack or supported it, large numbers (perhaps a significant majority globally) of Muslims opposed the war as well as UN imposed sanctions on Iraq that followed – and which devastated the lives of millions of innocent Iraqis. Such opposition would be greatly magnified a decade later. By this stage, there were settled Muslim communities in Western countries with mosques acting as a key focal point, especially for males; from which would hail an increasing radicalisation. This duly occurred after September 11 2001 and the US/UK-led invasion of Afghanistan in October 2001, followed by the war on Iraq in March 2003, as Islamist activism intensified exponentially. London had since the Soviet invasion of Afghanistan become a major hub – Mark Curtis provides the reasoning for this as follows:

> Throughout this period, many jihadist groups and individuals found refuge in Britain, some gaining political asylum, while continuing involvement in terrorism overseas. Whitehall not only

tolerated but encouraged the development of 'Londonistan' – the capital acting as a base and organising centre for numerous jihadist groups – even as this provided a de facto 'green light' to that terrorism. I speculate that some elements, at least, in the British establishment allowed some Islamist groups to operate from London not only because they provided information to security services but also because they were seen as useful to British foreign policy, notably in maintaining a politically divided Middle East – and as a lever to influence foreign governments' policies' (Curtis, 2010, p. xv).

Avowedly Islamist – though not necessarily jihadist – groups such as the Muslim Association of Britain, the Muslim Council of Britain, the Islamic Human Rights Council, the Muslim Public Affairs Committee UK, Hizb ut Tahrir, and Al Muhajiroun went into overdrive as they campaigned and protested against the so-called 'war on terror' which they deemed to be a war *of* terror on Islam, and made significant forays into the media to put forward an explicitly Islamic world view. Some such as Al Muhajiroun and individuals linked to Al Qaeda went as far as to advocate a *jihad* against America and the West. For such groups, this marked a decisive shift away from the unholy alliance in favour of holy war.

Zionism, despite its prize of a state in the Middle East and its biblical justifications, is nevertheless a European phenomenon. As such, it is imbued with a European heritage, the most important of which is the enlightenment. Islamism, in stark contrast, rests on a belief system of a 7th century desert society which, despite some important advances in the sciences and knowledge in the middle ages, was never touched by the enlightenment and the age of reason. Steeped in unreason, superstition, and obscurantism, it has struggled to make sense of the world forged by enlightenment thinking for the simple reason that it lacks the intellectual tools to do so. This helps explain why despite the fact that those espousing or sympathetic to Islamism far outnumbering Zionists, they have been no match for them on the intellectual and political terrain.

What unites all Islamists in their concerns and campaigning is Palestine, whilst the importance and survival of Israel to Zionists is second to none: accordingly, this tract of 'holy land' forms the epicentre of the clash between Islamists and Zionists, to which we now turn.

PART II

ISLAMISM AND ZIONISM IN THE MIDDLE EAST

Chapter 2

Palestine/Israel: The Epicentre

Background

The conflict in the Middle East, whose core is Palestine-Israel, is fundamental to the conflict between Islamism and Zionism. What is important to stress – and a fact which is invariably downplayed – is that prior to the 20th century there is no history of serious conflict between Arabs and Jews in the region. Indeed, as is frequently pointed out, Jews fared far better under Islamic rule than under Christianity, most notably in Moorish Spain. Given this history, it was an exogenous political shock – the advent of Zionism – that altered this relatively benign equilibrium. Hostilities arose and intensified exponentially between Arabs/Muslims and Jews in the Middle East because of Zionist designs on Palestinian land and, importantly, well before the Balfour Declaration of 1917. Neville Mandel, in his study *The Arabs and Zionism before World War 1*, summarises the Arab case against Zionism thus:

> The main Arab arguments were that the Zionists sought a Jewish state in Palestine (which might extend as far as Iraq); that they retained their foreign nationality and did not become loyal Ottomans; that they did not integrate with the local population; that they were establishing independent institutions of self-government and self defence; that they preferred Hebrew to Arabic; that they possessed vast financial resources and thus the capacity to achieve their aims ... The period before 1914 therefore takes on new importance in terms of the Arab-Zionist conflict. The roots of Arab antagonism, and perhaps of the conflict, stretch back to it. Indeed it may be argued that the Balfour Declaration was not so much the starting point of the conflict as a turning point which greatly exaggerated an existing trend (Mandel, 1976, pp. 228, 231).

Indeed, as we saw in the previous chapter, Zionist intentions were remarkably clear from the outset: the first Zionist Congress in Switzerland, in 1897, called for a home for Jewish people in Palestine whilst a pamphlet published in the same year by the founder of socialist Zionism, Nahum Syrkin, made clear what this would necessitate – Palestine 'must be evacuated for the Jews' (cited in Pappe, 2006, p. 282). Thus, Zionism was an existential threat that was greatly feared by the indigenous people from its inception given that those eyeing up their land were Europeans who were generally much richer, far better educated, well organised, with the capability of acquiring superior weaponry – the history of colonisation shows these as the necessary requisites which enable relatively small numbers of colonisers to overpower any indigenous population which dares to resist. An indication of the worries felt by Palestinians in the early years of Zionist settlement was provided by Hafiz Bey al Said of Jaffa, the first deputy to raise the Zionist issue in the Ottoman Parliament, who cautioned in 1914:

> Were the Zionist danger not great, I would be the first to declare that we need Zionism here in this country. [But] it is otherwise, if the matter proceeds unrestricted, if the [Jewish] immigrant is entitled to buy [land] wherever he pleases ... If the government does nothing against the danger of Zionist immigration, it is quite possible that the new settlers will attract to themselves the lion's share of trade and land [in Palestine], and that they will outnumber the local population, nine-tenths of whom are ignorant of what knowledge and education are ...' (cited in Mandel, *op. cit*, pp. 183-184).

In the same year, Raghib Bey al Nashashibi declared: 'if I am elected as a deputy [to the Ottoman Parliament], I will dedicate all my energies day and night to remove the harm and danger awaiting us from Zionism and the Zionists – without, as has been said, harming the rights of our Ottoman [Jewish] brethren' (*ibid*, p, 185).

These worries and danger were to prove very real – leading ultimately to the expulsion of the majority of Palestinians from their land and the disappearance of Palestine from the map.

Serious confrontation broke out between Jewish Zionists and Palestinians after World War I, particularly following the

Palestine/Israel: The Epicentre

Balfour Declaration of November 1917 (see Weinstock, 1989 [1969], chs. 6-10). This was – and remains – one of the most fundamental grievances of Palestinians against Zionists and against the British 'Mandate Authority' which made the unjust promise of handing over a large proportion of the land of one people to another. Unjust because the recourse to a promise made in a holy text was always disqualified by the entirety of the Palestinian population, Christian and Muslim, both steeped in the teachings and doctrines of their own holy books, (but see below on religious claims to the land made in the Hamas Charter) and also by some Jews (in the main, secular anti-Zionists but also including religious groups such as Naturei Kartei).

In the present era (late 20th century/early 21st century), Palestine has increasingly become a 'Muslim issue' for Muslims in general and Islamists in particular. In this view, non-Muslim Palestinians have been airbrushed out: to all intents and purposes, Palestinians are Muslims whose oppression and seizure of land is a particularly heinous manifestation of a wider 'war against Islam'. Matters have not been helped by the silence of the small minority who are Christians (estimated at about 8 per cent of the West Bank population and 2 per cent of the Israeli population) (CIA World Fact Book) – the majority of Palestinian Christians have emigrated from Mandate Palestine. Part of the problem is that there is no Palestinian organisation which stresses the unity of all Palestinians: the PLO (and its largest constituent, Fatah) has nominally been a non-religious, nationalist, movement but has long been corrupted. The writer and activist Eqbal Ahmad – who had met Yasser Arafat a number of times in the 1970s at the latter's request – came to the following conclusion following a meeting in the mid-1970s: '[t]hey [the PLO leadership] listened respectfully ... Some gave lectures that were essentially ignorant ... I had seen enough. *They defeated themselves more than the Israelis did*' (emphasis added). Some 20 years later in 1996, following the Oslo Accords, Ahmad came to the following harsh judgement: 'Arafat and the people around him are thugs collaborating with Israel' (Ahmad, 2000, pp. 34, 36).

In an article written towards the end of his life, Edward Said (who had been a close ally of Eqbal Ahmad) similarly pulled no punches regarding the degradation of the PLO: '[a]s for the Oslo "peace process" that began in 1993, it has simply repackaged the occupation, offering a token 18 per cent of the lands seized in 1967 to the corrupt Vichy-like Authority of Arafat, whose mandate has essentially been to police and tax his people on Israel's behalf' (Said, 2001, p. 28).

One, rather neglected, aspect of Fatah's political corruption has been its leadership's opportunistic utilisation of Islamic rhetoric – a particularly glaring example of this was the speech made by Arafat's successor, Mahmoud Abbas, in Gaza in August 2005 after Israel's withdrawal from the strip. A beneficiary of this kow-towing to Islam has been Hamas which has always posited an 'industrial strength' version of the faith and its rise has accentuated the association of Palestine with Islam. Despite its detestation of Hamas and other smaller Islamist groups such as Islamic Jihad, Fatah has never properly challenged such an association.

The 'Islamisation' of the cause of Palestine became pronounced during the US-led invasions of Afghanistan and Iraq. For Islamists and their supporters, this was as noted above a key component of what was deemed to be a war against Islam waged by the West in general and the US in particular. However, wars in Chechnya and Kashmir were also included in this putative war against Islam though the fact that the perpetrators of these – Russia and India – are non-Western countries was not thought to have undermined this thesis. In Kashmir's case, however, as part of the province has long been 'liberated' – the territory known as 'Azad [Free] Kashmir' which is under the jurisdiction of Pakistan – it has not been such a campaigning issue for Islamists outside Pakistan. Chechnya, a much more recent conflict, has also not attracted any great campaigning zeal and we can conjecture as to why this might be the case. In contrast, the sense of injustice over Palestine has long been palpable throughout the Islamic world and beyond, flowing from the 1948 *nakba* and the systematic removal or, in modern parlance, ethnic cleansing of Palestinians from their land after the formation of Israel (see Masalha, 2012; Pappe, 2006).

Palestine/Israel: The Epicentre

So, to reiterate, it is the Palestine-Israel conflict that lies at the epicentre of the clash between Islamism and Zionism. For Zionists, Israel represents the culmination of the long-desired Jewish homeland that must be defended by all means necessary including a relentless struggle against those who would threaten it or even question its legitimacy. For Jewish Zionists who have not made the *aliyah,* Israel nonetheless holds a very special place, akin to a spiritual home or 'motherland'; in effect, a surrogate 'home land'. Accordingly, it is supported by financial transfers and by use of 'soft power' such as support in the media and the arts, and through lobbying of official channels. Thus, critics and opponents of Israel are deflected, parried, or harassed and power structures are influenced by carrots and sticks. Such, in sum, is the work of what has come to be known as the 'Israel Lobby' (Mearsheimer and Walt, 2007). No matter one's view of the Israel-Palestine conflict, it is indubitably the case that the Israel Lobby has been supremely effective. A simple, yet stark fact attests this: a small foreign country with a Jewish population of less than 6 million, strongly supported by about the same number of co-religionists in the USA (comprising 1.7 per cent of the population [Pew, 2010]) has managed to make itself become de facto a domestic issue for the world's most powerful country. No other country comes anywhere near as close to achieving this remarkable influence and, in consequence, no other country receives anything like the aid and political support that Israel garners from the US.

A crucial feature of this successful lobbying power is that dissenting voices on US support for Israel are rendered largely silent. The overwhelming majority of Congress views Israel as it were a home state; one can indeed argue that Israel is, in all but name, the 51st state.[12] Similarly, critical and dissenting

---

[12] This is attested by the fact that no leader is allowed to speak to the US Congress as regularly as the Prime Minister of Israel. Moreover, in his speech to Congress on 24th May 2011, Benjamin Netanyahu received 29 standing ovations by both Democrats and Republicans. This astonishing, quite unique, phenomenon is a crucial manifestation of the power of the Israel Lobby. This was acknowledged by Thomas Friedman, the *New York Times* columnist,

voices in the mainstream press and media and the arts are conspicuous by their absence. The one terrain in which critical voices and opinions are to be found is the academy but even here, the cost to any 'recalcitrant' can be extremely high[13]. The standard view of Israel in American academia is enormously supportive. In Western Europe, official support for Israel is also very strong and is underscored by the EU's granting it associate membership. Leading EU countries such as Britain, France and Germany view Israel as a natural and important ally and quietly tolerate or ignore its myriad breaches of UN resolutions and international laws and conventions. That said, the standing of Israel is very low. For example, in the BBC World Service's annual Country Rating Poll of 27 countries, Israel invariably comes near the bottom. In the 2011 poll, Israel was thought to have the most negative influence after Iran, North Korea, and Pakistan. The findings show that 'there have been significant increases in negative views of the country [Israel] among Americans (negatives rising from 31% to 41%) and Britons (from 50% to 66%) (BBC World Service Poll, 2011). These are, of course, two of the countries where official support for Israel is the strongest.[14]

---

well-known for his Zionist sympathies: 'I sure hope that Israel's prime minister, Benjamin Netanyahu, understands that the standing ovation he got in Congress this year was not for his politics. That ovation was bought and paid for by the Israel lobby' (Friedman, 2011).

[13] The case of the Jewish American academic Norman Finkelstein, renowned for documenting Israel's oppression of Palestinians, is a case in point: De Paul University denied him tenure in 2008 after strong lobbying by pro-Israel groups.

[14] The 27 countries are: Australia, Brazil, Canada, Chile, China, Egypt, France, Germany, Ghana, India, Indonesia, Italy, Japan, Kenya, Mexico, Nigeria, Pakistan, Peru, Philippines, Portugal, Russia, South Africa, South Korea, Spain, Turkey, UK, US. If more Muslim majority countries are included in the sample, Israel's rating would indubitably sink to last in every poll.

Palestine/Israel: The Epicentre

Though Zionism did not command majority support prior to World War 2, Jewish opinion was considered important in Western Europe with many Jews playing important roles in public life. Notwithstanding at times virulent anti-Semitism, Jews were part of the fabric of society. The reason why the Dreyfus Affair so scandalised France in late nineteenth and early twentieth century was because a French officer, who happened to be Jewish, was so blatantly discriminated against – despite showing strong loyalty to the French state and empire. The anti-Dreyfusard right were indeed afflicted by an irrational phobia of Jews. Despite this phobia, Ashkenazi Jews have long been part of European society: no matter the views of their detractors, they were/are Europeans (see Sand, 2010, for an extensive analysis of the origins of European Jews).

In stark contrast, Russia and Eastern Europe have been the true cradle of anti-Semitism with bouts of intense hostility, discrimination and oppression of Jews, to the point of murder in the form of pogroms (a Russian word meaning to destroy by violent means) and the widespread perception of Jews as unwelcome interlopers. Indeed, it would not have been altogether surprising if Nazi-style persecution of Jews had arisen in Russia rather than in Germany.

The situation of Muslims in Western Europe is entirely different. There was no component of the indigenous population in this part of the continent with a significant Muslim population: though the Moors had ruled Spain for nearly 800 hundred years, after the departure of the last Moor in 1492, the Muslim population that remained was, following Charles V's edict of 1526, either forced to convert to Christianity or be expelled from the peninsula (Miller, 2008, p. 2). This contrasts with Eastern Europe where Ottoman rule led to widespread conversion to Islam and, after the collapse of the Ottoman empire at the end of the First World War, there were significant pockets of Muslims on this side of the continent (apart from European Turkey, this included Albania, Kosovo, and parts of Bosnia-Herzogovina; there are also Muslims of the Caucasus region of Russia and of the former Soviet Union, many of whom have their origins in the Mongolian Khans). Importantly, because the Ottomans were fierce rivals of the European powers, and considered peculiarly alien because of their religion (all the European powers were Christian), Islam was never fully accepted as a European religion.

These contrasting histories – and views – of Jews and Muslims in Europe have left a legacy on the political struggle between Islamism and Zionism in the West. Shorn of caveats and somewhat crudely stated, we can aver that Jews have long been part of the Western fabric, notwithstanding the bouts of discrimination and oppression. Moreover, they have enormously influenced European and North American societies in practically every aspect – be it intellectually, artistically, politically, and economically. As such, they can be deemed as 'insiders'. Muslims by contrast have not had anything like the same impact on Western society. True, Arab/Muslim science and literature has had some influence but this does not detract from the general hypothesis of their having a marginal impact, particularly in the modern era.

Importantly, in the West, there has been a layer of influential non-Jews who have been attracted to Zionism and hence have shown strong support for both the *idea* and *reality* of Israel. This is especially true for Christians attracted to the biblical prophecy of the 'restoration' of Jews to Palestine; what would in the 20th century be termed Christian Zionism. This includes, for example, powerful British leaders in the late nineteenth century such as Benjamin Disraeli, David Lloyd George, Lord Shaftesbury and, later, Winston Churchill (Masalha, 2007, p. 91 ff.). As such, this ideological support precludes those gentiles who supported a Jewish homeland because of their anti-Semitism.[15] Indeed, there is good reason to think that, at least in part, Arthur Balfour's support for a Jewish state stemmed from his anti-Semitism of which there is no doubt as evidenced by his forthright views during the introduction of the 1905 Aliens Bill to curb the influx of immigrants from eastern Europe: 'the

---

[15] Though Churchill also displayed anti-Semitism when he described Leon Trotsky's 'schemes of a world-wide communist State under Jewish domination' (cited in Weinstock, 1989 [1969], p. 96).

undoubted evils that had befallen upon the country from an immigration that was largely Jewish' (cited in Egremont, 1980, p. 205). A Jewish state would serve the purpose of stemming this 'undoubted evil' as it would be a magnet for Jews to leave Europe and venture forth to their 'own' state and 'homeland'; precisely the desired goal of both anti-Semites and Zionists.

More recently, particularly in the US, there is a powerful layer of Christian Zionists who strongly support Israel for biblical reasons (see chapter 5). This affinity has, of late, tempered the two millennia hostility between Christianity and Judaism – and doubtless contributed to the hybrid term that emphasises their purported commonality (whilst also conflating Zionism with Judaism), that is, 'the Judeo-Christian tradition'.

Again, in stark contrast, there has been no such constituency of Western non-Muslims who have passionately advocated support for the Muslim (or Arab) world view and cause, no matter how diffuse or disparate. In Britain, for example, there has existed an 'Arabist' tendency but, apart from the fact of it being miniscule, it has been devoid of any ideological conviction but rather based on cold strategic considerations to serve the empire or, in the post-colonial era, to serve economic and geopolitical interests. Importantly, its influence has been insignificant. The Zionist narrative has been utterly dominant and given added cogency by the conflation of anti-Zionism with anti-Semitism. Such a sleight of hand has been most effective in inducing silence, self-censorship, or deflecting criticism in regard to Israel and its numerous breaches of international laws noted earlier.

This is not to deny that critiques of Zionism and Israel have been mounted – sometimes robustly – in official channels as well as in the mainstream media. But these have invariably been made by non-Muslims stirred by a sense of justice on the issue, in particular of the seemingly perennial Israeli oppression of Palestinians. They have thus not been motivated by any allegiance either to the global *umma* or to 'Arabism'. Similar critiques have rarely emanated from Islamist sources: unable to counter pro-Israel views and policies, they have largely been rendered impotent, bitter, and resentful. Moreover, their strict adherence to doctrines and *weltanschauung* embedded in the holy book has prevented them from seeking and acquiring the means of properly analysing the world around them. In its place has arisen the glib, simplistic, explanation of Western support for Zionism and the supposed enmity towards Islam as clear manifestations of a generalised 'war on Islam'. In keeping with lack of systematic analysis, little attempt is made to establish whether this hypothesis is correct, to discover evidence which challenges its assumptions so as to offer a more nuanced and convincing explanation.

From this sharp dichotomy, it is safe to conclude that Islamists – with few supporters and lacking the intellectual and political wherewithal – have been no match for Zionists on the ideological battleground in the West. In every field touching on the issue, Jewish Zionists have been vastly superior to Muslims and Islamists. Yet, as the plight of Palestinians has worsened over the years – particularly since the first Intifada of 1987 – sympathy for their cause has risen. Take Britain for example: research by Greg Philo and Mike Berry (2011) shows a noticeable and sustained bias in media coverage in favour of Israel. However, in 2002, an opinion poll showed that sympathy for Palestinians was running at twice that for Israel (ICM Research, 2002 – see chapter 6 for details) – but this has not altered the pro-Israel bias of the media and the political establishment. Just as a compass needle's default position points to the North, the polity's and media's default position points to an unwavering, favourable, stance on Israel.

In his film, *The War You Don't See*, the writer and documentary maker John Pilger asked the Head of Newsgathering at the BBC, Fran Unsworth, in a section discussing Israel's killing of nine activists on a Turkish flotilla (on May 31st 2010) bound for Gaza: 'who is the Palestinian equivalent of Mark Regev?' [the spokesperson for the Israeli government]. The question was fair and important: Pilger's argument was given that the BBC generously allowed the views of the Israeli government to be aired, via a state propagandist, then in all fairness it ought to air the views of a Palestinian equivalent of Regev. Unsworth's response that 'it is not our job to appoint a Palestinian spokesperson' whilst being obviously true did not address the fundamental bias that was displayed in regard to the reporting of the attack on the flotilla – and which corroborated the work of Philo and Berry. Indeed, Pilger should also have asked her why no spokesperson for the Turkish government was called upon given that the nine activists killed were Turkish.

The problem, however, is that – notwithstanding any alleged ingrained bias on the part of the BBC – there is simply no Palestinian equivalent of Mark Regev. A spokesperson on behalf of Fatah/ Palestinian Authority which polices the West Bank would not at all be to the satisfaction of Hamas, the Islamist rivals to Fatah, which has nominal control of Gaza. This highlights one important consequence of the internecine rivalry among the two dominant Palestinian organisations: the absence of a unified voice. Of course, this should not prevent media organisations from seeking opinions from the different Palestinian viewpoints, but part of the reason for the compass needle of the media failing to shift away from Israel is that the other party in the conflict has been utterly ineffectual in applying pressure on media organisations. So the default position, buttressed by powerful lobbying by pro-Israeli individuals and groups, remains intact – adding to the generalisation of Zionists and Israel being within the Western sphere, whereas Arabs and Islamists are deemed to be the 'other'.

Israel and Hamas: from collaboration to confrontation

The importance of the 'holy land' is naturally of profound importance to Muslims and Jews in general and to Islamists and Zionists in particular; as indeed it is to Christians of all denominations. Islam and Palestine are intimately linked in their religious significance for Muslims: the al-Aqsa mosque (*al Masjid al-Aqsa*) in Jerusalem is the first place that Muslims directed their prayers to in the early 7th century, and Jerusalem is the third most important holy place after Mecca and Medina. If one place marks the spot of religious tensions between Jews and Muslims, it is the Dome of the Rock, also in Jerusalem, where the prophet Mohommed is thought to have ascended to heaven to meet Allah – adjacent to the spot where Jews believe the Old Temple of Solomon was built. But, perhaps surprisingly, such tensions had not been particularly great prior to the 20th century. Contrast this with myriad regions that have been fought over by neighbouring peoples or by imperial rivals. What is, however, true is that where recourse is given to religion as the link between a people and a tract of land, reason tends to be abandoned and, beneath the surface of tranquillity, lurk eddies of potential strife.

Muslims were conquerors of the holy land in the early 7th century and, until the Christian crusaders brought Palestine under their banner in the 11th century, had lived in reasonable harmony with Jews and Christians; though Muslims, to all intents and purposes, had superior status. Christian rule after the crusades, followed many centuries later by the colonisation of Arab/Muslim lands, was thought by many Islamists to have been the precursor of Zionist colonisation by European Jews. From this view, we can infer that Ottoman rule of Arab land is not accorded quite the same degree of animosity.

An early precursor to Hamas (discussed below) was the Izz ad-Din al-Qassam movement of the 1930s – named after the religious scholar who launched a jihad against British colonial rule and European Zionist settlers (Milton-Edwards, 1996, p. 11 ff.). But the efforts of al-Qassam and, indeed, of the Palestinians in their entirety (including the Arab revolt of 1936-38) could not prevent the creation of Israel in 1948, with the ensuing loss of 57 per cent of the land; which subsequently increased to 78 per cent after the Six Day War of 1967, with the remaining 22 per cent coming under Israel's military occupation. In this period, the leadership of the Arab world was firmly under the nationalists, led by Gamal Nasser of Egypt. The crushing of Nasser's army in 1967 and occupation of large tracts of Arab land dealt a mortal blow to Arab nationalism in general and 'Nasserism' in particular. Humiliated and discredited, it underwent a steady decline. In this vacuum, the alternative politics of Islamism (or political Islam) began to gather strength.[16] However, it was in Iran and not in the Arab world where the apogee of Islamism was reached, albeit of the minority Shia variety as Islamists throughout the world gained heart and confidence from the overthrow in 1979 of the Western-backed, nominally secular, Shah dictatorship.

In Palestine, Islamism had historically been weak – indeed prior to the rise of Hamas, Palestinian politics were largely non-religious, a characteristic which rubbed off on society at large. The Islamist movement's banner in Palestine as elsewhere in the Arab world was carried by the Muslim Brotherhood; its Palestine branch was set up in 1946. The key goal of the Brotherhood was to establish Islamic states as part of a single *umma* and, to this end, the means of its politics were naturally infused with religious doctrines.

During the 1980s, the Palestinian Islamic Jihad group splintered off from the Muslim Brotherhood because of the latter's refusal to oppose Israeli occupation – as the name implies, the group's aim has been to wage a *jihad* against Israel and reclaim Islamic land from the Jewish people. Also, in opposition to the Brotherhood, Islamic Jihad was supportive of the Shia revolution in Iran, thinking of it as a model that ought to be emulated in Palestine. It claims that its actions sparked the first intifada in 1987 when, for the first time, political Islam became a serious player in Palestinian resistance to the occupation. Israel, however, responded by repressing the organisation including the arrest and deportation of several of its leaders (Milton-Edwards, 1996, pp. 116-123). It is a small organisation, but has gained considerable impact and notoriety by carrying out suicide bombings in Israel from 1996; and by launching rocket attacks into northern Israel from the Gaza strip. In October 2011, nine Islamic Jihad fighters were killed

---

[16] Note that though Nasser and his successor Anwar Sadat were devout Muslims, their politics – which cannot properly be described as secular as is normally the case – were not infused with religious ideology, and nor did they advocate the creation of an Islamic state. Accordingly, the term 'Arab nationalist' offers the best approximation for their politics.

by Israeli attacks on Gaza after the organisation had resumed firing rockets into Israel after a period of relative calm. Though retaining independence, it is ideologically close to Hamas which, soon after its formation, has dominated Islamist politics in Palestine.

Hamas is by far the most important Palestinian Islamist organisation, having its roots in the Muslim Brotherhood (Abu-Amr, 1993). It was founded on 14th December 1987, six days after the explosion of the first intifada. Up till that point, as noted, the Brotherhood had avoided confrontation against the occupying Israeli forces, concentrating instead on the spread of Islamic ideology and on undertaking much needed welfare work on the ground. This was known as the strategy of 'preparing the generations'; one which would take much time and ideological work to build an army capable of fighting a formidable enemy (Hroub, 2010, p. 13) . For the non-religious nationalist groups, this was de facto abstentionist, even cowardly, that did nothing to take the struggle forward. But the Islamists could legitimately reply that the terrorist tactics of their critics, including the notorious hijacking of aeroplanes, did far more harm than good. But the enormity and depth of the intifada jolted the leadership to alter its hitherto relatively serene path and join with the Palestinian masses in confronting the Israelis.

For a new political entity to succeed, it has to offer something which chimes with significant numbers of those whom it purports to represent, and which is lacking among the existing dominant political forces. In Hamas's case, this was selfless, corruption-free welfare work on the ground which proved appealing when combined with the new emphasis on *resistance*. This is made clear by the choice of the name 'Hamas' – which in Arabic means 'zeal' and is also the acronym for *Haraqat al-Muqawama al-Islamiyya,* or the Islamic Resistance Movement. Hamas calls for a jihad against the Israeli occupiers, something it had avoided in its previous incarnation, and offers an avowedly Islamist programme. But we can reasonably conjecture that this was not what attracted ordinary Palestinians to its banner, that is to say, support was given despite its religiosity rather than because of it. That said, as Abu Amr (1993, p. 18) makes clear: 'Hamas did benefit from an 'atmosphere of oppression, deprivation, and hopelessness [that] contributed to the spread of an Islamic climate. The PLO factions ... [were] sensitive to this shift ... [as evidenced by] the increased use of religious expressions and Quranic verses in the statements issued by the UNLU [Unified National Leadership of the Uprising]'.

Indeed, as noted earlier, in August 2005, after Israel's withdrawal from Gaza, Fatah leader Mahmood Abbas made explicit reference to Koranic verses in his speech in Gaza to mark the event; of the sort which any political leader with a secular outlook would refrain from doing.

Hamas's political and religious beliefs are enunciated in its Charter, drafted in August 1988, 9 months after its formation (see Hamas Covenant [Charter], 1988). It uses verses from the Koran and *hadith* as justification for its beliefs. This document has rightly gained notoriety as can be evidenced from some of its key points: its *leitmotif* is that Islam is uncompromisingly opposed to Judaism and Zionism. In the section 'Structure and Formation', Article 3 states:

> The basic structure of the Islamic Resistance Movement consists of Muslims who have given their allegiance to Allah whom they truly worship.

Article 6 expounds on this:

> The Islamic Resistance Movement is a distinguished Palestinian movement, whose allegiance is to Allah, and whose way of life is Islam. It strives to raise the banner of Allah over every inch of Palestine, for under the wing of Islam followers of all religions can coexist in security and safety where their lives, possessions and rights are concerned.

Article 7 utilises a notorious *hadith (al-Bukhari)* to realise Allah's promise:

> The Day of Judgement will not come about until Muslims fight the Jews (killing the Jews), when the Jew will hide behind stones and trees. The stones and trees will say O Muslims, O Abdulla [servant of Allah], there is a Jew behind me, come and kill him. Only the

Gharkad tree would not do that because it is one of the trees of the Jews.

Article 11 mirrors – and counters – the 'Promised Land' to the Jews:

> The Islamic Resistance Movement believes that the land of Palestine is an Islamic Waqf [endowment] consecrated for future Muslim generations until Judgement Day. It, or any part of it, should not be squandered: it, or any part of it, should not be given up.

The religious significance of Palestine to Muslims is stated in Article 15:

> It is necessary to instil in the minds of the Muslim generations that the Palestinian problem is a religious problem, and should be dealt with on this basis. Palestine contains Islamic holy sites. In it there is al-Aqsa Mosque which is bound to the great Mosque in Mecca in an inseparable bond as long as heaven and earth speak of Isra' (Mohammed's midnight journey to the seven heavens) and Mi'raj (Mohammed's ascension to the seven heavens from Jerusalem).

Article 22 provides a bizarre recourse to conspiracy theories – the most absurd nonsense put out by a political organisation purporting to liberate its people from subjugation:

> With their money, they took control of the world media, news agencies, the press, publishing houses, broadcasting stations, and others. With their money they stirred revolutions in various parts of the world with the purpose of achieving their interests and reaping the fruit therein. They were behind the French Revolution, the Communist revolution and most of the revolutions we heard and hear about, here and there. With their money they formed secret societies, such as Freemasons, Rotary Clubs, the Lions and others in different parts of the world for the purpose of sabotaging societies and achieving Zionist interests. With their money they were able to control imperialistic countries and instigate them to colonize many countries in order to enable them to exploit their resources and spread corruption there.

Article 32 continues with the conspiracy theme by stating:

> '[t]heir plan is embodied in the "Protocols of the Elders of Zion" – which is, of course, the notorious forgery.[17]

Article 27 acknowledges the legitimacy of the PLO but does not support its non-Islamic ideology: accordingly, Hamas never joined the PLO, nor accepted its leadership:

> That is why, with all our appreciation for The Palestinian Liberation Organization - and what it can develop into - and without belittling its role in the Arab-Israeli conflict, we are unable to exchange the present or future Islamic Palestine with the secular idea. The Islamic nature of Palestine is part of our religion and whoever takes his religion lightly is a loser ... The day The Palestinian Liberation Organization adopts Islam as its way of life, we will become its soldiers, and fuel for its fire that will burn the enemies.

In an attempt to explain its profoundly reactionary nature, Khaled Hroub (2010, p. 36) argues that:

> The Charter was written in early 1988 by one individual and was made public without appropriate general Hamas consultation, revision or consensus to the regret of Hamas's leaders in later years. The author of the Charter was one of the 'old guard' of the Muslim Brotherhood in the Gaza strip, completely cut off from the outside world. All kinds of confusions and conflations between Judaism and Zionism found their way into the Charter to the disservice of Hamas ever since, as this document has managed to brand it with charges of 'anti-Semitism' and a naive world view.

He points out that Hamas published documents in 1990 which

---

[17] Beverly Milton-Edwards (1999[1996], p. 189) makes the important point :'[t]hat the themes in the Hamas covenant which demonise Jews in Islamic terms are bolstered by Western anti-Semitic sources is ironic given that the organisation is dedicated to offering an Islamic rather than Western, secular-inspired solution to the conflict with Israel'.

distanced themselves from what had been included in the Charter and which emphasise that its struggle has been against Zionists and Zionism, not against Jews and Judaism (*ibid.*, p. 37). But this attempt to minimise the naïve and indeed pernicious nature of the Charter will not do. The obvious question to ask is this: if the Charter is indeed thought to be burdensome and naïve by the Hamas leadership, why not abandon it? Issuing other documents that ameliorate the Charter only provides a thin veneer for its ugly contents and will fail to convince anyone but the most resolute apologist of the sincerity of this manoeuvre. If there are indeed Hamas members unhappy with the problematic nature of the Charter, then why have they not campaigned to abolish it, or to thoroughly re-write it, or at least distanced themselves from it? In an interview with Hamas leader Khaled Meshal by Robert Pastor of Columbia University, who asked him about the Hamas Charter, 'Meshal replied that it is a piece of history and no longer relevant, but cannot be changed for internal reasons' (cited in Adas, 2010). This cryptic response suggests that at least an important element (perhaps the majority) of the leadership adheres to the goals of the Charter, hence has prevented it from being scrapped.[18] It ineluctably leads to the judgement that the persistence of the Charter demonstrates the profoundly reactionary nature of Hamas's goals. Not surprisingly, aside from Islamists around the world, we can aver that the movement has attracted little meaningful solidarity from those sympathetic to the Palestinian cause.

What is underplayed but of great importance is that despite Hamas's unremitting hostility to Israel, and its espousal of an Islamic state on the land of historic Palestine, Israel – rather than being concerned – *quietly and indirectly supported its precursors*. Though *prima facie* this seems paradoxical, there are good reasons as to why Islamist politics were appealing to Israel. The political reasoning behind this was evident in the

---

[18] Perhaps because of the damage the Charter has done, it is not available on the Hamas website.

1970s when, as Andrew Higgins of the *Wall Street Journal* explains:

> The Israeli government officially recognized a precursor to Hamas called Mujama Al-Islamiya, registering the group as a charity. It allowed Mujama members to set up an Islamic university [the only university in Gaza] and build mosques, clubs and schools. Crucially, Israel often stood aside when the Islamists and their secular left-wing Palestinian rivals battled, sometimes violently, for influence in both Gaza and the West Bank ... the cleric [Sheikh Yassin, founder of the Mujama and, later, Hamas] and Israel had a shared enemy: secular Palestinian activists. After a failed attempt in Gaza to oust secularists from leadership of the Palestinian Red Crescent, the Muslim version of the Red Cross, Mujama staged a violent demonstration, storming the Red Crescent building. Islamists also attacked shops selling liquor and cinemas. The Israeli military mostly stood on the sidelines (Higgins, 2009, p. W1).

This reasoning has also been provided by David Shipler but he provides evidence to show that the Israeli military did more than 'stand on the sidelines':

> Politically speaking, Islamic fundamentalists were sometimes regarded as useful to Israel because they had their conflicts with the secular supporters of the PLO. Violence between the groups erupted occasionally on West Bank university campuses, and the Israeli military governor of the Gaza strip, Brigadier General Yitzhak Segev, once told me how he had financed the Islamic movement as a counterweight to the PLO and the Communists. "The Israeli Government gave me a budget and the military government gives to the mosques," he said. In 1980, when fundamentalist protestors set fire to the office of the Red Crescent Society in Gaza, headed by Dr Haidar Abdel-Shafi, a Communist and PLO supporter, the Israeli army did nothing, intervening only when the mob marched to his home and seemed to threaten him personally' (Shipler, 1987, p. 177).[19]

---

[19] In fact Fatah tried to cooperate with the Muslim Brotherhood but was told that this would require 'the complete Islamization of the PLO, including the elimination of the PLO's left wing. "The Muslim Brotherhood leadership

The motive behind Israeli support for Islamists is also supported by Palestinians – for example, Rema Hammami of Bir Zeit University, Ramallah, has argued that:

> Until the Intifada, there was an objective coalition of interest between al Mujama'a and the Israelis in thwarting PLO hegemony. A number of Israeli security experts admitted that the Islamists were allowed to flourish as a tactical means to undermine Palestinian nationalists. The movement's rhetoric and literature (until the Intifada) posed "communists" as the main threat to their social and political project (Hammami, 1999, p. 15).

Zaki Chehab (2007, p. 20) makes similar claims:

> The Israeli decision, despite obvious second thoughts, to grant the licence to the Islamic Compound ... was an indicator of what would become unannounced, but official, Israeli policy. The Israeli government perceived its staunch enemy to be the nationalist and secular PLO and, by allowing Islamist rivals to flourish, believed that opposing Palestinian groups would do its work on the ground in a way that did not necessitate active Israeli involvement.

In an article written at the beginning of 1989, Lisa Taraki sheds yet more light on this neglected phenomenon:

> ... which has some currency in the occupied territories ... that the Israeli intelligence services have incited or at least encouraged Hamas to sow discord and disunity among Palestinians. The history of the relationship between the Muslim Brethren and the national movement, and the long-held suspicion on the part of the movement that the Brethren were encouraged by occupation authorities help give credence to this interpretation (Taraki, 1989, p. 32).

---

urged Fatah to purge its ranks of Marxist elements, to be aware of the futility of secularism, and to cooperate closely with the Islamic groups'" (Dreyfuss, 2005, p. 207).

Palestine/Israel: The Epicentre

In her defence of this assertion, she cites the Israeli journalist Yehuda Litani who, in the *Jerusalem Post*, September 8th 1988, stated:

> 'until [a] few years ago, some Israeli officials thought the best way to fight the PLO was to encourage the Moslem fundamentalists in the territories. Some of the fundamentalist groups did receive help and encouragement from the Israeli authorities ...' *(loc. Cit)*.

Actually, rather than 'some years ago', the support for Islamists occurred up till the beginning of the intifada. As Philip Wilcox, head of the US Consulate in Jerusalem at the time, states: '[t]here were persistent rumors that the Israeli secret service gave covert support to Hamas, because they were seen as a rival to the PLO' (cited in Dreyfuss, 2005, p. 208).

In an interview with the Italian newspaper *Corriere della Sierra* in December 2001, PLO leader Yasser Arafat gave credence to this view by unequivocally stating 'Hamas is a creature of Israel, which, at the time of Prime Minister Shamir, gave them money and more than 700 institutions, among them schools, universities, and mosques'. He further claimed that former Israeli Prime Minister Yitzhak Rabin admitted support for Hamas to him, which he described as a 'fatal error' (cited in Dreyfuss, *op. cit.*, p. 209).

So there appears to be persuasive evidence that Israel was providing resources and tacit support to Islamists before and at the beginning of the first intifada; doubtless to the embarrassment of both parties. In fact, this is entirely consistent reasoning on the part of the Israeli state: any colonial or occupying power will endeavour to implement a 'divide-and-rule' approach which, as we saw in the previous chapter, may require forging 'unholy alliances' so as to weaken the resistance to its rule and Israel has been no exception in this regard. Though the PLO, the dominant nationalist movement, had not provided much effective opposition, compounded by a corrupt political culture under the dictatorial leadership of Yasser Arafat, the stated goal of a democratic, unitary, non-sectarian state[20] in historic Palestine for all who lived on the land, was a threat to Israel as a Jewish state and provided, in principle, a unifying banner to all Palestinians, no matter their religion or ethnicity. In principle, this was also an appealing scenario to the few Jewish Israelis who had become disillusioned with Zionism. All this naturally was quite unpalatable to Zionists of all persuasions. Accordingly, it would be to Israel's advantage to break PLO's dominance over Palestinian politics and, to this end, the advent of Islamists in general and Hamas in particular, provided a welcome opportunity. Israel well-understood that Hamas's politics were deeply alienating to Christian Palestinians and non-religious Palestinians from a Muslim background: like its Islamist counterparts elsewhere that were utilised by the British and the Americans, Hamas could, therefore, be seen as a fifth column in the heart of the nationalist Palestinian body politic.

If Hamas's politics were alienating to broad swathes of the non-Muslim, non-religious Palestinian population, they were complete anathema to all Israeli Jews. A Palestinian organisation whose *raison d'être* was to bring about the Islamisation of the entirety of historic Palestine was naturally the worst nightmare for all Zionists but was also intolerable for those Jews prepared to oppose the discriminatory basis of the Zionist state. So, from this perspective, Hamas served Israel well.

Echoing Yitzhak Rabin's view that supporting Hamas was a 'fatal error', Avi Shlaim (2000, p. 459) argues that such divide and rule tactics 'backfired disastrously' when the first intifada radicalised Hamas so that its actions went beyond the law – from throwing stones to use of firearms and, from 1994, recourse to suicide bombings. But this would (or ought) not be the objective view of hard-line Zionists (notably Benjamin Netanyahu, leader of the Likud party and 'ultra-Zionists' such as Yisrael Beitenu [Israel Our Home] led by Avigdor

---

[20] Ghada Karmi (2007, p. 240) points out that Yasser Arafat only once used the term 'secular state' but soon retracted it.

Lieberman) who gained great political support from Hamas's increasing use of violence and terror – which later included rocket attacks from the Gaza strip after Israel's withdrawal in 2005. That said, in 2006, months after the Palestinian elections, Israel's view of Hamas's victory in the elections to the Palestinian Authority was resoundingly clear: it bombed Gaza. This would prove to be the precursor to an even greater assault some two and half years later. Israel and Palestinian Islamists had become irreconcilable enemies.

When, in December 2008, Israel launched a military offensive against Hamas in Gaza (to which they gave the name 'Operation Cast Lead') 94% of Jewish Israelis 'strongly supported the action' (cited in Ben Meir, 2009)[21] – an assault that led to about 1400 deaths including 341 children and massive destruction of the strip (Goldstone Report, 2009, p. 106).[22] A Report of the United Nations Fact Finding Mission on the Gaza Conflict in September 2009 (otherwise known as The Goldstone Report) found that Israel had committed war crimes and possibly crimes against humanity. This attack was supposedly an act of self-defence against Hamas rockets yet '[f]rom 28 June 2004, when the first fatalities from rocket fire were recorded, to 17 June 2008, 21 Israeli citizens, including two Palestinian citizens of Israel, two Palestinians and one foreign worker were killed inside Israel as a result of rocket attacks and mortar fire' (Goldstone Report, 2009, p. 457). Such a stark contrast led to a widespread belief (including among

---

[21] In stark contrast, 85 per cent of Israeli Arabs *opposed* it (*loc. Cit.*).

[22] According to the Government of Israel, during the military operations there were 4 Israeli fatal casualties in southern Israel, of whom 3 were civilians and one soldier, killed by rockets and mortars attacks by Palestinian armed groups. In addition, 9 Israeli soldiers were killed during the fighting inside the Gaza strip, 4 of whom as a result of friendly fire (Goldstone Report, 2009, p. 11). Disregarding the distinction between oppressor and oppressed, and the enormous disparity in the death toll (1400 Palestinians compared to 13 Israelis), the Goldstone Report deemed Hamas also to have committed war crimes.

those who were sympathetic to Israel) that Israel's response had been 'disproportionate'.

We can sum up the political consequence of Hamas's policies as the further cementing of Israeli control and hardening of its stance on Gaza. On the one hand, the suicide bombings gave Israel the pretext to build a 'separation barrier' (referred to by Palestinians as a colonial or apartheid wall) that ate into even more territory of the Palestinians and, on the other, the rocket attacks led to the devastation of Gaza. In Israel itself, the hard-line stance was not challenged in the least: Zionism had become harsher still, fulfilling the advocacy of Jabotinsky's 'Iron Wall'. In this military battle between Zionism and Islamism, Zionism had clearly come out on top – but Israel's moral standing suffered gravely.

Throughout the world, including in the West, there was much sympathy for Gazans and outrage at Israeli attacks on innocents – but very little, in many quarters, for Hamas which was still shunned as a terrorist group by Western powers and viewed as being not much better than Al Qaeda.[23] There was even the sense that Israel had the right to defend itself from Hamas acts of terrorism but that it had used disproportionate power. That is to say, global hostility to Israeli aggression did not translate into appreciable support for Hamas.

A crucial factor in the appeal of Hamas's politics to Palestinians in the occupied territories was its refusal to support the Oslo Accords of 1993, and its refusal to recognise Israel – the very policies most unacceptable to Israel and its sponsor the

---

[23] The Israelis, however, have long understood that Western governments often pay lip-service to the wishes of their populations in regard to foreign policy. This was succinctly summed up the former Labour MP Lorna Fitzsimons who, after losing her seat in the 2005 elections, became a PR agent for Israel. Speaking at a conference for Israel's leaders in 2010 she assured them they didn't have to worry about the British people's growing opposition to their policies because 'public opinion does not influence foreign policy in Britain. Foreign policy is an elite issue' (cited in Fisk, 2010).

Palestine/Israel: The Epicentre

USA. Because it did not support Oslo, it did not, in 1996, contest elections to the body set up by the Accords, the Palestinian Authority (PA). But, sensing the disillusionment with the Oslo process and with Fatah, which controlled the PA, Hamas decided to contest the elections in 2006. This was astute political judgement for, to the surprise of all the key players, it won a remarkable victory in free and fair elections. For Israel, Hamas had done its job rather too well: it had certainly become a strong pole of attraction to large numbers of Palestinians, thereby fissuring the legitimacy and unifying umbrella of the PLO under the tutelage of its largest faction Fatah. But, on the downside, its raison d'être had become resolute resistance to Israel, something which had been abandoned by the nationalist elements, and this was quite intolerable to Israel. Naturally, considerable back-pedalling ensued: the democratic legitimacy of Hamas was cast aside as it was relentlessly denigrated as a terrorist organisation with which absolutely no negotiations would take place. The subtext was clear: Hamas must now be crushed.

In this endeavour, Israel was supported by the 'Quartet' (USA, EU, Russia, and the UN) which imposed sanctions against a democratically elected organisation. But, importantly, Israel also received backing from Fatah (who refused to relinquish control of the PA's security forces) and who had become de facto Israel's agents in the occupied territories. Further important assistance came from Egypt by its closure of the Rafah crossing to Gaza as it suited President Mubarak that Hamas be removed, given its links with the Muslim Brotherhood in Egypt, an organisation which the dictator had long feared as a serious threat to his rule.

Indeed, prior to the bombing of Gaza in December 2008, Israel had consulted with both Egypt and Fatah as is evidenced by a Wikileaks cable sent from the US embassy in Tel Aviv, reported in the *New York Times* on June 19th 2011. In a June 2009 meeting between Defence Minister Ehud Barak and a US congressional delegation:

Barak made clear in these meetings that he feels the Palestinian Authority is weak and lacks self-confidence, and that Gen. Dayton's training helps bolster confidence. *He explained that the GOI [Government of Israel] had consulted with Egypt and Fatah prior to Operation Cast Lead* [emphasis added by RH], *asking if they were willing to assume control of Gaza once Israel defeated Hamas. Not surprisingly, Barak said, the GOI received negative answers from both. He stressed the importance of continued consultations with both Egypt and Fatah – as well as the NGO community – regarding Gaza reconstruction ...*

This explains why both Mubarak of Egypt and Mahmoud Abbas of Fatah retained a diplomatic silence when Operation Cast Lead commenced. The hope for the three, in this unholy alliance, was that Hamas would be swept aside in Gaza by the Israeli assault. Though Fatah told the Israelis that it would not 'assume control of Gaza', this was clearly disingenuous given the bloody battle it had waged with Hamas after the 2006 elections for precisely the control of Gaza and West Bank under Israel's tutelage. However, contrary to their hopes and expectations, Hamas remained intact and in firm control of Gaza though it is unclear whether its popularity was strengthened as a result. Certainly, the mantle of resistance to Israel had unequivocally passed to Hamas as Fatah became increasingly discredited by its collaborationist stance. Indeed, in the conflict between Israel and Hamas, Fatah appeared to have come out worst.

True, there was widespread condemnation of Israel's attack – leading to the UN's Goldstone Report which, as already noted, concluded that Israel had committed war crimes but, as we saw, support for the assault among Jewish Israelis was overwhelming so that 'ultra-Zionism' was shored up. To reiterate: Hamas's ideology, means and ends, were an affront to even those Israelis who had become disillusioned with Zionism, the *soi disant* liberals and 'post-Zionists'. The clash between Islamism and Zionism provides a clear motif: both reinforce each other, providing grist for each other's mills.

For all its faults, Hamas has not gone along with Israel's diktats, in keeping with its emphasis on resistance, which has added to its credibility among many Palestinians, including those not enamoured with its religiosity. Globally, however, Hamas's campaign of suicide bombings and rocket attacks significantly weakened the justice of the Palestinian case. Hamas's attempts to explain these acts as retaliatory measures against Israeli killings of innocent Palestinians and use of the Islamic doctrine of *jihad* in justification fell on deaf ears. Post 9/11, this became the case *a fortiori*.

Moreover, despite the fear that suicide bombings in particular instilled among Israelis, the tactic played politically into Israel's hands as it relentlessly used the argument that, like the US, it was confronting Islamic terrorism. A cold political calculation might lead to the judgement that the price paid in terms of fatalities was more than offset by the political gain. Furthermore, year on year, the casualties inflicted by Israel on Palestinians were enormously in excess of the reverse, a stark fact that was invariably ignored in the West. Of far greater prominence was that the 'terrorist' tag once more became pinned onto Palestinians and so facilitated the reversing of the roles of coloniser/colonised and aggressor/victim.[24]

The Israeli state, the global Israel Lobby, and its supporters had in combination played a superb role in shielding Israel from significant harm and in this they were helped inordinately by the absence of opposition from Palestinians on the ideological and propaganda front. Yet, for all the 'hard' and 'soft' power at Israel's disposal and the ineptitude of the Palestinian leaderships (be they Hamas or Fatah), the thorny problem of pacifying a colonial people persisted. We can surmise that it was this that led to the Israeli academic Arnon Soffer, in an article to the *Jerusalem Post* in 2004, to proffer the following gory advice:

> So, if we want to remain alive, we have to kill and kill and kill. All day, every day ... If we don't kill, we will cease to exist ... Unilateral separation doesn't guarantee 'peace' – it guarantees a Zionist-Jewish state with an overwhelming majority of Jews (Cited in Pappe, 2006, p. 248).

---

[24] This role reversal was highlighted in a book edited by Edward Said and (in retrospect, most surprisingly) Christopher Hitchens in 1988 with the title *Blaming the Victims*.

Dangerous Liaisons

The Marxist historian and biographer, Isaac Deutscher, soon after the Six Day War of 1967, provided a famous, poignant, parable (in a talk to an Israeli audience) to describe the essence of the Palestine-Israeli conflict:

> A man once jumped from the top floor of a burning house in which many members of his family had already perished. He managed to save his life; but as he was falling to the ground, he hit a person standing down below and broke that person's legs and arms. The jumping man had no choice; yet to the man with the broken limbs he was the cause of his misfortune. If both behaved rationally, they would not become enemies. The man who escaped from the blazing house, having recovered, would have tried to help and console the other sufferer; and the latter who might have realized that he was the victim of circumstances over which neither of them had control. But look what happens when these people behave irrationally. The injured man blames the other for his misery and swears to make him pay for it. The other one, afraid of the crippled man's revenge, insults him, kicks him and beats him up whenever they meet. The kicked man again swears revenge and is again punched and punished. The bitter enmity, so whimsical at first, hardens and comes to overshadow the whole existence of both men and to poison their minds.
>
> You will, I am sure, recognize yourselves (I said to my Israeli audience), the Israeli remnants of European Jewry, in the man who jumped from the blazing house. The other character represents, of course, the Palestine Arabs, more than a million of them, who have lost their lands and their homes. They are resentful; they gaze from across the frontiers on their old native places; they raid you stealthily, and swear revenge. You punch and kick them mercilessly; you have shown that you know how to do it. But what is the sense of it? And what is the prospect?
>
> The responsibility for the tragedy of European Jews, for Auschwitz, Majdanek, and the slaughters in the ghetto, rests entirely on our western bourgeois 'civilization', of which Nazism was the legitimate, even though degenerate, offspring. Yet it was the Arabs who were made to pay the price for the crimes the West committed towards the Jews. They are still made to pay it, for the 'guilty conscience' of the West is, of course, pro-Israeli and anti-Arab. And how easily Israel has allowed itself to be bribed and fooled by the false 'conscience money'.

Palestine/Israel: The Epicentre

A rational relationship between Israelis and Arabs might have been possible if Israel had at least attempted to establish it, if the man who jumped from the burning house had tried to make friends with the innocent victim of his descent and compensate him. This did not happen. Israel never even recognized the Arab grievance. From the outset Zionism worked towards the creation of a purely Jewish state and was glad to rid the country of its Arab inhabitants. No Israeli government has ever seriously looked for any opportunity to remove or assuage the grievance ...' (Deutscher, 1967, p. 36).[25]

Setting aside all its inherent limitations, this parable seems *prima facie* illuminating and the bravery in speaking in such a candid and uncompromising manner to an Israeli Jewish audience is impressive. But there is a fundamental problem with it: it is a gross misrepresentation. Deutscher is suggesting that the Palestinians were the unfortunate, *accidental*, victims of another people fleeing persecution and genocide. Alas, a moment's reflection tells us that this reasoning is false to the point of being wilfully so. This was not an 'accident' but the outcome of a colonial-settler plan foretold with great clarity and honesty by its chroniclers going back to Herzl: the innocent Palestinian Arabs had long been the target of the Zionists – they were fully aware of it but too weak to provide much resistance. In other words, there is no justification grounded in justice (the 'Biblical mandate' most certainly does not provide this) as to why the suffering, displaced, Jews of Europe should then go on to displace an indigenous people of another land. As we have seen, the majority wished to settle in Western Europe or North America, but was prevented from doing so. In fact, Deutscher's parable unwittingly provides succour for the Zionist narrative;

---

[25] With a similar sentiment, in his book *Pity the Nation*, Robert Fisk provides a quote from Shlomo Green, a Jewish refugee from the Nazis upon learning that his home in Israel was taken from a Palestinian family in 1948: 'It is a tragedy of both our people ... I think the Arabs have same rights as the Jews and I think it is a tragedy of history that a people who are refugees make new refugees ... I don't know that we Jews did this tragedy – but it happened' (cited in Fisk, 1990, p. 12).

as such would never convince Arabs in general and Palestinians in particular.

A far better ethical stance, one firmly rooted in justice, was provided ten years before the creation of the State of Israel, in 1938, by another historian and political activist, Christian Arab George Antonius. Knowing full well the implications, for the indigenous people, of the creation of a Jewish state, Antonius, in *The Arab Awakening,* provides a clear refutation of Deutscher's reasoning:

> The treatment meted out to Jews in Germany and other European countries is a disgrace to its authors and to modern civilisation; but posterity will not exonerate any country that fails to bear its proper share of the sacrifices needed to alleviate Jewish suffering and distress. To place the brunt of the burden upon Arab Palestine is a miserable evasion of the duty that lies upon the whole civilised world. It is also morally outrageous. No code of morals can justify the persecution of one people in an attempt to relieve the persecution of another. The cure for the eviction of Jews from Germany is not to be sought in the eviction of Arabs from their homeland; and the relief of Jewish distress may not be accomplished at the cost of inflicting a corresponding distress upon an innocent and peaceful population (Antonius, 2000 [1938], p. 411).

In the midst of the 1948 war, with Jewish forces in the ascendant, Hannah Arendt bravely issued a sober warning, one which doubtless would have infuriated Zionists given that it emanated not from a Palestinian or Arab, but from a Jewish woman:

> And even if the Jews were to win the war, its end would find the unique possibilities and the unique achievements of Zionism in Palestine destroyed. The land that would come into being would be something quite other than the dream of world Jewry, Zionist and non-Zionist. The 'victorious' Jews would live surrounded by an entirely hostile Arab population, secluded into ever-threatened borders, absorbed with physical self-defense to a degree that would submerge all other interests and activities. The growth of a Jewish culture would cease to be the concern of the whole people; social experiments would have to be discarded as impractical luxuries;

political thought would center around military strategy ... And all this would be the fate of a nation that ... no matter how many immigrants it could still absorb and how far it extended its boundaries (the whole of Palestine and Transjordan is the insane Revisionist demand) ... would still remain a very small people greatly outnumbered by hostile neighbors (Arendt, 2007, [1948], p. 326).

With typical candour, David Ben-Gurion also clearly understood the Arabs' (and Palestinians') bitter enmity towards Israel, in a famous remark he made to the Zionist leader Nahum Goldmann, a few years after the creation of Israel:

> Why should the Arabs make peace? If I was an Arab leader I would never make terms with Israel. That is natural: we have taken their country. Sure, God promised it to us, but what does that matter to them? Our God is not theirs. We come from Israel, it's true, but two thousand years ago, and what is that to them? There has been anti-Semitism, the Nazis, Hitler, Auschwitz, but was that their fault? They only see one thing: we have come here and stolen their country. Why should they accept that? They may perhaps forget in one or two generations' time, but for the moment there is no chance. So it's simple: we have to stay strong and maintain a powerful army. Our whole policy is there. Otherwise the Arabs will wipe us out (cited in Goldmann, 1978, p. 99)[26].

The injustice of 'stealing their country' has still not been forgotten by Palestinians, millions of whom remain as refugees – many, as in the words of Mona Hamzeh – 'in their own land' (Hamzeh, 2001). To keep hold of the land and ensure not being 'wiped out', the Israeli state has indeed remained strong with a powerful military, which it has utilised frequently to wage myriad battles and wars with not only the dispossessed Palestinians but also with its Arab neighbours. What is beyond dispute – which Ben-Gurion would doubtless concur with – is that this profound injustice remains the epicentre of the conflict

---

[26] Though Goldmann does not provide the date of this remark, it is likely to be in 1955 or 1956.

between Israel and the Arabs and that between Zionists and Islamists.

Chapter 3

Israel and the Shia Islamists of Iran and Hezbollah

The greatest Islamist opponents of Zionism and Israel are not Hamas but the Islamic Republic of Iran and, especially, the Lebanese Shia group Hezbollah. However, just as the present hostility between Hamas and Israel had been pre-shadowed by a de facto alliance, so too was there an alliance of sorts between Israel and Iran in the 1980s. As we noted in chapter 1, Ayatollah Khomeini was strongly supportive of the Palestinians and railed against the 'Zionist regime'. But this was little more than posturing given that the new Islamic regime was far more concerned by two of its neighbours: Afghanistan which had come under Soviet occupation, and Iraq with whom it would wage a bloody war during the 1980s. That said, the relationship between Israel and Iran is not only pivotal to the region but of immense importance globally. This chapter examines how this relationship has evolved since the Iranian revolution before turning to the fierce clash between Israel and Hezbollah, Iran's Shia ally in Lebanon.

Israel and Iran: from discreet collaboration to confrontation

Though Shia comprise only about one tenth of all Muslims, in terms of opposition to Israel and Zionism, they have, since the 1980s, been by far the most outspoken. The roots of this policy stance and determination lie in the aftermath of the Iranian revolution of February 1979 and the ensuing hostility between the new Islamist regime of Ayatollah Ruhollah Khomeini and the US and Israel. Under the Shah, Israel had managed to forge close ties with Iran and naturally wished to re-activate them. This seemed *prima facie* wishful thinking given that Khomeini was deeply hostile to Zionism and Israel, and sympathetic to Palestinians. But, in reality, this was largely rhetorical as Iran was prepared to set aside principle for pragmatism so as to realise geo-political gains. The reason for this was the long-term rivalry and distrust between Iran (Shia Persians) and the Arab world (largely Sunni). Muslims they may all largely be but this did not provide sufficient cause for the erosion of mutual suspicion and for the forging of a unified Pan-Islamic bloc. In particular, both the Shah and Khomeini were fearful of Iraq as a dominant force in the Middle East – though having a Shia majority, its ruling elite under Saddam Hussein was Sunni. This fact needs stressing as it provides a major blow to the thesis by myriad Islamists of a de facto perpetual war on Islam by the US in cahoots with its Western allies and Israel. So, in 1998, Ayman Zawahiri and Osama Bin Laden called for a 'jihad against Jews and crusaders' (Wright, p. 259) but conveniently neglected the fact that Muslims were unendingly engaged in attacks on each other and that Iranian leaders feared their Arab co-religionists so much that they would be prepared to make alliances of convenience with the very 'crusaders and Jews' (meaning the US and Israelis) whom they wished to wage jihad against. Nonetheless, with aspirations of spreading the revolution, of a Shia vision of 'Pan Islamism' and ultimately of leading the Islamic world, the Iranian Ayatollahs had to tread carefully, that is to say, mask their dealings with Israel. Such a double game would ultimately prove extremely difficult.

The US too was playing a double game: whilst attempting to forge a dialogue with Iran after the fall of the Shah and the subsequent hostage crisis in the 1980s, they did not object when another strong man in the region whom they were nurturing as an ally – Saddam Hussein –launched an attack on Iran in September 1980. The reasoning behind this was that the Iranian revolution risked the spread of anti-Western Islamism. This was based on the judgement that unlike the Islamist movements and regimes that the US and UK had nurtured and supported and used as a battering ram against nationalist and leftist forces throughout the 20th century (highlighted in chapter 2), Khomeini's regime could not be won over to the Western camp. However, such a turn of events caused much concern to the US's closest ally, Israel, which did not wish to see a victorious and militarily strengthened Iraq. Consequently, to counter this unappealing vista, Israel attempted vigorously to forge closer links with Iran. Despite the denunciations made by Khomeini against Israel, Israeli leaders took the view that it was preferable – even necessary – to maintain a reasonable *modus vivendi* with Iran as a buffer against Iraq. Since its creation, a key foreign policy goal of Israel has been to prevent Arab unity with its threat of strong and meaningful support for the Palestinians. The Camp David Peace Agreement with Egypt in 1979 greatly assisted in this regard as the Arab world's largest and most important country had been effectively neutralised: to sweeten the pill, the US began to channel large sums of aid to Egypt. Attention turned to Iraq and Syria as potential threats, notwithstanding that the former was nominally in the US camp. Thus, Israel's attempts to fashion a reasonable relationship with Iran were based on the presumption that the Islamist regime's opposition to Zionism in principle would be outweighed by geopolitical realities – events of the 1980s did appear to offer support for this reasoning. Be that as it may, this was certainly an unholy alliance at its most extreme.

A comprehensive study of Israel-Iran (and US) relations since the Iranian revolution has been undertaken by Trita Parsi in *Treacherous Alliance* (2007) which the first part of this chapter draws on. Parsi (pp. xv-xvi) makes the important observation about Israel and Iran's relations in the 1980s:

Ironically, when Iran's leaders called for Israel's destruction in the 1980s, Israel and the pro-Israel lobby in Washington lobbied the US *not* to pay attention to Iranian rhetoric. ... The Iranian government in turn, has pursued a double policy throughout this period: in the 1980s Iran made itself the vocal regional supporter of the Palestinian cause yet its rhetoric was seldom followed up with action, since Iran's strategic interest – reducing tensions with Israel and using the Jewish state to re-establish relations with the US – contradicted Iran's ideological imperatives.

As an example of Iran's double game, in 1980, '[t]he Ayatollah declared August 17 Quds (Jerusalem) day and urged Muslims worldwide to demonstrate on that day in support of the Palestinians. In reality, however, the celebrations of Quds Day demonstrated Iran's unwillingness to deliver concrete support to the Palestinians' (*ibid*, p. 85). In the same vein, '[o]n August 14 1980, the Iranian Foreign Ministry called for an end to oil sales to countries that supported Israel. After much fanfare, the threat was never acted upon' (*ibid.,* p. 95).

Iran made other negative gestures towards Israel such as attempting to expel it from the UN knowing full well that this was a pipe dream though it played well to the Palestinian and Arab gallery. It sponsored a children's drawing/writing contest in numerous Islamic countries on the theme of 'Israel must be erased from the earth'; it pledged to send Iraqi prisoners-of-war to fight Israel in Lebanon; and proposed the creation of an Islamic army to force Israel out of the occupied territories. Parsi argues that Iran's anti-Israel stance was 'to alleviate Arab threats to Iran or at least make it more costly for Arab governments to support Iraq' (*ibid.,* pp. 101-102). But all of this was to no avail given that, precisely because such rhetoric was popular with the Arab masses, the Arab governments took fright and supported Saddam even more (*loc. cit.*).

As stressed above, throughout the 1980s, Israel was anxious to maintain good relations with Iran, as it had previously done with the Shah. It pursued the 'periphery doctrine' whereby Iran (a geographically peripheral country) was viewed as providing a counterbalance to the hostile 'core' (in close geographical proximity) of Arab countries. This was an entirely rational approach given the animosity between Shia Iran and the Sunni Arabs, in view of Iran's claims to the leadership of the Muslim world and desire to export its Shia revolution. Unlike so many in the West, the Israelis fully understood this sharp religious-political antagonism – and wished to take advantage of it. Given that for both Iran and Israel, Sunni Arab states were deemed to be enemies, there was certainly the potential for at least a working relationship, if not a warm embrace.

Matters were greatly helped in this endeavour by Iraq's attack on Iran in September 1980 on the pretext of an alleged Iranian assassination attempt on Iraq's Foreign Minister, Tariq Aziz, which led to an 8 year long war costing some one million lives. Iraq was bankrolled by the Gulf States – in particular by Saudi Arabia and Kuwait – of which the US, though remaining ostensibly neutral, quietly approved (*ibid,* p. 98). What was doubtless galling for the Iranians was that not only the PLO but also Islamists supported their fellow Arabs and not Iran in the war. Olivier Roy points out the reason for this. During the war, Khomeini coined the slogan 'the road to Jerusalem goes through Karbala [in Iraq]', meaning that before fighting Israel, we must defeat Saddam Hussein. 'It is precisely for this reason that Sunni Arab Islamic movements (the Muslim Brotherhood, for example) have refused to support Islamic Iran against the conservative Arab regimes, even though the latter repress them' (Roy, 2007, p. 85)

However, rather than Israel finding itself more dependent on Iran, it was the latter that suddenly found itself in desperate need of Israel – so as to access US arms. After the Americans were evicted from Iran, following the revolution of 1979, US-Iran relations became frozen: the US refused to deliver to Iran armaments ordered by the Shah. Moreover, much of Iranian military hardware was American and the US also refused to supply spare parts. Hence, Iran resorted to using Israeli intermediaries – albeit discreetly as open relations with Israel would undermine Iran's standing and credibility with its Arab neighbours. Given the mutual enmity between Shia Iran and Sunni Arab states, such a view might be thought as over-sensitive – but what was decisive was that both Islamic camps did not recognise the legitimacy of Zionism. Parsi (*op. cit.,* p. 104) indicates Israel's reasoning thus:

At the height of Iran's ideological zeal, Israel's fear of an Iraqi victory, its dismissal of the dangers of Iran's political ideology, and its efforts to win Iran back and revive the periphery doctrine all paved the way for Israel's policy of arming Iran and seeking to defuse tensions between Washington and Tehran ... A majority of Israeli officials, including Yitzhak Rabin, continued to believe that Iran was a "natural ally" of Israel.

Deputy Defence Minister Mordechai Zippori stated, soon after Iraq invaded Iran: 'Israel has the possibility to extend significant aid to Iran and enable it, from the logistical point of view, to continue its war with Iraq. Of course this cannot take place as long as there is no serious change in the extremist Iranian regime' (*ibid.,* p. 105). But it did take place without any change in the nature of the regime as Israel negotiated with Iran the sale of arms and spare parts. The Iranian arms dealer, Ahmed Haidari, estimated that some 80 per cent of weapons bought by Iran immediately after its war with Iraq began, originated in Israel. Between 1980-83, Iran purchased over $500 million worth of arms from Israel – mostly paid by delivery of Iranian oil to Israel (*ibid.,* pp. 106, 107).

In the midst of the Iran-Iraq war, on 7th June 1981, Israel fighter jets destroyed the Iraqi nuclear reactor at Osirak. According to Ari-Ben Menashe, who was involved in Israel-Iran contacts, Israeli officials discussed the attack with their Iranian counterparts – Iran had apparently launched an unsuccessful attack on the facility in September 1980, soon after the outbreak of war. He claimed that Iran had provided Israel with photographs and maps of the plant and agreed to permit Israeli planes to land in Tabriz in the case of an emergency. Though top secret and despite Iranian denials, Iraq suspected collusion and accused the Iranians of fighting Israel's war. Later, the PLO protested at what it thought were Iranian double standards towards the Palestinians (*ibid.,* p. 107). But Defence Minister Ariel Sharon went public with the collaboration in May 1982 admitting that Israel had indeed supplied Iran with arms and ammunition because Iraq was 'dangerous to the peace process in the Middle East' ... and to "leave a small window open" to the possibility of good relations with Iran in the future'. His hope was that this would naturally further alienate and isolate Iran from the Arab world and increase its reliance on Israel. Unsurprisingly, Khomeini was furious with this breach of the secret pact and denied the allegations (*ibid.,* p. 108).

But this did not derail the collaboration as the war with Iraq dragged on and Iran's need for weapons remained strong. Hassan Karoubi, a close confidant of Khomeini's, explained the reasoning to Israelis in 1985:

> America can rescue Iran from its difficult position. We are interested in cooperating with the West. We have common interests and wish to be part of the West. A defeat in the war with Iraq would turn Iran into a Soviet satellite ... unless America and

Israel and the Shia Islamists of Iran and Hezbollah

Israel discreetly intervened ... Our region and yours, can expect a physical threat from the Soviet Union. We fear the Soviets and the Left in our country' (*ibid.,* pp. 118-119).

The upshot was that Iran received missiles from Israel in return for putting pressure on Hezbollah to release four American hostages – the prelude to the Iran-Contra scandal whereby then US President, Ronald Reagan, acknowledged that, despite an arms embargo on Iran, the US had secretly sold arms to Iran and transferred the proceeds to the Contras in Nicaragua fighting the democratically elected Sandinista government. Whilst Israel's Abba Eban bullishly stated 'it's our right to sell arms to Iran', the Iranians were again embarrassed: the head of the Iranian Parliament Rafsanjani unambiguously declared 'we have never negotiated with Israel ... for arms purchases' (*ibid.,* pp. 124-125).

Whilst Iran publicly claimed there was a chasm between itself and Israel, the Israelis continued to offer olive branches. Thus, in October 1987, Defence Minister Yitzhak Rabin stated 'Iran is Israel's best friend and we do not intend to change our position in relation to Tehran, because Khomeini's regime will not last forever' (*ibid.,* p. 128). But Rabin's adviser Yossi Alpher provided the logic to the olive branches and rationale for the 'periphery doctrine':

Iraq is getting stronger every day by acquiring chemical and non-conventional arms that threaten us. There is a reason to see to it that Iran can continue confronting and diverging the Iraqi forces ... Beyond that, Iran has oil, Iran has Jews and all these are good reasons for renewal of connections with Iran, without any relation to the governing regime (*ibid.,* p. 131).

But Eliezer Tsafrir (head of the Mossad in Iran and Iraq, in the 1960s and '70s) provided a more sobering assessment: '[h]owever ideological and Islamic, everything Iran was doing was nationalistic, and even similar to the Shah' (*ibid.,* p. 129).

After Ayatollah Khomeini's death in 1989, Iran attempted to tone down its rhetoric and improve relations with the west and the Arab states – but it never attempted to forge any sort of alliance with Israel. At the same time, it refrained, as ever, from providing Palestinians with meaningful support. Indeed it was alienated by the anti-Shia Palestinian Muslim Brotherhood's support for Iraq in the war against Iran.[27] Though Iran remained hostile to Israel, it adopted a rather more detached stance as expressed by Mohsen Mirdamadi, former member of the Foreign Relations Committee of the Iranian Parliament:

> Our position was to respect whatever solution the Palestinians agreed to. If the Palestinians would agree to a two-state solution, we would not protest. We wouldn't support it, but neither would we object to it. But the policy of not objecting was in essence a policy of indirectly supporting it' (*ibid.*, p. 134).

The political dynamic had, however, changed significantly at the beginning of the 1990s which would lead to Israel's *volte face* on Iran. The defeat of Iraq in February 1991 and the collapse of the Soviet Union at the end of the same year meant that two of Iran's greatest perceived enemies had been neutralised. Accordingly, the need to have even surreptitious links with Israel would be greatly reduced. Israel understood this clearly so that from advocating a policy of rapprochement and cajolement, Iran became a serious threat which must be countered. Ephraim Sneh, Labor Member of the Knesset, pithily argued that 'Iran is a dangerous combination – a regime that wants our destruction that may get nuclear capacity' (Parsi, *op. cit.*, p. 162). Israel now wanted the US to take action against Iran arguing that Iran presented a danger not only to Israel but to the entire western world. The Israel Lobby, led by AIPAC (American Israel Public Affairs Committee), went into overdrive; its crowning achievement being the Iran Libya Sanctions Act passed in 1996 (*ibid.*, pp. 163, 188). This was accompanied by the US ratcheting up its denunciations of Iran. Ineluctably, Iran and Israel began to pull apart – this was the

---

[27] Otherwise known as *Mujama*, it was, in fact, ordered not to support Khomeini by Saudi Arabia, its main source of funds. But, as noted in the previous chapter, a splinter group – Islamic Jihad – broke away from the Brotherhood by proclaiming support for the Iranian revolution (Milton-Edwards, 1996, pp. 119-120).

post-Oslo period and Iran began to support the Palestinian rejectionist Islamist group Hamas – who, in turn, reciprocated thereby quietly forgetting Iran's Shi-ism.

After being elected President in August 2005, Mahmoud Ahmadinejad intensified the venomous rhetoric against Israel; a marker that there would be no going back to clandestine negotiations. In October 2005 he made the incendiary assertion '[t]his regime that is occupying Quds [Jerusalem] must be eliminated from the pages of history' (*ibid.,* p. 1). He followed this up by questioning the Nazi Holocaust, something that no previous Iranian leader had done, and, by so doing, also greatly alienated many Europeans: '[t]oday, they have created a myth in the name of Holocaust and consider it to be above God, religion, and the prophets ... If you [Europeans] committed this big crime, then why should the oppressed Palestinian nation pay the price? ... You [Europeans] have to pay the compensation yourself' (*ibid.,* p. 264).

Trita Parsi uses the reasoning provided by a senior Iranian official (whose name is not provided) to point out that the rhetoric had strategic motives:

> [P]eople close to Ahmedinajad favoured putting into question issues Israel had managed to settle over the past two decades: Israel's legitimacy and right to exist, the reality of the Holocaust, and the right of European Jews to remain in the heart of the Middle East. Such an approach, they argued, would resonate with the discontented Arab street and reveal the impotence of the pro-US Arab regimes, which would be in equal parts pressured and embarrassed (*loc. cit.*).

In actual fact, Ahmedinajad's outburst played to Israel's claim that Iran was a danger that needed to be tackled; an argument which the Europeans too began to warm to. Thus, Israel and its lobby further intensified pressure on the US to take military action against Iran, to destroy its nuclear installations, just as they had relentlessly pushed for – and got – war against Iraq (Mearsheimer and Walt, 2007, chs. 8, 10). That this did not happen is in good measure due to the USA being tied up in Afghanistan and Iraq: a third war might have broken the back of the US military and severely jeopardised these two campaigns.

Crucially, however, the core reason for going into war against Iraq – weapons of mass destruction – was soon shown to be demonstrably false, so that a similar false pretext for waging war on Iran would provoke even more global outrage and opposition and, indubitably, a most ferocious response from Iran – including attacks against US forces in Iraq. Such a vista was indeed sobering for some in the Bush administration and in the US defence establishment – many of whom were warning against another war. Thus, on September 27 2007, *The Boston Globe* reported that:

> The Army's top officer, General George Casey, told Congress yesterday that his branch of the military has been stretched so thin by the war in Iraq that it cannot adequately respond to another conflict - one of the strongest warnings yet from a military leader that repeated deployments to war zones in the Middle East have hamstrung the military's ability to deter future aggression.

In the seemingly inexorable build up to another destructive war, a *deus ex machina* appeared: a report by the US intelligence agencies in 2007 clearly stated that Iran had given up its nuclear weapons programme in 2003 (Dombey and Ward, 2007). This provided much proverbial ammunition – and relief – for those in the Bush administration and the military wishing to avoid involving the US in another disastrous imbroglio.[28]

Curiously, however, no Western leader or the IAEA pointed out the elephant in the room: Israel's denunciations of Iran's nuclear programme ranked of the highest hypocrisy. Here was a state which refused to sign up to the Non-Proliferation Treaty (NPT), never had any nuclear inspections – and had amassed (notwithstanding evasions and denials) a large arsenal of nuclear weapons – but ceaselessly called for military action from the country which had the largest stockpile of weapons to destroy nuclear installations of a country which had joined the

---

[28] Gabriel Kolko (2009, p. 121) points out that the US lost a simulated war game with Iran in August 2002 and 'it would lose again as the Iranian military has become far more potent'.

NPT and which did not possess nuclear weapons. The fact that Iran argued its right, under the NPT, to develop nuclear power for civilian purposes was wilfully ignored; moreover nuclear inspectors were not to be trusted, and nor was the report by US intelligence agencies. The only acceptable remedy was that meted out by Israel to Iraq's Osirak plant in 1981, against a myriad of international laws and conventions.

This stark hypocrisy was also almost never commented on by the media and leaders in the West, who simply internalised the double standard. The presumption was clearly that Israel had legitimate reasons to develop and stockpile nuclear weapons – and could be trusted with them – to deter aggressor states in its vicinity. By comparison, Iran could not be so trusted, and so had no right to develop its own similar deterrent against a state that was unremittingly hostile to it. This is one instance of a catalogue of double standards that rankles so many, not least Islamists. It has naturally been a gift to the latter's politicking and propaganda against the West in general and Israel in particular. Iran's strategy, however, has also been to underplay the fact of Israel's nuclear arsenal – presumably to ward off any inference that Iran is using this as reason to develop its own nuclear weapons. That said, in April 2010, at the opening of the First International Conference on Disarmament and Non-Proliferation held in Tehran, President Ahmedinajad asserted that Israel's nuclear arsenal is safeguarded by the United States, while Iran is prevented from establishing its peaceful nuclear energy program (*Haaretz*, 2010). But, unsurprisingly, the conference and Ahmedinajad's speech, was largely ignored by the Western media.

Be that as it may, the threats and sanctions against Iran continued – even under the Obama regime. In October 2011, the US Attorney General Eric Holder provided details of a plot by an Iranian agent to assassinate the Saudi ambassador to the US. In a thinly veiled threat, President Obama warned Iran of dire consequences and further isolation, meaning the ratcheting up of sanctions and – analogous to what the US did to Iraq in 2003 – using the plot as a pretext for launching a war. Though these are likely to be piped up charges, and bluster to boot, Israel and the lobby would naturally have been delighted; and this might well indeed have been the prime motivation for the US President going public with such a flimsy, implausible, plot in the run up to the 2012 presidential election. Julian Borger set out a list of probing 'unanswered questions' regarding this assassination plot in *The Guardian* – suggesting it had the ring of a far-fetched Hollywood thriller. However, his question 8 was particularly poignant: '[c]ould the alleged plot be provocation by an outside agency seeking to start a conflict between Iran and its enemies?' (Borger, 2011).

As if choreographed, almost immediately after the 'Iran plot', in November 2011, the IAEA issued a report which suggested that Iran's nuclear programme could be used for weapons production (*BBC News,* 2011). Again, bellicose voices came out of Israel and the US asked for yet more sanctions against Iran – with the EU and Japan nodding in agreement. But, again, Iran rejected the IAEA findings and dismissed the threat of sanctions – adamantly adhering to the line that its nuclear ambitions were solely for civilian use. The ratcheting up of tensions raises the probability of a conflagration to dangerous levels as was pointed out by two former CIA analysts, Ray McGovern and Elizabeth Murray, in an article of 30th December 2011:

> '[a]n accident, or provocation, could spiral out of control quickly, with all sides — Iran, the U.S. and Israel making hurried decisions with, you guessed it, "unintended consequences" ... or Intended Consequences'? (McGovern and Murray, 2011).

What might the consequences – intended or unintended – be following an Israeli strike against Iran? First, it will be thought by Iranians and many others besides, including almost the entirety of the masses of Arab and Muslim worlds, as being sanctioned by America; the level of anger and protest would be enormous, accompanied by vigorous demands for swift and decisive retribution. Iran will, of course, immediately retaliate, with every possibility of being assisted by Hezbollah (see next section) and strikes against American ships in the Strait of Hormuz and its closure cannot be ruled out; as well as likely strikes against oil wells in the gulf. Inexorably, the price of oil will escalate and global stock markets tumble. Uprisings by the Shia in Bahrain and Saudi Arabia will be inevitable and Iran will naturally seek closer alliances with China and Russia who would doubtless be offered oil at a heavily discounted price for providing Iran with some kind of diplomatic shield. The world economy, stagnant since 2008, will trip up further, triggering anger in Western heartlands – and this time, the ire of protestors will be aimed directly at Israel. The Israel Lobby will naturally use its immense power and influence to steer opinion against Iran but, after the fiasco of Afghanistan and Iraq, the likelihood of such manipulation succeeding for a sustained period is remote. And what of the aftermath? In all likelihood, Iran's rulers will expel IAEA inspectors, leave the NPT and move quickly towards the 'North Korean solution', that is, acquire nuclear weapons as deterrence against further strikes on it. Indeed, precisely such a scenario would be highly appealing to hardliners in the regime whose position would indubitably be strengthened.

Such a state of affairs – admittedly a small fraction of the true ramifications of an Israeli war of aggression against Iran – has certainly concentrated the minds of many in the American establishment despite the gung-ho views of Israeli hawks and the Israel Lobby in America. A new approach took hold at the beginning of 2012. In January, President Obama changed tack and ordered the postponement of joint US/Israel military exercises scheduled for April 2012 so as not to be drawn into any Israeli attack on Iran (see Porter and Lobe, 2012). In the same month, US Defence Secretary Leon Panetta stated that Iran has not yet decided to make a nuclear bomb, and cautioned against an Israeli strike (Birch, 2012). This was followed up by General Martin Dempsey, chairman of the U.S. Joint Chiefs of Staff, who averred that it would not be 'prudent' for Israel to launch a strike on Iran's nuclear facilities at this time, as it would cause instability in the Middle East and that sanctions are starting to influence Iran. He also thought Iran to be a 'rational actor' who has not yet decided whether to make a nuclear weapon (Mozgovaya, 2012). In April 2012, *Forbes* published an article with the heading 'Attacking Iran would push the US back into recession' (Fontevecchia, 2012). Without explicitly stating so, it was indubitably dawning on many key American players that Israel's and the Israel Lobby's threats against Iran were harming America's interest; in an election year, this was certainly concentrating the minds of some of the leading lights in the Obama administration

Further signs of cooling over Iran's nuclear programme came in May 2012 when the hawkish, pro-American, head of the IAEA, Yukiya Amano had talks in Tehran – which he described as 'positive' – with Iran's top nuclear negotiator, Saeed Jalili, with the aim of obtaining better access for his inspectors (*BBC News,* May 2012). This was soon followed by a meeting between Iran's nuclear negotiators and six world powers: China, France, Britain, Russia, the United States (the permanent members of the UN security council) and Germany (known as 'P5+1'). Oddly enough, the latter meeting was held in Baghdad at Iran's request; perhaps as a reminder to America and its allies of the folly of the invasion based on a pack of lies about Iraq's 'weapons of mass destruction'. Unsurprisingly, there was deadlock on the key issue of P5+1's demands for Iran to stop nuclear enrichment altogether. Iran has always insisted that it has the right to do so, for civilian purposes, under the NPT (Reynolds, 2012). Yet, the very fact of the talks took immediate military threats off the agenda – much to the disappointment to the Israeli and American hawks.

The grave consequences of an Israeli strike also affected the thinking of ordinary Israelis, who are normally most enthusiastic about their country's military adventures. An opinion poll conducted in February 2012 by the University of Maryland showed that only a small minority (19 per cent) supported an Israeli attack on Iran without US support; whilst 42 per cent support such a strike with American backing; and 34 per cent opposed any strike (UMD Newsdesk, 2012). It seemed that many Israelis were paying heed to the blunt advice proffered by *Haaretz* journalist Gideon Levy that 'Israelis should be afraid of their leaders, not Iran' (Levy, 2012).

Furthermore, the minds of several leading figures in the Israeli military and security establishments also became concentrated, as evidenced by quite unprecedented, forthright, criticisms of a pre-emptive strike against Iran. Perhaps the most brazen was by Yuval Diskin, who retired as head of the Shin Bet domestic intelligence service in 2011. In April 2012, he launched a blistering attack on Benjamin Netanyahu and Ehud Barak: 'I have no faith in the prime minister, nor in the defense minister ... I really don't have faith in a leadership that makes decisions out of messianic feelings' (cited in Williams, 2012). This followed a similarly blunt view by the former head of the Mossad, Meir Dagan, that attacking Iran was 'the stupidest idea I have ever heard of' (cited in Sherwood, 2012). Also in April 2012, in an interview with *Haaretz*, IDF's Chief of Staff Lt. Gen. Benny Gantz made a sobering assessment – with implied criticism of Netanyahu and Barak – to the effect that he did not think that Iran will develop nuclear weapons:

> If the supreme religious leader Ayatollah Ali Khamenei wants, he will advance it to the acquisition of a nuclear bomb, but the decision must first be taken. It will happen if Khamenei judges that he is invulnerable to a response. I believe he would be making an enormous mistake, and I don't think he will want to go the extra mile. I think the Iranian leadership is composed of very rational people (*Haaretz*, 2012).

What is 'rational' for Iran is highly debatable. In an interview with PBS' Charlie Rose in November 2011, Ehud Barak was asked whether he would strive for nuclear weapons had he been in Iran's shoes. Barak's response was remarkably candid: '[p]robably...I don't delude myself that they are doing it just because of Israel. They have their history of 4,000 years. They look around, they see the Indians are nuclear, the Chinese are nuclear, Pakistan is nuclear...Israel allegedly has it (military nuclear capability)' (cited in *YNetnews.com*, 2011). Similar sentiments had been expressed by the influential Israeli military theorist Martin van Creveld as far back as 2004 in an article for the *New York Times*: '[h]ad the Iranians not tried to build nuclear weapons, they would be crazy' (van Creveld, 2004).

Whilst a 'hot war' has not yet materialised, there is evidence of a covert war being waged by Israel against Iran, with likely assistance from the Americans (for example, a US spy drone crashed into Iranian territory in December 2011) involving assassinations of Iranian nuclear scientists, explosions at military bases, and the spread of computer worms. The extent of American involvement was revealed in June 2012 by David Sanger of the *New York Times* who reported that President Obama had ordered a wave of cyber attacks against Iran's nuclear facilities using cyberweapons ('Stuxnet' and 'Flame' worms) jointly developed with Israel (Sanger, 2012).

Saeed Dehghan argues, seemingly uncontroversi-ally, that a covert campaign aimed at disrupting Iran's nuclear and missile programmes represents an alternative to aerial bombing raids or full scale war and so, despite its illegality, is a better approach owing to fewer casualties and less confrontation with supporters of Iran, such as Russia and China (Dehghan, 2012). Though it is difficult to predict with any certainty the likely outcome of the Iran-Israel clash, we can be sure that irreconcilable hostility will remain: Israel desperately desires the removal of the Shia Islamist regime and will use all its resources to achieve this. A unilateral strike – or a joint one with the Americans – cannot be ruled out.

The consistent barrage of US and Israeli threats against Iran and the latter's refusal to wilt has given great credibility to the Islamic Republic throughout the Islamic world, including in Sunni majority countries. Muslims of all denominations across the globe have taken heart from the fact no Islamic country has dared to resist US pressure in such an uncompromising manner. Perhaps they could be excused for turning a blind eye to Iran's dalliance with Israel in the 1980s, given the subsequent firmness of the turnaround of policy and of practising what they preached. But there has been a profoundly damaging aspect to this clash, that is, that the Iranian regime has used this very real existential threat to bolster support at home and remain entrenched in power. This has doubtless undermined the efforts of democratic and progressive forces to topple the regime and bring about a new democratic order. As highlighted in chapter 1, in the past the US and UK supported Islamist groups and regimes *against* progressive forces; but since the mid-1990s, they have threatened and tried to isolate Iran, yet one of the most important consequences of this has been to bolster the Islamist regime and give it a pretext to crackdown on dissidents demanding democracy and freedoms, accusing them of being

Western lackeys.

Israel and Hezbollah: from confrontation to cold peace

In chapter 1, we quoted David Ben-Gurion regarding the 1948 Arab-Israeli War: 'the Arabs: they are such incompetents, it is difficult to imagine'. We might generalise this statement to assert that incompetence and impotence have been the lamentable history of Palestinian and Arab dealings with the ideology of Zionism and the State of Israel. That said, there are two exceptions to this devastating generalisation, which even the tough-minded Ben-Gurion would surely concede. The first is the early period of the 1973 October (Yom Kippur) War where the Egyptian and Syrian forces performed well by genuinely surprising the Israelis and making serious gains before the tide was quickly turned – partly because of later military incompetence but also because of US military aid to Israel (Golda Meir later acknowledged this by her gloomy admission: '[t]he war was a near disaster, a nightmare that I myself experienced and which will always be with me ... I found myself as Prime Minister, in a position of ultimate responsibility at a time when the state faced the greatest threat it had known') (cited in O'Ballance, 1979, p. 330).

The second is Israel's conflict with the Lebanese Shia group Hezbollah, the one Arab organisation whose history has been characterised by competence, determination, and potency. Hezbollah managed to do what no other Arab regime or group had done: to remove Israel by force from occupied land. After some 18 years of a guerrilla campaign, in 2000, Israel was forced to withdraw from South Lebanon. Hezbollah followed this up by inflicting real damage on Israel and its hitherto exalted military in the war of July/August 2006; including taking the battle into Israel itself by a sustained barrage of shelling.

After being evicted from Jordan in 1970, the PLO had set up its base in Beirut and launched raids into Israel from south Lebanon. In the midst of civil war, which had broken out in 1975, Israel invaded and occupied southern Lebanon in 1978 and armed Lebanese militias to fight PLO guerrillas. In 1982, following the murder of its ambassador to London, Israel invaded much of Lebanon, including Beirut. The invasion duly removed the PLO from its Lebanese redoubt but at the cost of killing some 20,000 people. Ostensibly to prevent the return of the PLO, Israel occupied southern Lebanon. An iron law of military occupation is that it engenders resistance – including armed resistance. This duly occurred and with great alacrity in south Lebanon; the key protagonists were, however, not Palestinians but Lebanese Shia Muslims, including what would become the *Hezbollah* or party of god. Whilst the leaders of Christian and Sunni Muslim groups gave support to Israel's attack on the PLO, as they felt threatened by the PLO's increasing power and influence in Lebanese politics, the Shia largely sympathised with them and resolutely opposed Israel's assault – the casualties of which were from all of Lebanon's confessional communities. In response to foreign occupation, on 23rd October 1983, Iranian-backed Islamists unleashed suicide bombers against the US marine barracks in Lebanon killing 241, mostly marines; this was followed by a suicide bombing on a French military compound that killed 58 paratroopers (Fisk, 1990, p. 515). Resistance to Israel and its international allies had begun in earnest as the US and French pulled out. From this devastating attack would emerge Hezbollah.

Hezbollah's politics have not been as codified as Hamas's. It openly declared its existence when it provided a de facto outline of a programme in a short 'open letter to the downtrodden in Lebanon and in the world' in 1985, taking inspiration from the Iranian revolution. The principal goals are laid out in a section 'Our Objectives':

> Let us put it truthfully: the sons of Hizballah know who are their major enemies in the Middle East – the Phalanges, Israel, France and the US. The sons of our *umma* are now in a state of growing confrontation with them, and will remain so until the realization of the following three objectives:
> (a) to expel the Americans, the French and their allies definitely from Lebanon, putting an end to any colonialist entity on our land;
> (b) to submit the Phalanges to a just power and bring them all

to justice for the crimes they have perpetrated against Muslims and Christians;
    (c) to permit all the sons of our people to determine their future and to choose in all liberty the form of government they desire. We call upon all of them to pick the option of Islamic government which, alone, is capable of guaranteeing justice and liberty for all. Only an Islamic regime can stop any further tentative attempts [at] imperialistic infiltration into our country (Hezbollah, 1985).

Special emphasis is given to Israel in a section headed 'The necessity for the destruction of Israel':

We see in Israel the vanguard of the United States in our Islamic world. It is the hated enemy that must be fought until the hated ones get what they deserve. This enemy is the greatest danger to our future generations and to the destiny of our lands, particularly as it glorifies the ideas of settlement and expansion, initiated in Palestine, and yearning outward to the extension of the Great Israel, from the Euphrates to the Nile.
    Our primary assumption in our fight against Israel states that the Zionist entity is aggressive from its inception, and built on lands wrested from their owners, at the expense of the rights of the Muslim people. Therefore our struggle will end only when this entity is obliterated. We recognize no treaty with it, no cease fire, and no peace agreements, whether separate or consolidated.
    We vigorously condemn all plans for negotiation with Israel, and regard all negotiators as enemies, for the reason that such negotiation is nothing but the recognition of the legitimacy of the Zionist occupation of Palestine. Therefore we oppose and reject the Camp David Agreements, the proposals of King Fahd, the Fez and Reagan plan, Brezhnev's and the French-Egyptian proposals, and all other programs that include the recognition (even the implied recognition) of the Zionist entity (Hezbollah, 1985).

So, like its mentor Iran, Hezbollah does not recognise Israel, but unlike Iran, it has not sought to broker deals with it. As a resistance movement formed in response and in opposition to Israel's occupation of Lebanon, it has remained firmly wedded to this nationalist goal. As such, it has not attempted to spread Shia Islamic uprisings in other countries, including in Palestine, despite its fervent desire for the liberation of Palestine, especially the holy city of Jerusalem.

Israel launched major air strikes against Lebanon in 1993, 1996, 1999, and 2000 – targeting infrastructures such as bridges and power stations, killing scores, and displacing hundreds of thousands. But, rather than curbing resistance to the occupation, such assaults intensified support for Hezbollah (Blandford, 2007, p. 8). Particularly under the leadership of Hassan Nasrallah (who became its secretary general in 1992) relentless, escalating, and carefully coordinated attacks were carried out on the Israeli army – from 19 in 1990 to 300 a month in 1999/2000 (*loc. cit.*) that eventually forced Israel to withdraw from southern Lebanon in May 2000. Indubitably, Hezbollah proved itself a formidable adversary of Israel.

Nasrallah has always affirmed Hezbollah's rejection of Israel as laid out in the open letter. Thus, in 1993, in an interview with Robert Fisk for a Channel 4 documentary, he stated: '[i]f the whole world were to recognise Israel, we never would. Israel is built on land owned by other people and taken from them by force' (Fisk, 1993). Accordingly, Hezbollah has strongly voiced support for the Palestinians. Though it has provided support to Hamas, the latter, as we saw in chapter 2, has been singularly ineffective against Israel. A further distinction is that, unlike Hamas, Hezbollah has been willing to work with other groups, including those whom it fought in the 1980s which are secular-minded such as the Syrian National Social Party and the Communist Party. More recently it has forged an alliance with Michel Ayoun's Christian group the Free Patriotic Movement (Noe [ed.], 2006, p. 379). In line with not calling for an Islamic Republic, it has rather stressed non-Islamic, non-religious issues such as 'economic exploitation and underdevelopment, iniquities in the political system, personal freedom and opportunity and ... security' (Norton, 2009 [2007], p. 102). Again, unlike Hamas, Hezbollah has not resorted to terrorist attacks. As Judith Palmer Harik points out:

> Highly conscious of the fact that accusations of terrorism would be used by the Israelis to try and halt the war of attrition being waged against them, Hezbollah leaders adopted and pursued a military strategy against Israeli military forces inside Lebanon's borders in which attacks against civilians to demoralize the government – a

common definition of terrorism – had no place. Instead, guerrilla warfare techniques were used by the Party of God to achieve its primary mission – the removal of an illegal occupation. This strategy significantly undercut Israel's capacity to generate outrage against Hezbollah as a terrorist organisation ...' (Harik, 2005, p. 2).

Thus Israel's forays into Lebanon to root out a Palestinian group, the PLO, led to the unintended consequence of fomenting a movement which is not Palestinian but offers tough opposition and unalloyed support for the Palestinian cause. As former Prime Minister Ehud Barak admitted, in July 2006: '[w]hen we entered Lebanon ... there was no Hezbollah. We were accepted with perfumed rice and flowers by the Shia in the south, It was our presence there that created Hezbollah' (cited in Norton, *op. cit.*, p. 33). Writing in 2003, the Israeli researcher Daniel Sobelman gave a sober assessment of the significance of Hezbollah and the 'new rules of the game' which confronted Israel:

> Because Hizbollah possesses the technical means to ignite the northern border [of Israel] with its enormous firepower potential, the tendency exists to consider Hizbollah as a perpetual threat to Israeli security. Indeed, the most common image of Hizbollah in Israel is an organization in anticipation of the opportunity to unleash its strategic capabilities. Thus, without an examination of whether this image is accurate or exaggerated, Hizbollah has been transformed into a key deterrent factor, a regional player whose response to regional developments must be taken into account by Israel (Sobelman, 2004, p. 10).

Though Hezbollah was funded, inspired by and took the lead from Iran's ayatollahs it has, nevertheless, in significant respects furrowed its own path, showing considerable independence of thought. The crucial reason for this is the society in which it resides: whereas Iran is an overwhelmingly Shia Muslim country, Lebanon is a multi-confessional society. In recognition of this, Hezbollah has had to tone down its shia Islamism – so whilst it desires a society and polity based on the Shia version of the Sharia, it recognises that this is not acceptable to significant sections of Lebanese society –

including elements of the Shia population. Thus, its democratic impulse has curtailed its religious dogma so that on the electoral terrain, Hezbollah has long suppressed the ideas embedded in its Open Letter of 1985. But, like Hamas and its charter, it has not explicitly abandoned it and replaced it with a programme more in line with its subsequent thinking and practice.

Even in a society where almost the entirety of the population are believers, nothing so curbs the monopoly desires of one sect's clerical establishment than the fact that large layers are of a different religious hue. Indoctrination into one strain of a faith powerfully inoculates one from switching allegiance to another – thus precluding Sunni conversions to Shi'ism and vice versa. In Islam's case as a whole, this is facilitated by the prohibition on apostasy. In a multifaith country such as Lebanon, with democratic pretensions, there is unsurprisingly little voluntary switching of faith; hence scant possibility of the religious dogmas of any one confession being widely accepted and so becoming laws of the state passed by a democratically elected parliament. In fact, Nasrallah has consistently acknowledged this: thus in September 1992, soon after becoming secretary-general, in an interview with the Lebanese magazine *Al Watan al-Arabi*, he gave the assurance:

> Regarding the project of the Islamic Republic, I can assure you that we will never propose this option per se in Lebanon, neither [*sic.*] through statements, slogans, or speeches ... We have never proposed the idea of imposing an Islamic Republic on Lebanon by force, and will not do that in the future ... This [Islamic] government would not be able to govern according to Islamic principles, or indeed survive, in the absence of overwhelming popular support (Noe [ed.], 2006, p. 90).

In the immediate aftermath of the war with Israel in the summer of 2006, Nasrallah made a similar pronouncement:

> [T]his country cannot take the form of on Islamic state, a Christian state, a Shia Islamic state, a Sunni Islamic state, a Maronite Christian state, or an Orthodox Christian state. In order for this country to be united and solid, and in order for us to be able to build a state in it that is capable of protecting the country, its

society, and its people's rights, and that is capable of serving them and preserving their dignity, there must be consensus (*ibid.,* p. 401).

So, given these constraints, in its political approach and manoeuvrings, Hezbollah has parked much of its religious zealotry in the sphere of general rhetoric. Indeed it is the one Arab movement that approximates most closely to Vietnamese resistance (albeit on a smaller scale) to the Americans during the 1960s and 1970s: principled opposition to the invading and occupying army and diligence in attempting to provide for the needs of the population in the most inhospitable of circumstances (see, for example, Maclear, 1989 [1981], ch. 15). It is thus not only a potent guerrilla force but also an effective welfare organisation in which non-religious themes and issues have been at the forefront. Hezbollah does not resort to the typical Islamist refrain that strictly following the edicts of the faith will deliver one to paradise – so that the challenges of daily life are soothed over, in the hope of a fulfilling afterlife. On the contrary, it has actively sought to deal with problems in the present life, particularly the depredations caused by an occupying power.

After the removal of Israel from Lebanon (with the exception of the disputed Shebaa Farms area), it appeared that Hezbollah's *raison d'être* and *casus belli* had also been removed. Whilst the Lebanese government did not call for its disarmament and recognised the legitimacy of Hezbollah as a resistance movement against any future Israeli assaults, Hezbollah would inevitably devote attention away from its guerrilla activities and focus more on 'normal', civilian, politics. The 'destruction of Israel' may have been a foundational objective but the reality was that this was no more than bluster and anger at repeated Israeli attacks on, and occupation of, Lebanon. Unsurprisingly, no serious attempt was made to bring this about; in its stead there has been modest assistance afforded to Palestinian groups.

Yet tensions with Israel remained acute and matters came to a head in the summer of 2006, when Hezbollah captured two and killed eight Israeli soldiers. Israel responded with a ferocious bombardment, of not only Hezbollah positions in South Lebanon, but targets throughout Lebanon. It would later emerge that Israel had planned the assault months in advance so that the capture of Israeli soldiers was the pretext that was needed (Urquhart, 2007) with the goal (backed by the US and much of Europe) of completely destroying Hezbollah. In the ensuing 34-day war, Israel killed some 1,200 Lebanese (including 1,000 civilians) and wreaked widespread destruction throughout Lebanon. But Hezbollah was not broken – indeed by general consensus put up an extremely tough fight the likes of which Israel had not before encountered from an Arab force, surpassing that of Egyptian and Syrian armies in 1973. It was this that led Brigadier General Guy Zur, a month after the fighting had stopped, to concede that Hezbollah was 'by far the greatest guerrilla group in the world' (cited in Norton, *op. cit.* P. 140). What was underplayed at the time – and still is to a certain extent – was that Hezbollah's performance had punctured the seeming invincibility of the Israeli military and genuinely *frightened* Israelis – notwithstanding the fact that the overwhelming majority (95 per cent) of Israelis thought their governments' action was justified (*BBC News*, 2006). True, the damage done to Israel and lives lost was a small fraction of that of Lebanon: 158 killed including 41 civilians (Urquhart, 2007). Apart from the death and destruction, nearly a million Lebanese had been displaced; in comparison some 300-500,000 Israelis had been displaced, fleeing thousands of rockets into northern towns and cities of Israel. But this represented a significant proportion of the Israeli population so that no one, at least in Northern Israel, felt safe, given Hezbollah's firepower and ability to take the fight to Israel. Naturally enough, immediately after the war, Hezbollah began to re-arm in earnest. The sense of foreboding and shift in the balance of power was provided in 2010 by Michael Oren, Israeli ambassador to the US: 'The Syrian-Iranian backed Hizbullah poses a very serious threat to Israel ... Hizbullah today now has four times as many rockets as it had during the 2006 Lebanon war. These rockets are longer-range. Every city in Israel is within range right now, including Eilat' (*Jpost.com*, 2010).

Though statistics are not available, one would expect that

many Israelis either left the country in the aftermath of the war or hedged their bets by acquiring a foreign passport, a phenomenon that has become rife. Gideon Levy of the Israeli paper *Haaretz* provides a plausuble explanation: 'if our forefathers dreamt of an Israeli passport, there are those among us who are now dreaming of a foreign passport ... The foreign passport has become an insurance policy against a rainy day. It turns out there are more and more Israelis who are thinking that day may eventually come' (cited in Davidson, 2011).[29] The prospect of another war with Hezbollah would have doubtless concentrated many Israeli minds and convinced some to make for the exit door before that rainy day arrived.

A 'cold peace' has duly held since the 2006 war but, despite the fact that Israeli occupation has long ended, the prospect of resumption of hostilities the two parties remains a very real possibility, that is to say, this element of the clash between Islamism and Zionism remains very much 'live' and extremely dangerous, with potential for a more widespread conflagration. The war between Israel and Hezbollah was thought by many in Israel and the US (including George W Bush, who gave Israel the green light) as, in the words of Ephraim Sneh, Israel's deputy defence minister, 'a prelude to the greater war with Iran' (cited in Parsi, 2007, p. 15). Though this has, thus far, not materialised, given the venomous animosity between the Islamist and Zionist regimes, such a destructive, destabilising scenario cannot be ruled out. Should it happen, the hostility between Islamists and Zionists will be felt the world over, not least in the West, accentuating already poisonous relations

---

[29] Davidson notes that the United States has issued over half a million passports to Israelis and a quarter million additional applications are pending. Germany runs second with 100,000 passports given to Israeli Jews and 7,000 new ones issued yearly (*loc. cit.*). Such a reversal of *aliyah* is of increasing concern to the Israel government which is why, in early 2012, it launched an advertisement campaign in America in order to induce Israelis settled in the US to return home – but the tactics used appeared to have alienated both Israeli and American Jews (*RT* [Russia Today], 2012).

Dangerous Liaisons

between Jews and Muslims.

Chapter 4

Israel and Sunni Islamists

Introductory remarks

As stressed in chapter 1, no matter their hue, Islamists are united – at least as a normative stance – in their opposition to Zionism and the state of Israel. Unlike Shia Islamists, however, the various sects and regimes of the dominant Sunni Islam[30] have not translated the theory much into practice. As such, there has not been a Sunni equivalent to the state of Iran or the Hezbollah. Indeed, the most important Sunni Islamist state, Saudi Arabia – in whose territory are the two most important cities of Islam (the House of Saud proclaims itself as the 'Custodian of the Two Holy Places') – has been characterised, particularly since 1973, by a distinct lack of any real resistance to Zionism and, as a corollary, a disdainful posture on Palestine[31]. In fact, it has been far more agitated by the Iranian Shia regime – for example, following the release by Wikileaks of US diplomatic cables in 2010, *Reuters* reported:

---

[30] There are, of course, various other smaller sects but for the purposes of this book, they are largely irrelevant – though see the discussion on the Sufism of Feisal Rauf in chapter 5.

[31] In April 2012, however, the Saudi regime made a small gesture of protest against Israel when Saudi Prince Nawaf Bin Faisal, chairman of the Arab Council of Youth and Sports Ministers, announced during the council's meeting in Jeddah that 'all companies that have sponsored the marathon in Jerusalem, including Adidas, will be boycotted' (Farouk, 2012). It is interesting to note that the second biggest investor (with 7 per cent of the voting shares) in Rupert Murdoch's News Corporation is Saudi Prince Alwaleed bin Talal (Sylt, 2012). News Corp (which owns the right wing American Fox News TV channel) is, of course, strongly pro-Israel; a stance which Alwaleed has seemingly not attempted to alter.

King Abdullah is reported to have 'frequently exhorted the U.S. to attack Iran to put an end to its nuclear weapons program'. 'Cut off the head of the snake', the Saudi ambassador to Washington, Adel al-Jubeir, quotes the king as saying during a meeting with General David Petraeus in April 2008 (Mohammed and Colvin, 2010).

It is true that under dictatorial Arab regimes, Islamists were suppressed and where any Islamist grouping dared to embark on an uprising, it was ruthlessly put down – the classic example of this was the crushing of Syrian Islamists in Hama by Hafez el-Assad in 1982. Accordingly, overt solidarity with Palestinians and active opposition to Israel was difficult unless it was officially sanctioned. That said, Islamists in Egypt were infuriated by the September 1978 Camp David Peace Treaty between Egypt and Israel – the first Arab country to recognise the Jewish state, for which Israel returned the Sinai peninsula – which saw the abandoning of any support for Palestinians in return for an annual American stipend for the Egyptian military. Some cynics viewed this as the Egyptian army being paid not to fight. The upshot was that members of Al-Jihad group assassinated the architect of the Treaty, Anwar Sadat. Unsurprisingly, his successor Hosni Mubarak clamped down hard on the Islamists (and indeed on all opposition) though, in subsequent years, he allowed a gradual infusion of Islam into the Egyptian polity and society. But two shibboleths remained untouched: a 'cold peace' with Israel, and the freezing of support for Palestine.

If the 1967 Six Day War was a mortal blow to Arab nationalism, Camp David marked its funeral rites: thereafter, Arab nationalism would not be able to offer even a pretence of progressive, non-religious politics, that it had done so in the 1950s under Nasser. The alternative Baathism of Iraq and Syria had degenerated into brutal, dictatorial regimes. In the vacuum created, Islamism would become an increasingly dominant force. But, as we have seen, it was the Shia version which broke through with great effect in Iran in 1979 and which would have a profound impact on the Arab world in which Islamists also made the running: Hezbollah in Lebanon, Hamas in Palestine, the FIS in Algeria, whilst the Muslim Brotherhood quietly expanded its influence and reach in Egypt and Tunisia, Islamist regimes took control in Sudan and Yemen. Beyond the Arab world, the mujahideen in Afghanistan (with American, Pakistani, and Saudi backing) overthrew the Soviet occupiers and its puppet regime. General Zia ul-Haq, who so enthusiastically funded the Afghan jihadists, became a de facto Islamist leader as he proceeded to Islamise Pakistan.

But the ascendancy of Sunni Islam did not translate into an intensification of a clash with Zionism. Whilst the rhetoric against Israel was certainly always harsh, there was an absence of concrete measures of support for Palestinians. The approach of 'preparing the generations' adopted by the Brotherhood in Palestine in the 1970s and much of the 1980s (see chapter 2) appeared to apply writ large to all Sunni Islamist groups. A notable exception was the Jihadist terror group, Al Qaeda, to which we now turn before proceeding to discuss the non-terror Sunni groups, specially the Muslim Brotherhood.

Israel and the jihadist terrorists of Al Qaeda

Since 9/11, in numerous instances, Al Qaeda leaders have emphasised the fundamental importance of Palestine and of American support for Israel as a decisive motivating factor for their jihadist terrorism. Curiously enough, Al Qaeda has not taken its jihad into Israel or the occupied territories: the clash with Israel and Zionism has been at the level of rhetoric. For Israel, Al Qaeda is merely another manifestation of Islamic terrorism akin to Hamas and Islamic jihad whom they have had to deal with over many years; and as such Al Qaeda terrorism has been utilised to gain empathy and sympathy in America and Europe with the refrain 'what you are now suffering, we have suffered for many decades; we have common interests in defeating our common enemy'.

The magnitude of the Israel-Palestine conflict for the jihadi terrorists has been well-understood by American intelligence agencies. Thus, the former head of CIA's Bin Laden unit, Michael Scheuer, ridicules the argument peddled by many politicians and thinkers that jihadist terrorism is motivated by a hatred of the 'American way of life':

> 'Bin Laden has been precise in telling America the reasons he is waging war on us. None of the reasons have anything to with our freedom, liberty, and democracy, but have everything to do with US policies and actions in the Muslim world' (Scheuer, 2004, p. x).

Another former CIA officer, Brue Riedel, in his book on Al Qaeda, hones in on the key reason:

> [T]he Arab conflict with Israel, especially the perceived grievances of the Palestinian people, is the all-consuming issue for the terrorists ... Muslims feel a profound sense of wrong about the creation of Israel and that infuses every aspect of al Qaeda's thinking and activities and has become the rallying cry used to convince the ummah of the righteousness of al Qaeda's cause. The organization's two key leaders, [Ayman] Zawahiri and [Osama] bin Laden, decided to become terrorists because of efforts to negotiate a peaceful solution to the Arab-Israel conflict that would leave Israel in the heart of the Muslim world (Riedel, 2008, pp. 5, 11-12).

Osama bin Laden's jihadist politics were forged in Afghanistan in the 1980s – the reasoning for which was made with great force by a Palestinian preacher and former guerrilla, whom Bin Laden greatly admired, Abdullah Azzam. Azzam argued that 'Afghanistan takes precedence over the Palestinian struggle against Israel. The war in Afghanistan was intended to bring forth an Islamic state ... whereas the Palestinian cause has been appropriated by various groups, including "Communists, nationalists, and modernist Muslims" who were fighting for a secular state' (Wright, p. 102). Some six months before the Soviet defeat in Afghanistan, the first intifada erupted in Palestine (in December 1987 – see chapter 2) but, despite his long standing angst over Palestine, Bin Laden was reluctant to participate in the intifada against Israel. This is because 'he envisioned moving the struggle to Kashmir, the Philippines, and particularly Central Asian republics where he could continue the jihad against the Soviet Union ... The vanguard he would create was primarily to fight against communism'. Such a vanguard was duly created in August 1988 and given the name of *Al Qaeda* (the base) (*ibid.,* pp. 131, 133). Thus, even after a major uprising by the Palestinians was taking place, Bin Laden was not motivated to fight his jihad against Israel or its protector, the US – which had, of course, been his major ally in the jihad against the Russians.

But Bin Laden would later state, somewhat unbelievably, that the US had always been his enemy – a hatred that began in 1982 'when America permitted the Israelis to invade Lebanon and the American Sixth Fleet helped them' ... As I looked at those demolished towers [high rises] in Lebanon, it entered my mind that ...' (*ibid.,* p. 151). So the destruction of the WTC towers in New York can ostensibly be traced to American support for Israel. Another crucial turning point for Bin Laden which further pitted him against the Saudis was Saudi Arabia's support for the 1993 Oslo Accords (Riedel, *op. cit.,* p. 52).

The first attempt to blow up the WTC towers occurred in February 1993; the mastermind of which plot was a blind sheikh, Omar Abdur Rahman, financially backed by Bin Laden. America's 'Jihadist blowback' had commenced in earnest. The perpetrator of the attack – in which six people were killed and more than a thousand injured – was Ramzi Yousef, a product of the Al Qaeda training camp in Afghanistan. Lawrence Wright points out that Yousef, who was not particularly devout, hoped that his act of terror would lead to the killing of 250,000 people, equivalent he thought of the pain the Palestinians had suffered because of American support for Israel (Wright, pp. 176-178).

It was, however, from about the mid-1990s that Bin Laden and Al Qaeda began to explicitly organise jihad against America and Jews/Israel (Al Qaeda tended to use these interchangeably, so often made no distinction between Jewry and Zionism and, therefore, resorted to classic anti-Semitism). Thus, in August 1996, Bin Laden issued a 'Declaration of jihad against the Americans occupying the land of the two holy sanctuaries' which begins:

> Each of you knows the injustice, oppression, and aggression the Muslims are suffering from the Judeo-crusading alliance and its lackeys. The blood of Muslims ... is flowing in Palestine, Iraq, and

Lebanon (the awful images of the Qana massacre[32] are still present in everyone's mind) ... (cited in Kepel and Milleli (eds.), 2008, p. 47).

In an interview Bin Laden gave to the CNN's Peter Arnett in March 1997, he declared that '[w]e believe that the American army in Saudi Arabia ... came ... in support of the Israeli forces in occupied Palestine, the land of our Prophet's night journey' (*ibid.*, p. 52).[33]

In February 1998, Bin Laden issued a fatwa with five other leading jihadists (including his key ally and present leader of Al Qaeda, Ayman Al-Zawahiri, described as 'emir of the Jihad group in Egypt') under the banner of the 'World Islamic Front'. It was entitled 'Jihad against Jews and Crusaders' and provided three key justifications:

> First, for over seven years the United States has been occupying the most sacred Islamic lands, the Arabian peninsula, plundering its riches, dictating to its rulers, humiliating its people, terrorizing its neighbors, and turning its bases in the peninsula into a spearhead with which to fight the neighboring peoples ... Second, despite the great devastation inflicted on the Iraqi people by the crusader-Zionist alliance, and despite the huge number of those killed, and which is approaching a million, the Americans are once again trying to repeat the horrific massacres ... Third, if the war aims of the American are religious and economic, they also have the effect of serving the Jews' petty state and diverting attention from its occupation of Jerusalem and murder of Muslims there (*ibid.,* p. 54).

---

[32] This was the attack by Israel on a UN refugee camp in Qana, Southern Lebanon, in April 1996 which killed over 200 civilians.

[33] American troops arrived in Saudi Arabia after Saddam Hussein' s invasion of Kuwait in the summer of 1990 and did not officially leave until the start of the second war against Iraq in 2003. But Bin Laden and Al Qaeda were well aware that the US continued to yield enormous influence on the House of Saud which they detested.

Israel and Sunni Islamists

The fatwa then issues the following exhortation:

> Killing the Americans and their allies – civilians and military – is an individual duty for every Muslim who can do it in any country where it proves possible, in order to liberate al-Aqsa Mosque and the holy sanctuary [Mecca] from their grip, and to the point that their armies leave all Muslim territory, defeated and unable to threaten any Muslim land (*ibid.,* p. 55).

Some six months later, on 7th August 1998, US embassies in Nairobi, Kenya and Dar Es Salaam, Tanzania were attacked killing some 200 people. This was followed, in October 2000, by an attack on the American warship USS *Cole* in Aden, Yemen, that killed 19 sailors. Fourteen months after 9/11, Bin Laden issued a 'letter to America' in which he answers the question 'why are we fighting and opposing you?' He provides various reasons, the first of which is 'you attacked us in Palestine', which is then elaborated upon:

> Palestine, which has sunk under military occupation for more than 80 years. The British handed over Palestine, with your help and your support, to the Jews, who have occupied it for more than 50 years; years overflowing with oppression, tyranny, crimes, killing, expulsion, destruction and devastation. The creation and continuation of Israel is one of the greatest crimes, and you are the leaders of its criminals. And of course there is no need to explain and prove the degree of American support for Israel. The creation of Israel is a crime which must be erased. Each and every person whose hands have become polluted in the contribution towards this crime must pay its price, and pay for it heavily (Bin Laden, 2002).

Ayman Zawahiri naturally concurred with this view arguing that the creation of Israel has been 'the West's most evil act' (he, like Bin Laden, forgets the decisive role of the Soviet Union as highlighted in chapter 2) and views his path of jihadist terrorism from his participation in the 1981 plot to assassinate Anwar Sadat for his negotiating the Camp David Treaty with Israel (Riedel, *op. cit.,* p. 129). For Zawahiri, 'what led us to the conclusion that "jihad is the only solution" was the brutality and injustice of the new Jewish crusade, which treats the Muslim community with utter contempt' (cited in Kepel and Milleli (eds.), *op. cit.*, p. 195).

Gilles Kepel poignantly describes the Islamic universalism of Palestine for jihadists and their recourse to 'martyrdom [that is, suicide] operations' to expose Palestinian oppression; the apotheosis of which were the 9/11 attacks:

> By the beginning of the millennium, jihadists had only to invoke the word "Palestine" in order to stigmatize Israel and its Western supporters as oppressors of Muslims. Transcending the suffering of local Palestinians, the word became synonymous with martyrdom – a legitimate response of the Islamic community, whether Shiite or Sunni. The grand narrative of martyrdom became part of their self-representation, and martyrdom operations were now seen as the best way to bear witness to the reality of oppression, and the only way to inflict meaningful harm upon Islam's powerful enemies. Suicide attacks – once an exception – were on their way to becoming the norm (Kepel, 2008, p. 102).

Whether Palestinians themselves approved of such operations in their name, or the conflation of their oppression with that of the whole of the Muslim world (Christian Palestinians seemingly did not exist), was of no consequence to the Al Qaeda jihadists. Jihadism implied, indeed necessitated, raising the banner of Palestine in violent attacks, whether suicidal or not. What is, however, most significant is that despite Israel/Zionism being such a *casus belli* for its jihad, Al Qaeda did not attack any target in Israel. Indeed, even in the post-2003 invasion of Iraq, as Patrick Cockburn highlights, 'the local franchisee, though never under the control of Bin Laden, was more interested in butchering Iraqi Shia than in killing American soldiers ...' (Cockburn, 2011). Moreover, after fleeing Afghanistan, it has set up franchises not only in Iraq but also in Yemen, North Africa, Somalia and Nigeria (where the jihadist group Boko Haram has close affinity with Al Qaeda), but not in Palestine. Clearly, there has been considerable divergence between what Al Qaeda's leaders preached and what has been practised by its jihadists.

Michael Scheuer (2004, p. 229) points out that, in regard to Palestine, there was a widespread belief that Bin Laden was an

'Osama-come lately'; and that he and Al Qaeda were cynically using Palestine to advance their jihad. One Al Qaeda leader, Abu-Ubayd al-Qurashi, did, however, argue that 'an attempt must be made to penetrate the borders with Palestine and bring in weapons. Military operations must be carried out against the Zionists, their sponsors, and their domesticated clients' (cited in *ibid.*, p. 77). Around the time of 9/11, Israeli intelligence agencies thought that Al Qaeda had indeed infiltrated the occupied territories and expected attacks on Israel; moreover, a number of Palestinians have served with, and been trained by, Al Qaeda (Gunaratna, 2003, p. 200). In 2002, Al Qaeda expanded its presence in Lebanon so as to be close to the Israel-Palestine conflict but, whilst desiring to launch attacks inside Israel, refrained from doing so[34] on the grounds that such attacks were all but impossible because of the refusal not only by Lebanon but also by Jordan, Syria, and Egypt – ostensibly to please Washington and Israel – to provide the group a contiguous safe haven (Scheuer, *op. cit.*, p. 229). Scheuer, however, argues that the October 2002 attacks on an Israeli hotel and charter airline in Mombasa, Kenya, and the November 2003 attacks on two synagogues in Turkey represented Al Qaeda launching an anti-Israeli war (*loc. cit.*). However, such a 'war' was short lived as, thereafter, Al Qaeda's attacks on Israeli targets did not materialize.

In regard to the Arab uprisings, it is manifestly clear is that the overwhelming victors have, so far, been non-violent Sunni Islamists of an electoral bent whilst the influence of Al Qaeda has been negligible. Indeed, the Muslim Brotherhood has sharply been at odds with Al Qaeda. In 2007, for example, the Brotherhood's Executive Bureau member Mahmud Ghozlan condemned Bin Laden's speeches calling for Jihad and argued that Al-Qaeda did nothing but divide the Muslim world, and stressed the futility of Al-Qaeda's bombings: 'they only helped occupation to expand in the world and took the lives of

---

[34] There was one famous planned attack that was thwarted, involving the 'shoebomber' Richard Reid (Gunaratna, 2003, p. 201).

thousands of innocent civilians, most of them are Muslims' (Ikhwanweb, 2007). Matters are in a state of flux but the second part of this chapter examines the Brotherhood and other Sunni Islamist parties and their stance on Israel and Zionism which, as we shall see, in rhetoric at least, matches that of Al Qaeda.

Muslim Brotherhood

The issue of Palestine to the Muslim Brotherhood, the most important Sunni Islamist organisation (founded in Egypt by Hassan al Banna in 1928) was of profound importance in its early years, as Thomas Mayer points out:

> [I]t was over Palestine that the Society [of the Muslim Brethren] vowed time and again to fulfil its religious duty through military means. The Ikhwan [Brotherhood] regarded Palestine as an Arab and Islamic country, and the Jews – all of them taken to be Zionists – as enemies of Islam and pawns of imperialism. To defeat these enemies and defend Palestinian Arab rights, the Society called for a Holy War (jihad) in Palestine (Mayer, 1982, p. 100).

During the Arab revolt of 1936 in Palestine, the Brotherhood conducted a propaganda campaign for Palestinian Arabs, organised fund raising and initiated protests in Egypt. With only about 800 members it was, unsurprisingly, ineffectual. By 1947, however, total membership had swelled to perhaps one million including 12-25,000 active members in Palestine. But the goal of jihad had been set aside as the group became avowedly apolitical focusing its activities on religious education, sending lecturers to mosques, developing educational programmes for illiterate people, raising the standard of living for Islamic families, and building clinics for the poor (*ibid.,* pp. 103-105). After the UN vote for the partition of Palestine was passed on 29 November 1947, military clashes broke out: Richard Mitchell points that 'after the formal opening of hostilities in May [1948], a number of minor engagements [by the Brotherhood] occurred, which seem to have been no more than harassing missions directed at Zionist positions and of little note, except for contributing to the Arab defence of Jerusalem and Bethlehem ...' (Mitchell, 1993 [1969], pp57-58). Mayer draws stark attention to the fact that '[a] Society which succeeded in recruiting to its ranks many thousands of members in less than two years was incapable of organising even one military unit for the liberation of Palestine', but he acknowledges that the Brotherhood's influence was crucial in drawing Egypt into a full scale military intervention in Palestine which can be construed as the realisation of its campaign for a Holy War (Mayer, *op. cit.*, pp. 105-106, 111). Though it was no such thing, it was certainly a pitiful failure as Palestine was duly partitioned with the bulk of the land being allocated to, and much else besides seized by, Israel.

Despite the centrality of Palestine, the Brotherhood was never again to attempt to 'fulfil its religious duties through military means'. It was proscribed by the Egyptian government in December 1948, but continued to work underground – its subsequent trajectory was to consolidate its base in Egypt and gain footholds in other Arab countries. The rise of Gamal Abdel Nasser was, however, a grave setback for Islamists of all persuasions. An assassination attempt in 1954, which was blamed on the Brotherhood, led to their organisation being dissolved, several leaders executed, and members jailed or exiled. A key Ikhwan theorist, Sayyid Qutb, denounced American support for Israel because of 'Truman, four million votes, Zionist pressure, Jewish gold, and Zionist influence' (Mitchell, *op. cit.*, p. 227) and proceeded to describe Egypt as 'jahiliya' (pre-Islamic ignorance) which must be struck down – meaning that the regime must be overthrown and replaced by an Islamic state. For such a brazen challenge, he was hanged in 1966 (Kepel, 2003, pp. 30-31). The Brotherhood then began to set roots in other – mainly Arab – countries. In any case, regardless of being outlawed, the ideological terrain in Egypt for Islamism became very tough given the popular support for Nasserism; moreover the 1956 Suez crisis and the aborted war, a humiliating defeat for Britain, France, and Israel, saw Nasser's standing reach dizzying heights not only in the Arab world but throughout the developing and post-colonial world.

Though the 1967 Six Day War marked a crushing and fatal blow to Nasser, the surprisingly good performance by the

Egyptian military in the 1973 October War allowed his successor, Anwar Sadat, a breathing space – one consequence of which was that the regime allowed Islamists to organise on a social basis and for exiled members of the Brotherhood to return. Indeed, Sadat encouraged the socially conservative Islamists and considered the Gamaat Islamiyya as close allies – so much so that the British ambassador to Cairo, Sir Richard Beaumont, thought that Sadat wished to use the Brotherhood as a 'counter-weight to left-wing forces' (Curtis, 2010, p. 109). His strategy was that 'in exchange for political support, he allowed the Islamist intelligentsia considerable cultural and ideological autonomy and gave the devout bourgeoisie easier access to certain sectors of the newly privatized economy. It was up to these favoured Islamists to hold the line against more radical groups whose goal was to subvert society' (Kepel, *op. cit.*, p. 83). However, the Camp David Accords were rejected by all Islamists – quite simply, the recognition of, and agreement with, Israel was a red line they would not cross. As noted, Camp David cost Sadat his life. Whilst the jihadi terrorists were relentlessly chased and rooted out, the moderates were quietly increasing their influence over areas of society open to them. In 1985, during the Mubarak era, Egyptian TV broadcast nearly 14,000 hours of Islamic broadcasts by preachers closely linked with the Brotherhood. Among their targets were secular intellectuals who brought 'religion into disrepute'. Alcohol was banned in several states as the regime quietly allowed Islamists to campaign on issues of morality, culture, public manners, and daily life. Indeed, the Brotherhood campaigned for the repeal of all legislation that they thought conflicted with Sharia law; this was putting into effect its clarion call of 'Islam is the solution'. In the 1990s, the Brotherhood took control of the professions including the law, medical, dentistry, engineering, and pharmacy (*ibid.*, pp. 281, 277).[35] The 1992 Egyptian earthquake

---

[35] As a flavour of the Islamist atmosphere in Egypt during the Mubarak era, Robert Fisk of *The Independent* describes an encounter with an Egyptian professor of Islamic thought, Nasr Hamid Abu Zeid, who 'had been declared an apostate by a Cairo court, deprived of his university professorship, and

further provided kudos for the Islamists. As Chris Hedges reported for the *New York Times*:

> To the chagrin of Government officials, fundamentalists quickly filled the void in disaster relief, opening shelters and providing medical aid in some areas within hours of the disaster. The earthquake killed 552 people, injured nearly 10,000 and left 3,000 families homeless. 'The earthquake was a godsend for the fundamentalists in different ways,' said Mohammed Sid Ahmed, a leading political commentator. 'They have portrayed the event as God's vengeance on a corrupt society. But more important, they have used it to show that they can provide services while the Government is ineffective' (Hedges, 1992).

Pressure was, therefore, mounting on the dictatorship to allow the Islamists into the political fold and this helps to explain why, despite being a banned group, members of the Brotherhood were allowed to stand as candidates for parliament as 'independents'. Owing to their effective and sustained work in the community, in the 2005 election, they won (or were allowed to win) 20 per cent of the seats (Bates, 2011). Despite such advances, the Brotherhood remained largely silent on its self-professed 'religious duty' towards Palestine. Accordingly, and notwithstanding the harassment, it never mounted any challenge to the Camp David Treaty or to Israel.

The cause of Palestine and the need to be seen resisting Israel was most crucial to the Jordanian branch of the Brotherhood, which includes many Palestinians. This was reflected in their 1989 election slogan 'the Islamic movement believes that the liberation of Palestine is the most important and sacred duty ... The soil of Palestine is Islamic and belongs to the Muslims for eternity' (cited in Pargeter, 2010, p. 198). Such electioneering never translated into any meaningful action nor threatened King Hussein's firm pro-US, pro-Israeli stance.

---

shamelessly hounded out of Mubarak's Egypt in 1995 ... Nasr Abu Zeid's sin was his belief that the Koran must be subject to reinterpretation, that centuries of Islamic scholarship needed to be re-studied' (Fisk, 2012).

A more concrete promise was made by the Supreme Guide of the Brotherhood, Mehdi Akef, in 2006, during Israel's war with Hezbollah: he promised to send 10,000 fighters to Lebanon to fight alongside the Shia group which was gaining enormous popularity amongst the Sunni faithful. But, typically for the Ikhwan, this was merely bluster to raise its profile (*ibid.,* p. 199).

Israel and the Islamists in the Arab Spring

When the fruit-seller Mohammad Bouazizi set fire to himself on 17th December 2010 in front of the governorate of Sidi Bouzid in Tunisia, it would have been impossible to predict the epoch-making events which would unfold in the Arab world. This was the start of the 'Arab Spring' which is still raging at the time of writing though the epithet 'Arab Awakening' – coined by George Antonius in the late 1930s (see chapter 2) – rather better encapsulates the profound and seemingly irreversible change that has been set in store. Arabs had woken up and, in Shelley's thunderous words from his revolutionary poem *The mask of anarchy*, risen 'like lions after slumber, in unvanquishable number'. For progressives, the initial omens were good: the revolutionaries in Tunisia and, soon to be followed in enormous numbers, in Cairo's Tahrir Square were largely young, modern, and secular-minded, fighting to shake off their 'chains to earth like dew', for a world full of freedoms that have been long available to citizens of the secular Western democracies, thereby giving true meaning to the Square in which they waged their struggle to bring down the despot Mubarak.

But, a demiurge appears to have tarnished this appealing vista: few predicted the enormous gains made by the Islamists – for whom Sharia law necessarily trumps democratic man-made laws and curtails myriad of freedoms. The Muslim Brotherhood in Egypt and its affiliate in Tunisia, the Ennahda [Al-Nahada] Party, were the winners of their respective elections; whilst the biggest surprise was the astonishing success of the Saudi-style Salafists in Egypt. Thus, in the parliamentary (People's Assembly) elections in Egypt held over three phases in late 2011 and early 2012, the Brotherhood's Freedom and Justice

Party (under the umbrella of *Democratic Alliance*, with three smaller parties) won 38 per cent of the vote and 45 per cent of seats; the *Islamist Bloc* (Salafists led by Al-Nour Party) won 25 per cent of the vote and 28 per cent of seats; whilst the Al Wasat Party won nearly 4 per cent of the vote and 2 per cent of seats. Thus, the Islamists won nearly 70 per cent of the vote and 72 per cent of seats (El Din, 2012). It is important to stress that the Salafists *opposed* the uprising against Mubarak (Al-Nour Party spokesperson Nader Bakar stated that the Salafists' refusal to join the enormous 25 January 2011 protest against Hosni Mubarak had been a 'positive step' because, otherwise, 'the Americans would have ordered Mubarak to massacre them all' [*Jadaliyya*, 2011]).[36] But the Salafists' position stemmed from their beliefs. Marwan Bishara points out that '[t]he rapprochement between Islamism and democracy was rejected by the Saudi-supported Salafis and other fundamentalist groups across the region who insisted on the literal interpretation and implementation of the Shari'a in future Islamic states or in a grand pan-Islamic caliphate' (Bishara, 2012, p. 206).

The Brotherhood's support for protests against Mubarak had been lukewarm and was wound down after the dictator's fall after which it proceeded to work amicably with the military junta (describing itself as the Supreme Council of the Armed Forces [SCAF]) that took power. Indeed, many at the forefront of the revolution blamed the 'political Islamists for empowering the military and being sucked into an electoral game designed to give the old regime a facade of democratic legitimacy' (Shenker, 2012). Mariz Tadros (2012, p. x) writes that '[b]y February 2012, there were clear indicators that the Brothers' policies had served to undermine social cohesion, deepen gender inequalities and significantly narrow the parameters

---

[36] In contrast, the secular, liberal 'Nasserist' candidate Hamdeen Sabbahi, who came third in the first round of the presidential elections in May 2012, stated that he would 'tear into pieces the peace treaty signed between Egypt and Israel in 1979' and 'would not recognize a Zionist entity that usurps Arab land' (*Egypt Independent*, 2012).

through which contentious issues can be discussed'. It is no exaggeration to think that this was the most right wing, reactionary, electoral outcome that any popular revolution has produced.

In the Tunisian Constituent Assembly elections of October 2011, by far the largest party is the Islamist Ennahda Party with 37 per cent of the vote and 41 per cent of the seats; no other party polled more than 9 per cent (Tunisialive.net, 2011). To offset an uprising, the Moroccan King Mohamed VI ceded some of his powers to a democratically-elected parliament. The elections took place in November 2011 and, once more, an Islamist party – Justice and Development Party (modelled on the Turkish AKP) – won most seats (107 out of 395) giving it the right to form the government (*BBC News*, 2011).

The Arab Spring seemed quickly to give way to an 'Islamic Summer': the avowedly secular Egyptian novelist and activist Alaa Al Aswany – who had countered the Brotherhood's clarion call of 'Islam is the solution' with the alternative 'Democracy is the solution' which chimed so well with the demands of the revolution, proceeded to write an article as early as July 2011 with the title 'Did the Egyptian revolution go wrong' (Al Aswany, 2011). With Islamists in the ascendancy, no matter the precise path each post-revolutionary Arab country would take, relations between the Arab world and Israel would inevitably feature prominently on the international sphere.

The euphoria in the Arab world and beyond was conspicuous by its absence in Israel. Long portraying itself as 'the only democracy in the Middle East', Israeli leaders have been distinctly lukewarm at the prospect of democracy flourishing among their neighbours and near-neighbours. Thus, in a speech to parliament in November 2011, Prime Minister Benjamin Netanyahu made his feelings about the Arab spring clear: 'Arab countries are "moving not forward, but backward" and support from the US and European countries was naïve. The Arab spring was becoming an "Islamic, anti-western, anti-liberal, anti-Israeli, undemocratic (*sic*) wave "' (cited in Sherwood, November 2011). In truth this response is hardly surprising: knowing full well that in rhetoric at least, Islamists had always been relentlessly hostile towards Zionism, Israeli leaders prefer the dictatorial devils they have long known rather than risk power transferring to democratically elected governments that might be dominated by Islamist parties given the possibility that, under popular pressure, the latter's harsh rhetoric might translate into meaningful action. That said, Israel – along with the US and the EU – have long been perfectly happy with the anti-democratic Islamists of the House of Saud and various Gulf states. But the tide of history could not be stopped: post-revolutionary governments with a strong Islamist component is the new reality and with it resides the possibility of an intensification of the clash between Islamism and Zionism.

What, then, has been the view of the rising Islamists regarding Zionism and the cause of Palestine they have long cherished? Buoyed by its tremendous electoral success, the Muslim Brotherhood's Freedom and Justice Party (FJP) began to use its muscle in the new parliament. In March 2012, there was unanimous support for a report by the Arab Affairs Committee of parliament that called for the expulsion of Israel's ambassador in Cairo and for the halting of gas exports to Israel. The report also declared that 'Egypt will never be a friend, partner, or ally of Israel' and described Israel as the nation's 'number one enemy' and endorsed Palestinian resistance 'in all its kinds and forms against Israel's aggressive policies' (Hendawi [for AP], 2012).

Also in March 2012, following Israel's attack on Gaza in which it killed 25 Palestinians, the FJP issued a statement which pulled few verbal punches:

> Israel must fully realize that Egypt, whose people have bravely erupted against and toppled the tyrannical corrupt regime which provided it with constant and direct support, will not under any circumstances accept such Israeli actions and deliberate violent escalation ... which put the entire region at risk and threaten international relations, stability and security ... the FJP calls on the Supreme Council of the Armed Forces ... to denounce this escalation ... and that post-revolutionary Egypt will stand solidly by her besieged brothers in Gaza ... The party also asserts that the siege Israel has been imposing on Gaza is no longer acceptable under any justification, which requires full and permanent opening

of the Rafah border crossing ...' (FJP, 2012).

Immediately after the fall of Mubarak, Israel's former ambassador to Cairo, Yitzhak Levanon, requested permission from his superiors in the Foreign Ministry to establish a dialogue with the Muslim Brotherhood. This showed foresight notwithstanding the fact that the Brotherhood would not likely have agreed to the idea; in any case, Foreign Minister Avigdor Lieberman blithely rejected the request (Ben-Meir, 2012). Plainly, the Israeli government hoped that the post-Mubarak junta would manage to channel the revolution into safe waters away not only from the secular revolutionaries that drove out Mubarak but also from the dangerous hands of the Islamists. But such self-delusion did not last long.

The overwhelming success of Islamists certainly concentrated Israeli minds so as to temper Lieberman's rejectionist stance. Recognising which way the wind was blowing, in January 2012, the Israel Foreign Ministry put out a positive feeler to the Islamist-dominated parliament:

> '[w]e send the new parliament our wishes of constructive and fruitful work for the well-being of the Egyptian public. We trust Egypt will continue to uphold the importance of peace and stability in our region' (cited in Gedhalyahu, 2012).

Foreign Ministry spokesman Yigal Palmor stated 'Israel has not closed the door to anyone ... we will be happy to engage in dialogue with anyone who is ready to negotiate with us' (cited in al-Tabaei, 2012). The response (provided to the Cairo paper *Asharq Al-Awsat*) from the Muslim Brotherhood spokesman Mahmoud Ghazlan was blunt: 'the [Muslim Brotherhood] group does not have any willingness to engage in dialogue with Israel. This decision has been taken and our position is consistent and clear, and is not currently open to discussion' (cited in *ibid.*).

After their success in the parliamentary elections, the salafists of Al-Nour Party issued a statement in December 2011 which also eschewed dialogue with Israel: '[t]he party strongly objects [to] normalization and dialogue attempts and establishing relations with an entity which wants to wipe off our identity, occupies our lands, imposes a siege on our brothers and strongly supports our hangers'. Regarding Camp David, Al-Nour provided a surprisingly moderate statement: 'it will honor the treaty but will seek to revise certain clauses' (cited in Kais, 2011).

The rhetoric of the leader of Tunisia's Ennahda Party, Rashid Al-Ghannouchi (who had returned from his long exile in London) was just as coruscating as that of the Egyptian Brotherhood. Speaking to *Quds Press* on the Israeli assault on Gaza in March 2012, Ghannouchi offered his opinion on Israel and Palestine:

> Aggression against the Palestinians is not something new as this is the nature of Israel; it grew up on aggression and cannot exist without it. The more that its victims are determined to resist, the more it increases its aggression, because the Israeli entity is going through an ageing process and sees that the only way to restore its confidence and the confidence of its sponsors and supporters is through increasing its aggression ... What can the revolutions offer the Palestinian cause? These revolutions are still concerned mainly about their domestic affairs. However, indications are that an important transformation is starting to appear; capitals in the Arab Spring countries have received Palestinian leaders of the resistance, with representative offices being opened in a number of cities, but the main concern of the Arab revolutions is essentially internal at this stage (Middle East Monitor, 2012).

In response to criticisms that Islamists have gained power in Arab Spring countries because of a political deal with the West under which a concession about the Palestinian cause has been made, he retorted:

> This is nonsense being spouted by losers; those who have failed to compete with the Islamists at the ballot box have nothing better to do except to promote such myths. No one can deny the Islamists' support for the Palestinian issue; many of the other political groups sold [out] the Palestinian cause, but the Islamists are the ones who have returned the Palestinian issue to the forefront of events (*loc. cit.*).

Unsurprisingly, Israeli leaders began to show concern by such categoric statements. Thus, Amos Gilad, a top aide to Defence Minister Ehud Barak, admitted: 'I'm not hiding from you that we are concerned ... The leaders of the Muslim Brotherhood keep declaring, "We are committed to this peace". I am not so sure' (cited in Williams, 2012). Prime Minister Benjamin Netanyahu also admitted '[t]he Muslim Brothers will not show mercy to us, they will not give way to us, but I hope they will keep the peace in Egypt, I hope that every government there will keep the peace (agreement)' *(loc. cit.)*.

On the vital Camp David Treaty, the Muslim Brotherhood has, in fact, been tip-toeing around the issue. The architect of the treaty, former US President Jimmy Carter thought (in May 2012) that the Brotherhood may seek to modify but not annul it – he indirectly hinted at what might need modification: '[t]he Camp David accords were also supposed to guarantee the rights of the Palestinians, at Sadat's insistence, but that aspect had not been honored' (*Ynetnews.com*, 2012). Though hard facts are difficult to come by we can be sure that a very significant majority of the Brotherhood and its supporters, rather than seek to 'modify' it, would like to see the rescinding of the treaty – especially as the aforementioned report by the Arab Affairs Committee of parliament (endorsed by FJP deputies) regards Israel as Egypt's 'number one enemy'. Doubtless, however, there are genuine concerns about how the military might react should the Brotherhood clearly state that it would not adhere to the Camp David Treaty on the grounds that it was signed by a leader who had no democratic mandate. Ruffling the junta's feathers before it has been fully seen off is understandably not a tactically astute move. Similarly, the Brotherhood wishes to appear 'responsible' on the global stage and not wish to incur the wrath of the Americans. Indubitably, there are likely to be divergent views as to how to proceed: 'pragmatists' will argue that nothing must jeopardise the road to civilian rule and implementation of myriad social, political, and economic reforms; whilst those of a more principled persuasion will want the treaty that is reviled by so many Egyptians to be junked as soon as a civilian government fully replaces military rule.

Israel is naturally keeping a keen eye on developments

knowing full well that the treaty with Egypt has been a lynchpin of its security given the fright it received in the early stages of the 1973 October war which threatened the integrity of the Zionist state. Since 1979, despite its recurrent wars and skirmishes with Arab neighbours, and despite perennial tensions with Iran, Israel has felt secure and not unduly worried about its survival and, accordingly, has devoted relatively few military resources to its border with Egypt. This equilibrium will indubitably be broken now that Islamists are exercising power in Egypt, possibly to be followed in Syria in the event of the collapse of the Assad regime – the two countries which gave Israel such a fright in 1973. The stakes are consequently very high. Whilst the scrapping of the Camp David Treaty would not necessarily trigger threats of a 'hot clash', nonetheless, this sense of security Israel has felt since its implementation would be much diminished. There is every prospect that the border between Egypt and Gaza would be permanently opened with the ensuing infiltration of weapons into the strip. The risk of a serious conflagration between Israel and Hams and Islamic Jihad, akin to that of the 2008-09 conflict, would doubtless rise – but next time, far more damage might be inflicted on Israel by the Palestinian Islamists.

Moreover, an Egypt freed from the yoke of the military and under the rule of Islamists is not likely to remain quiescent for long in such a scenario – mass solidarity rallies calling for the Egyptian army to provide military support for the Gazans would be the order of the day. Furthermore, some Egyptians might take matter into their owns hands and take pot shots at Israelis in border areas as happened in August 2011 when gunmen attacked Israeli civilian buses near the Red Sea resort of Eilat, killing eight people. In response, the Israelis killed five Egyptian policemen that led to weeks of protest outside the Israeli embassy in Cairo, which was attacked, broken into and the protective wall around it destroyed – protestors called for the expulsion of the Israeli ambassador (*BBC News*, September 2011). The episode reveals a glimpse of the hatred for Israel felt by so many Egyptians, Islamists and secular alike, a hatred which has hitherto been prevented from being fully vented. It also points to the sort of catalyst that could ignite a full blown conflict.

Though the Islamists have apparently gained the most from the Arab Spring, the Arab revolutions have not at all been – unlike Iran in 1979 – 'Islamic revolutions'. Not even the Egyptian Brotherhood campaigned for an Islamic revolution – indeed, the unmistakeable motif has been that that they all are democratic, nationalist, uprisings. There is great uncertainty at the time of writing as to the precise trajectory of the Egyptian revolution: what is clear is that the *ancien régime* has been rather successful in reining back the thrust of the revolution, and the Supreme Court (comprised of Mubarak appointees) had the audacity, in June 2012, to annul the parliamentary elections. Nonetheless, the presidential elections did take place: in the first round, the Brotherhood's Mohamed Morsi came first followed closely by Ahmed Shafiq, the former Air Force chief who was Mubarak's last Prime Minister. On *Al Jazeera's Empire* programme, Marwan Bishara poignantly described this is as the 'power struggle between the two most organised and least revolutionary groups – the Muslim Brotherhood and the military' (Bishara, 2012). In the run-off, Morsi narrowly defeated Shafiq so that the first democratically elected President of of Egypt was a member of the long proscribed Muslim Brotherhood. His first speech as President regarding international relations affirmed that he would abide by existing international treaties, notwithstanding the fact that they were implemented and upheld by the previous military dictators:

> We came to the world with a message of peace. We will maintain international charters and conventions and the commitments and agreements Egypt has signed with the world. We will not allow ourselves to interfere in the internal affairs of any country in the same way that we will not allow any interference in our affairs (cited in *BBC News, 2012*).

But in an interview published by Iran's Fars news agency on 25th June 2012, Morsi provided a more revealing insight to his views: he said the issue of Palestinian refugees returning to homes abandoned in the 1948 Arab-Israeli war and the 1967 Six-Day War 'is very important ... all these issues will be carried out through cabinet and governmental bodies because I will not take any decision on my own'. What will be of undoubted concern to Israel and the US is Morsi's desire to improve ties with Iran: 'part of my agenda is the development of ties between Iran and Egypt that will create a strategic balance in the region' (*National Post,* 2012). This will undo the freezing of relations between Egypt and Iran after the Camp David Treaty, which has served Israel so well.

Furthermore, what is most interesting and relevant for our purposes is that on 14th June 2012, a week before the second round of the presidential election, the Brotherhood's 'Supreme Guide' Mohamed Badie gave a speech in which he raised the issue of Israel-Palestine shrouded in Islamic theology in a typically uncompromising manner:

> How happy would be the Muslims if all Muslim rulers made the Palestinian cause a pivotal issue, around which Muslims, rulers and the ruled, would line up ... [so that] the sole goal for all of them [would be] the recovery of al-Aqsa Mosque, freeing it from the filth of the Zionists, and imposing Muslim rule throughout beloved Palestine ... We say to our people and our brothers in Palestine that they need to make as their inspiration the removal the Zionist project from Palestine (all of Palestine): Unity, unity, persistence, persistence, reconciliation, reconciliation, and patience, patience. Make your motto and your starting point be in confronting the Zionists ... (Badie, June 2012).

He followed this up with another speech reported in *Al Wafd* in July 2012 in which he called on 'all Muslims to wage jihad with their money and their selves to free al-Quds [Jerusalem]' and for 'the freeing of prisoners'. He demanded the right of return of [Palestinian] refugees, and challenged the return of Jews from around the world to settle on Palestinian land, and asked all Muslims to unite behind this return of the refugees (cited in *Al Wafd*, July 2012).[37]

---

[37] My thanks to Fatih Kariem for the translations from the *Ikhwan* and *Al Wafd* websites .

Notwithstanding his promise to be a President for all Egyptians, with the concomitant requirement to be free from party loyalties – he resigned from the Brotherhood and from the Freedom and Justice Party prior to standing for President – Morsi is still seen as a loyal member of the Brotherhood and, accordingly, will be put under enormous pressure to dutifully follow the guidance of his Supreme Guide. How this translates into practical politics is, however, far from clear: what is certain is that such sentiments have never been those of the military.

In August 2012, President Morsi boldly moved against the military by dismissing the head of SCAF, Field Marshal Mohamed Hussein Tantawi and his chief of staff, Sami Anan. He followed this up by sacking the head of every service of the armed forces (Hauslohner, 2012). This appeared to mark a decisive shift in power away from the military in favour of the Brotherhood. Given the passive response by SCAF to this move against them, there is good reason to suspect that an undertaking was provided by Morsi that core military interests would be protected. That said, part of the Arab awakening is likely to be a full awakening of the issue of Palestine that has long been put in aspic by leaders and rulers of the region. It will be difficult for the Brotherhood to side-step the Camp David Treaty on a never-never basis; in fact, as we have suggested, both progressive and Islamist forces are likely to demand that at least some meaningful support is provided to the Palestinians. Beyond Egypt, the issue will remain a clarion call for Hezbollah given its resolute and principled opposition to Israel. So it would be entirely in keeping for it to use the banner of Palestine to maintain and garner support not only among Palestinians but throughout the Arab and Islamic world. What this unmistakeably indicates is that rather than being dampened, the clash between Islamism and Zionism in the Middle East is likely to intensify in the coming years. This is the sort of vista that is doubtless concentrating Israeli minds.

PART III

ISLAMISM AND ZIONISM IN THE WEST

Chapter 5

The Clash in the USA

Centrality of the Israel/Palestine conflict

The clash in Israel/Palestine has truly seeped into America where, outside Israel, the Zionist movement is strongest. Though tensions existed prior to 9/11, they have intensified considerably since then. In a book edited by Reza Aslan and Aaron Hahn Tapper (2011) examining the relations between American Jews and American Muslims (entitled *Muslims and Jews in America,* with 16 papers by 'moderate' Jews and Muslims, seeking to improve 'interfaith dialogue'), there is an overwhelming sense that by far the most important determinant of this relationship, and cause for mutual suspicion and distrust, is indeed the Israel/Palestine conflict. As Rabbi Amy Eilburg states '[m]ore often than not, the Israeli-Palestinian conflict plays a role when American Muslims and American Jews enter into a relationship with one another. Generally speaking, I have found this to be true to a greater or lesser extent even for Muslims and Jews who do not have direct personal or familial ties to Palestine or Israel' (Eilberg, 2011, p. 34).

Another Rabbi, Eric Yoffie (president of Union of Reform Judaism), makes clear in an address given to the convention of the Islamic Society of North America (ISNA) in 2007 that 'American Jews have a deep, profound, and unshakable commitment to the state of Israel. We Jews see assuring the security of Israel as one of our community's most important accomplishments, and we are maintaining her security as one of our most important priorities' (Yoffie, 2011, p. 124)[38]. The

---

[38] There is an interesting 'distancing from Israel debate' in the US, that is, whether the distance (or connection) felt by American Jews towards Israel has, over time, narrowed or increased. Miller and Dashefsky (2010, p. 161) summarise the findings of the research as: 'younger Jews are less connected, intermarried Jews are less connected, and the majority of Jews (even younger

unambiguous inference is that Jewish Americans are committed Zionists writ large, that is, the well-being of another country – Israel – is of supreme importance to their identity, and that this is a non-negotiable position. Despite receiving a standing ovation, this categorical statement by a moderate Zionist will, nonetheless, have alienated a good percentage of the audience, for whom Israel is the cause of the perennial plight of the Palestinians – but hardline Islamists (who would probably not have attended ISNA's convention) will indubitably have concluded that given the chasm on this core issue, there is little reason for them to attempt to forge meaningful relations with their Jewish Zionist counterparts.

In contrast to Rabbis Eilberg and Yoffie, hardline American Zionists have been busy vigorously campaigning against not only Islamic terrorism, Islamism, but, to all intents and purposes, against the Muslim presence in the US. Among examples of the conflict provided in the Aslan and Hahn Tapper collection, the latter's paper (based on primary research) on the conflict on US university campuses demonstrates the poisonous nature of this inter-communal rivalry in America's seats of learning: Hahn Tapper makes clear that Jewish Zionist students are systematically using their far superior power, resources, and influence to attack Muslims and Islamists who dare to support the Palestinian cause (Hahn Tapper, 2011).

However, an even more graphic example of a Zionist onslaught on Muslims and Islamists in America is provided in the paper by the Islamic scholar Omid Safi, a professor at the University of North Carolina. The topic of this is a DVD, some 28 million of which were distributed free of charge with newspapers such as the *New York Times* in September 2008 in 'swing states' (such as Colorado, Florida, Ohio etc.) prior to the Presidential elections that year in the hope of stopping the

---

Jews) support Israel'. They cite research which suggests that 'about 60% of younger adult Jews who are not Orthodox profess some attachment to Israel. While less attached than their elders, most younger adult Jews still view Israel positively' (*loc. cit.*).

election of Barack Obama. The DVD was entitled *Obsession: Radical Islam's War against the West*. Safi argues that *Obsession* is 77 minutes of propaganda footage with the message that Muslims are out to destroy Western civilisation: 'that attacks taking place in Iraq, Palestine, Chechnya, and Iran present a global Muslim conspiracy against Israel and "The West" ... Radical Islam is intrinsically linked to destroying the state of Israel'. He points that 'most of the figures who are paraded in the DVD, whether they are Jewish, Christian, or Muslim, are all passionate pro-Israeli speakers who have a long history of speaking out against Palestinians, Arabs, and Muslims in general' (Safi, 2011, p. 22). Indeed, the producer, Raphael Shore, is a Canadian-Israeli. Safi then asks '[w]hy are Jewish American and Jewish Israeli organizations deploying the same "othering" strategies that were leveled against Jews for millennia? And where is the voice of dissent from the Jewish community itself? Indeed "Obsession" has torn down bridges of dialogue between Muslim and Jewish groups across the country, connection that took years to establish' (*ibid.*, p. 30).

The producers of *Obsession* followed this up by making another film on the same theme: entitled *The Third Jihad* this attracted even more controversy. Michael Powell of *The New York Times* points out that the New York City police commissioner, Raymond W. Kelly, personally cooperated with the filmmakers – a decision which he subsequently thought a mistake. The film's thesis is 'the goal of "much of Muslim leadership here in America" is to "infiltrate and dominate" the United States – it was screened for more than 1,400 officers during training in 2010 and was shown on a "continuous loop" for between three months and a year to officers receiving antiterrorism training. The film, amid images of assassinations, bombings and executions, portrays many mainstream American Muslim leaders as closet radical Islamists, and states that their "primary tactic" is deception' (Powell, 2012).

The more such militant Zionists assert or imply that Muslims are a threat to US society, the greater the likelihood of an Islamist backlash. As Safi warns: '[w]e can either keep going down this slippery slope of accusations and blanket generalizations, or bond together and rise up to say "Enough!"'

(*ibid.*, p. 31). The 'rising up' might, however, lead to more than just the assertion of saying 'enough' by American Muslims: it can precipitate open conflict between Islamists and Jewish Zionists which might take some very ugly turns and further corrode relations between the two groups. What is clear is that for American Zionists, Palestine is, above all, an 'Islamic issue' – according with our view in chapter 2 that the issue of Palestine has been thoroughly 'Islamised'. This is not too surprising given the virtual absence of Christian Palestinians, and of Christians in general, making a robust and public stance in support of Palestinians (but see the section on Christian Zionism for exceptions to this generalisation).

There is, however, a profound difference between Islamists and Zionists in America. Jewish adherents of Zionism are, in the main, long-settled in the US, mainly Ashkenazi with European origins, thoroughly integrated in all aspects of society, and yield very significant power and influence in regard to their advocacy of Israel. A graphic example of the power of the Israel Lobby is provided in the memoirs of a former Secretary of State, George Shultz, relating to events of December 1982:

> In early December [1982]... I got word that a supplement was moving through the lame-duck session of Congress to provide a $250 million increase in the amount of U.S. military assistance granted to Israel: this in the face of Israel's invasion of Lebanon, its use of cluster bombs, and its complicity in the Sabra and Shatila massacres! We fought the supplement and we fought it hard. President Reagan and I weighed in personally, making numerous calls to senators and congressmen. On December 9, I added a formal letter of opposition saying that the supplement appeared to 'endorse and reward Israel's policies'. Foreign Minister Shamir called President Reagan's opposition 'an unfriendly act' and said that 'it endangers the peace process'. The supplement sailed right by us and was approved by Congress as though President Reagan and I had not even been there. I was astonished and disheartened. This brought home to me vividly Israel's leverage in our Congress. I saw that I must work carefully with the Israelis if I was to have any handle on congressional action that might affect Israel and if I was to maintain congressional support for my efforts to make progress in the Middle East (cited in Mearsheimer and Walt, 2007,

p. 46).

A more recent example – in April 2010 – is that of 76 US senators (more than three quarters of the total) including 38 Democrats, having signed a letter sponsored by the pro-Israel group AIPAC to Secretary of State Hillary Clinton implicitly rebuking the Obama Administration for its supposed confrontational stance towards Israel (Smith 2010).

In stark contrast, Muslims are largely recent immigrants or refugees: some two-thirds are foreign born (coming from an astonishing 68 countries with all the diversity this implies); most (25 per cent) who are US-born are African-American (Hahn Tapper, *op. cit.,* p. 75), so that almost the entirety of the Muslim population of America which is not African-American is first generation immigrant. Typically for recent settlers, they are superficially integrated, with very little power and influence – certainly in relation to US foreign policy. The population of American Jews is nearly three times that of Muslims but, as a proportion of the total US population, both are very small: 1.7 per cent is Jewish and 0.6 per cent is Muslim [Pew Forum, 2010]). However, the 'power differential' is truly enormous: a reality that needs to be borne in mind when considering the antagonisms between the two camps.

The context of 9/11

As noted in chapter 4, one of the core reasons for Al Qaeda's terror campaign was US support for Israel – a reason reiterated by Osama bin Laden on many occasions. Moreover, the binary opposition of support for Palestinians and opposition to Israel has been a defining principle of all Islamists, Shia and Sunni alike; jihadists or otherwise. For hardline Zionists, this has facilitated their relentless efforts to paint Islamists as irrational fanatics intent upon acts of terrorism to achieve their aims. The operating principle is: if individuals and organisations conducting such acts can be discredited, then so too can their cause, no matter how justified. Thus, questions relating to US imperialism, US foreign policy, including its unyielding support for Israel, can be conveniently side-stepped as indeed was the case in the aftermath of 9/11. In the mainstream, there was, to all intents and purposes, no effort to seek out the ultimate causes of the 9/11 attacks, to discern motivating factors. The 'why?' question regarding a crime is of vital importance in the search for the perpetrator: credible motivating factors providing a reasonable 'fit' to a crime frequently point to the likely offender. If the offender is deemed an irrational fanatic, motives are thereby rendered immaterial and, accordingly, he or she is considered insane and in need of psychiatric treatment. Yet, the 9/11 hijackers and their sponsors were not accorded the defence of insanity: they were, rather, deemed to have acted with careful planning and purpose – rooted in their religion, ideology, and sense of justice. That is to say, there were tangible reasons – no matter how unpalatable – for their suicidal, murderous, actions: what has long been termed 'blowback' emanating from US foreign policy.

In the case of 9/11, however, the 'why?' question was (and has been) wilfully neglected. It's as if the gravity of the crime precluded the need for a serious interrogation of the likely causal factors – *res ipsa loquitur* sufficed: no end could be justified through recourse to means which are deemed truly beyond the pale. The focus turned to – and remained fixated on – security failures, and the sheer evil nature of the suicidal hijackers, Al Qaeda, and its leader, Osama bin Laden. To prevent such an attack from recurring, no expense was spared in regard to tightening security and counter-terrorism measures. The absence of carefully ascertaining and analysing the motivating factors served Zionist purposes well: quite simply any examination of Israel and Israeli policies, and unrelenting American support for Israel, as key causes for Arab/Muslim anger and resentment – at the jihadist extreme of which were Al Qaeda terrorists – was perfunctorily set aside by the US government and the mainstream media. Yet, such blatant evasion of the underlying causes, in combination with the launch of the 'war on terror', aroused still more anger and frustration among large numbers of Arabs and Muslims including those residing in the US. But, as recent migrants and refugees, who chose to settle in the US, their response was muted and they were – and have been – powerless to challenge

The Clash in the USA

the official line.

A direct consequence of this frustration – highlighted in the remark by Omid Safi above – is that tensions between Islamists and Zionists have intensified. Since the attacks, Muslims have come under particular scrutiny and suspicion given that the perpetrators of 9/11, as well of terror threats thereafter, have been Muslims. As is the norm with new migrants, Muslims (excluding the 'Black Muslims' of the Nation of Islam) in America are politically weak having (at the time of writing) only one congressman, a black convert with a non-Muslim name, Keith Ellison. Because of US wars in Afghanistan and Iraq, and its firm support for Israel, many Muslim-Americans (like their co-religionists elsewhere) have harboured a deep resentment at US foreign policy believing it to be waging a war on Islam under the guise of a war on terror. At the extreme, this has led some to pursue a jihad and countenance committing acts of terror against US targets. Such Islamists have become America's public enemy number one.

This threat to the US has been greatly stressed and utilised by Zionists: they vigorously campaign for the US to take tough, uncompromising, actions against such Islamists both at home and abroad. As noted in chapter 1, since 9/11, Islamists have been the most determined and vociferous opponents of Israel and Zionism. By a sleight of hand, Zionists conflate Islamist regimes (notably Iran) and organisations (notably Hezbollah and Hamas) which are opposed to Israel as being also a threat to the USA and to the western world writ large. Moreover, this collapsing of US interests with those of Israel means those Muslim majority countries which are not Islamist but opposed to Israel (notably Syria under the Assad regime) are similarly viewed as a danger to the West. Contrariwise, those Islamist regimes that have a benign attitude to Israel (notably Saudi Arabia and the Gulf states) are quietly ignored. The rule adopted therefore is straightforward and rational: any individual, group, or regime that is critical of, or hostile to, Israel is to be relentlessly opposed. This has certainly been

American policy in the post 9/11 period.[39]

What is beyond dispute is that the 9/11 attacks brought Muslims in general, and Islamists in particular, to the forefront of US politics. Of crucial importance was – and remains – the fact that the hijackers were Muslims carrying out suicide attacks in the name of Islam which they believed was sanctioned by Islam.[40] This fact has deeply affected the American psyche and, accordingly, helped powerfully conflate Muslims and Islam with terrorism; a conflation that has been accentuated by the subsequent terror threats instigated by Muslims.

Immediately after the 9/11 attacks, this conflation was seized upon by Zionists: the charge was led by Israeli leaders. The *New York Times* reported that the former Prime Minister Benjamin Netanyahu was asked on the night of 11th September what the attack meant for relations between the United States and Israel. At first he revealingly replied 'It's very good' but

---

[39] Though 15 of the hijackers were Saudis and Bin Laden was also a Saudi citizen, the 9/11 Commission controversially concluded that there was no evidence of Saudi state involvement in the attacks or the funding of the hijackers (*BBC News*, 2004). Hence, the US took no action against its Saudi ally.

[40] There are, however, myriad 'conspiracy theories' which cast doubt on the official version of the events of 9/11. This is not the place to examine the nature and merits of these – one of the important authors to shed a highly critical light is David Ray Griffin. An opinion poll of 17 countries in 2008 found that only 46 per cent thought that Al Qaeda was responsible for the 9/11 attacks, 15 percent said the U.S. government, 7 percent said Israel and 7 percent said some other perpetrator. One in four people said they did not know who was behind the attacks (Reuters, 2008). I propose simply to adhere to the conventional view that the hijackers were Islamists who carried out suicidal attacks because of their grievances against US foreign policy. In fact, Al Qaeda's deputy leader, Ayman Al-Zawahiri accused Iran for spreading the 'lie' that Israel was responsible for the 9/11 attacks: '[t]he purpose of this lie is clear - [to suggest] that there are no heroes among the Sunnis who can hurt America as no-one else did in history ... Iranian media snapped up this lie and repeated it ... Iran's aim here is also clear - to cover up its involvement with America in invading the homes of Muslims in Afghanistan and Iraq' (*BBC News*, 2008).

then steadied himself by stating 'well, not very good, but it will generate immediate sympathy' ... the attack would 'strengthen the bond between our two peoples, because we've experienced terror over so many decades, but the United States has now experienced a massive hemorrhaging of terror' (Bennett, 2001). In the same vein, Prime Minister Ariel Sharon asserted the strong links between Israel and the United States, calling the assault an attack on 'our common values' and declaring, 'I believe together we can defeat these forces of evil' (*loc. cit.*).

We can aver that post 9/11 a simplistic but most effective ideological chain was stressed by Zionists that had widespread currency, especially in America: Muslim→Islamist→opposition to Israel→opposition to the US→opposition to the West. This is, of course, the setting out of Samuel Huntington's clash between Islamic and Western civilisations, as highlighted in the preface, where Israel/Zionism is firmly within the Western camp. Curiously enough, such an assertion of political identity to followers of a religion (Islam in this case) is akin to the same assertion made by millions of Muslims around the world in regard to Jews and Zionism. Whereas one considers Muslims in general to be Islamists the other considers Jews in general to be Zionists. *Ipso facto* such an assumption is utilised for the view that Jews support the policies and actions of Israel *tout court*. Needless to say, such a rigid schema in both cases makes reasoned debate and dialogue well-nigh impossible – a case of the deaf haranguing the deaf. This is another instance of the clash between Islamism and Zionism being particularly toxic in countries where both groups of people live as fellow citizens, invariably as small minorities in each case. Events of faraway lands dominate their lives to a pernicious extent, to the point of corroding individual and community relations. America, with its long history of a society disfigured by the ugly stain of race and the legacy of slavery, now has two small minorities with the ability to truly scar the body politic.

Thus, on one side, Zionist critiques of Islamism are summarily dismissed as illegitimate propaganda; more troublingly, dissenting remarks and views by Jews are similarly rejected. On the other side, Islamist critiques of Israel and Zionism are dismissed by the same logic; and Muslims are viewed to be sympathetic to terror attacks on Israel and the USA.

It is important to stress that the US-led war on terror has proved a self-fulfilling prophecy: attacks on Afghanistan and Iraq have provoked actual and planned Islamist terrorist attacks not only in these two countries but in parts of the West also as a manifestation of 'jihadist blowback'. The sight of Americans killing innocent civilians and using torture in Abu Ghraib, Bagram, and Guantanamo fuelled outrage and has given Islamists the world over an enormous fillip in their recruitment drive. Yet, the indiscriminate and sectarian attacks by Islamist terror groups have grievously besmirched Islam given that jihadists have relentlessly used Koranic doctrines in justification. This has deeply alienated non-jihadist Muslims and put them on the defensive whilst contemporaneously giving ammunition to those – especially Zionists and Christian fundamentalists – who strongly conflate Islamism with violence and terror and who, in turn, are the strongest advocates for the prosecution of the war on terror. A self-reinforcing mechanism has come into play: war on terror →Islamist terror →justification for continuing war on terror →justification for Islamist terror in response etc. An important outcome has been that Islam itself has been subjected to great scrutiny so there has also transpired considerable unease and negative views of Islam and Muslims throughout North America and Europe which has given added cogency to the arguments raised by Zionists and Neocons.

Such has been the legacy of 9/11 and the war on terror, which centrally provides the context to the clash with respect to what became known as the 'Ground Zero mosque' controversy to which we now turn.

The 'Ground Zero mosque' controversy

During the course of 2010, a great hue and cry occurred over the application by Muslim developers to build a mosque and Muslim community centre in the Manhattan district of New York. What troubled so many about this entirely legitimate application was that the proposed site at Park Place is two blocks from where had stood the twin towers, that is, from 'Ground Zero', and that the building in question had been damaged by the debris from the destruction of the towers. In normal circumstances, this would not have aroused much, if any, concern – but these are far from normal times. The building of a mosque – or indeed of anything explicitly Islamic – was deemed by detractors to be intolerable in the post-9/11 era notwithstanding the fact that the US constitution and law guarantee the developers the right to proceed with such a project.[41] As was pointed out, the Pentagon has a prayer space for Muslims (though this is not a mosque). At least two mosques exist near the vicinity of Ground Zero and the World Trade Centre had had several designated prayer rooms for Muslims.

The proposal (originally named Cordoba House, later changed to Park 51) appeared to be progressing smoothly, so much so that in December 2009 the *New York Times* published a supportive front page article on the project. A crucial reason for the preference of this particular site for the Islamic Centre is provided by Imam Feisal Abdul Rauf, the cleric leading the project: '[a] presence so close to the World Trade Center where a piece of the wreckage fell sends the opposite statement to what happened on 9/11 ... we wanted to push back against the extremists'. The article points out that two Jewish leaders (one a rabbi, the other the Director of the Jewish Community Center, which Rauf wants to model his Islamic Centre on) and two city officials including one from the mayor's office, support the project, whilst an FBI spokesman acknowledged that Rauf has worked with the FBI (Blumenthal and Mowjood, 2009). Later in the month, Laura Ingraham of *Fox News* interviewed the wife of Feisal Rauf, Daisy Khan, remarking 'I can't find many people who really have a problem with it ... I like what you're

---

[41] There is a wealth of material on this topic – Wikipedia's article in particular cites extensive sources from all sides of the conflict. Rather than going over details of the debate, our purpose in this chapter is simply to draw attention to the key political issues involved, which are germane to the thrust of this book.

trying to do' (cited in Elliott, 2010).

For almost six months after the publication of the *New York Times* article, the project did not arouse much interest. Matters, however, suddenly changed when a New York City community board unanimously approved the project. In an interview with *The Wall Street Journal* in May 2010, Daisy Khan explained 'we wanted to look at the legacy of 9/11 and do something positive ... to reverse the trend of extremism and the kind ideology that the extremists are spreading'; but then cautioned 'I am sure that there will be some people who are a little concerned' (cited in Rutkoff, 2010). Indeed, right at the moment of this interview, there were indeed some people expressing concern at the project, and would do so with great vigour.

Rupert Murdoch's *New York Post* then ran a story on May 6th 2010 under the heading 'Panel approves "WTC" mosque' (Topousis, 2010). On the same day it was picked up by a Jewish American woman, Pamela Geller, who is an extreme Zionist and hostile critic of Islam. Geller had revealed her views in a robust and forthright manner in an Israeli media outlet *Arutz Sheva 7* (Israel National News.com) in May 2008, exactly two years before she interjected against the Manhattan Islamic Centre:

> In Israel's sixty years, the Jews thrived. Free to pursue their dreams, the Jews flourished and their enemies seethed; Jews prospered, while their enemies plotted their annihilation. The end of the Third Reich was merely a *hudna*, a cessation of hostilities until the annihilationists could regroup, rearm, redeploy. But Israel succeeded and Islamic jihad failed in all but one thing. The enemies of the people of Israel succeeded in infecting the world politic with their vile Jew-hatred. Worse still, "enlightened," guilty, secular Jews sidled up to the enemy and worked their evil inside Israel, the US and other Western nations.
>
> It galls me that the Jews I fight for are self-destructive, suicidal even. Here in America (and the world over), Israel's real friends are in the Republican party and yet over 80% of American Jews are Democrats. I don't get it. The conventional wisdom on the Left is that Israel is an oppressor and her actions are worse than the world's most depraved and dangerous regimes. Chomsky, Finkelstein, Soros - these men are the killers.
>
> So I say to Israel, stand loud and proud. Give up nothing. Turn

The Clash in the USA

over not a pebble. For every rocket fired, drop a MOAB [Massive Ordnance Air Blast bomb]. Take back Gaza. Secure Judea and Samaria [West Bank]. Stop buying *Haaretz*. Throw leftists bums out. Stand straight and walk on. Be worthy of your ancestors (Geller, 2008).

Geller, a founder member (with Robert Spencer) of the group Stop Islamization of America, began a campaign to oppose the Islamic Centre. On 6th May, she posted a blog with the heading 'Monster Mosque Pushes Ahead in Shadow of World Trade Center Islamic Death and Destruction'; she later described the proposed centre as the 'Ground Zero Mega Mosque' (Geller, 2010a). As was subsequently pointed out by many, this was in fact not a mosque but an Islamic community and cultural centre (though the original plan did have a mosque in the building which, however, was later designated – in the midst of the controversy – as a 'prayer space'). But even if the project had been solely for a mosque, it would still, in all likelihood, have passed the planning regulations as there was felt to be a genuine need for further space in the Manhattan district.

The stark coupling of 'Ground Zero' with 'mosque' had astonishing emotive and political power, and proved highly effective in mobilising opposition to the project. But why should it have done so? After all, as already noted, two mosques already existed in the near vicinity and the World Trade Center had spaces for prayer spaces for Muslims (which admittedly were not equivalent to mosques). Moreover, New York has some 30 mosques in the city so these have become part of its landscape. The reason as to why this conflation proved so potent is surely because negative connotations associated with mosques have become embedded in the minds of many Americans since 9/11 – emanating from the destruction of the twin towers at Ground Zero in the name of Islam, whose holy places of worship are mosques. It was this simplistic, one-dimensional causality which Geller utilised and supercharged it by asserting that '[t]his is Islamic domination and expansionism. The location is no accident. Just as Al-Aqsa was built on top of the temple in Jerusalem' (Geller, 2010b). Her reference to the Al Aqsa mosque is very revealing notwithstanding the fact that the site of the proposed Islamic Centre is *not* where the twin towers had stood. Such an ideological underpinning and false analogy was of no concern to the public at large and nor indeed to the media – what truly mattered and gave enormous cogency and legitimacy was that her arguments genuinely resonated among many of the relatives of the 9/11 attacks (though, importantly, many relatives *supported* the project). For example, Debra Burlingame, co-founder of the group 9/11 Families for a Safe and Strong America told *Fox News*:

> This is a place which is 600 feet from where almost 3,000 people were torn to pieces by Islamic extremists ... I think that it is incredibly insensitive and audacious really for them to build a mosque, not only on that site, but to do it specifically so that they could be in proximity to where that atrocity happened (quoted in Green, 2010).

Indeed, many other 9/11 families who opposed the project also asserted that the developers were 'insensitive'. Leading Republican politicians such as John McCain, Newt Gingrich, and Rudy Giuliani as well some Democrats such as Howard Dean also came out strongly against the project.

Pamela Geller realised correctly that the 9/11 attack on New York was still a source of great angst for Americans and was intrinsically bound up with the religion of the hijackers, that is, Islam in the generic sense. The fact that different strands and traditions exist and are often in violent conflict with each other was deemed irrelevant. This powerful sentiment was not picked up by the developers and was later admitted as much by Sharif El-Gamal, one of the developers (see below).

Some influential Muslim commentators succumbed to the tidal wave of opposition and began also to speak out against the project and to argue that it should be moved elsewhere in the city. Thus, for example, Zuhdi Jasser, a founding member of the Center for Islamic Pluralism and President of the American Islamic Forum for Democracy, in Phoenix, told *CBS News* on the ninth anniversary of the 9/11 attacks:

> We Muslims should first separate mosque and state before

lecturing Americans about church and state ... American freedom of religion is a right, but ... it is not right to make one's religion a global political statement with a towering Islamic edifice that casts a shadow over the memorials of Ground Zero. ... Islamists in 'moderate' disguise are still Islamists. In their own more subtle ways, the WTC mosque organizers end up serving the same aims (as) separatist and supremacist wings of political Islam (*CBS News,* (2010).

In stark contrast, Mayor Michael Bloomberg strongly supported the project on the grounds of freedom of religion which the US constitution provides for. Given his well-known Zionist sympathies, this was a refreshing and principled stance, and unusual given that Zionist individuals and organisations were generally on the side of Pamela Geller.[42] Perhaps the most extreme statement was issued by the Zionist Organization of America in a press release with a revealing headline: 'Don't Increase Pain To Families Of 9/11 Victims Of Islamist Terror By Building Mosque Led By Extremist, Anti-U.S., Pro-Hamas Imam' (ZOA, 2010).

The media commentator, Fareed Zakaria, showed his displeasure at the oppositional stance of another major Zionist organisation to the project (the Anti-Defamation League) by returning the Hubert H. Humphries First Amendment Freedoms Prize which it had awarded to him in 2005. He made the novel point that '[i]f there is going to be a reformist movement in Islam, it is going to emerge from places like the proposed institute. We should be encouraging groups like the one behind this project, not demonizing them. Were this mosque being built in a foreign city, chances are that the U.S. government would be funding it' (Zakaria, 2010).

The Pakistani academic Akbar Ahmed, an Islamic studies

---

[42] But in December 2011, many New York Muslim leaders boycotted Mayor Bloomberg's annual 'interfaith breakfast', in protest at surveillance on Muslims with police attempting to infiltrate Muslim neighbourhoods and mosques – Bloomberg deemed such 'counter-terrorism measures' to be legal (*BBC News*, December 2011).

professor at American University in Washington, D.C., stressed that 9/11 is still a running sore for Americans – so Muslims need to act with great care. In an interview with *CNN* he cautioned:

> I don't think the Muslim leadership has fully appreciated the impact of 9/11 on America. They assume Americans have forgotten 9/11 and even, in a profound way, forgiven 9/11, and that has not happened. The wounds remain largely open ... And when wounds are raw, an episode like constructing a house of worship – even one protected by the Constitution, protected by law – becomes like salt in the wounds (*CNN*, 2010).

But, in the same piece, Ibrahim Hooper, a leading spokesman for The Council on American-Islamic Relations disagreed with Ahmed's analysis, instead arguing that Muslims should not back down simply because a vocal minority was complaining: 'I am not going to base my actions and my principles and my future on the ability of bigots to manufacture a controversy' (*loc. cit.*).

There was also the suggestion (albeit without hard evidence) that the vitriolic opposition to the Islamic Centre was generating support for Islamist extremists. An article in the *Voice of America* provides the views of Evan Kohlmann, senior partner of the New York-based security consulting firm Flashpoint Global Partners, who believed that radical Islamists see a propaganda and recruitment opportunity in the New York mosque controversy as well as other manifestations of anti-Muslim feeling:

> The reaction is, at least on the part of extremists, fairly gleeful – that America is playing into our hands, that America is revealing its ugly face, and that even if it doesn't further radicalize people in the Middle East, there's no doubt that it will radicalize a kind of a key constituency that al-Qaida and other extremists are seeking to covet, seeking to court, which is the small number of homegrown extremists here in the United States (quoted in Thomas, 2010).

In a nutshell, we can aver that the key motivating factor behind Pamela Geller's relentless campaign was her strong Zionist views – a crucial fact that was neglected in discussions about her and the campaign in the mainstream media. This is not to suggest that if she did not have such views, the campaign would never have gotten off the ground – certainly we could imagine, say, a Christian fundamentalist taking up the cudgel in a similar manner. But that did not happen – it took the indomitable will of a Geller, driven by a ruthless sectarian agenda with an evangelical zeal, to act as the catalyst and bring the issue into the public eye. Geller understood very clearly what we have stressed in this book: the most determined opponents of her cherished views on Zionism are, in the main, Islamists so *ipso facto* they must be attacked and rooted out mercilessly. For a New Yorker, it was far better to point to their threat to the USA rather than to Israel – but this only partially masked her underlying beliefs and motives.

There is good reason to think that ordinary New Yorkers and Americans were not particularly enamoured by Geller's pro-Israel agenda and barely disguised racism (she argues that black South Africans are conducting a genocide against Whites: '[t]he genocide of white South Africans is heating up' [Geller, 2010c]) yet were highly sympathetic to her arguments against the proposed centre and indeed to her tirades against Muslims in general and Islamists in particular. In this, her campaign proved a stunning success. Why should this be so?

No matter her motives, it is incontrovertible that Geller's remarks in an interview with *New York Times* that the proposed centre was an 'outrage' and 'deeply offensive' proved extraordinarily effective (Barnard and Feuer, 2010). In a an interview for *CNN* in August 2010, she was asked 'do you agree that the terrorists who attacked us on 9/11 were practicing a perverted form of Islam, and that is not what is going to be practiced at this mosque'? Her response was uncompromising: 'I will say that the Muslim terrorists were practising pure Islam, original Islam. The Turkish prime minister ... said to Obama there is no extreme Islam. There is no moderate Islam. Islam is Islam. It was pure Islam' (*CNN* Transcripts, 2010). No matter that she distorted the meaning of Prime Minister Erdogyan, her judgment again would have convinced a significant constituency of Americans (and we might aver that Al Qaeda members doubtless also believe that they preach and practice a 'pure' form of Islam).

These core messages proved decisive, resonating among and permeating through broad swathes of US society. From small beginnings as a local issue, concerns about the proposed centre reverberated throughout the US and quickly followed around the world. Geller's campaign provides a good case study of what Malcolm Gladwell has famously described as the 'tipping point' whose three pre-requisites – the 'law of the few', 'stickiness factor' and 'power of context' – were duly obtained (Gladwell, 2000)[43]. Evidence of the success was borne out by opinion polls showing that a large majority of Americans opposed the building of the Islamic Centre on Park Place. A CNN poll conducted in August 6-10, at the height of the furore, found that *68 per cent of Americans opposed the project whilst 29 per cent supported it* (CNN, 2010). An Economist/YouGov poll in August 2010 showed a similar disparity: *58 per cent opposed; 18 per cent in favour* with the remainder undecided (*Economist*, 2010). In both – and other – polls more Republican voters were opposed than Democrats.

These astonishing poll percentages against a project by the most benign Muslims imaginable attempting to improve the image of Islam in the US surely indicate that very large numbers of Americans now have serious reservations about Islam. This is attested by a Gallup poll in January 2010 which showed that Islam is by far the most negatively viewed religion in America: 31 per cent view it as 'not favourable at all'; whilst 23 per cent view it as 'not too favourable' (the respective

---

[43] Thus, Pamela Geller was exceptional ('the law of the few') in her drive and determination to spread the message about the proposed Manahattan Islamic Centre; her systematic conflation of 'Ground Zero' and 'mosque' proved enormously 'sticky', that is, the message had a huge impact as it easily stuck in the minds of millions of people ; and finally the context of 9/11, Manhattan, New York, and indeed the USA, was crucial to the effectiveness of her campaign which quickly reached the tipping point from obscurity to global prominence.

figures for Christians are 4 and 4 per cent and for Jews 15 and 10 per cent). Similarly, 43 per cent admit to feeling at least "a little" prejudice towards Muslims – far more than the number who say the same about Christians (18%), Jews (15%) and Buddhists (14%) (Gallup.com, 2010). This theme was developed by Samuel Huntington in a work on American national identity, which followed his controversial 'clash of civilisations' thesis (briefly elaborated upon in the preface). Huntington argues that:

> Muslims, particularly Arab Muslims, seem slow to assimilate ... The difficulties [regarding their assimilation] also may stem from the nature of Muslim culture. Elsewhere in the world, Muslim minorities have proved to be "indigestible" by non-Muslim societies ... In some circumstances, the desire of Muslims to maintain the purity of their faith and the practices of their religion may lead to conflicts with non-Muslims (Huntington, 2005, pp. 188, 189)[44].

What was understated was the fact that the developers (including Feisel Rauf and Daisy Khan) are, in fact, keen for Muslims to integrate into American society. This is attested by the following remark by Rauf, which is most unusual for an imam: '[w]hile Muslim minorities must surely enjoy the right to practice their religion, these communities should also attempt to adapt to the society in which they live, in particular when such a community's majority is non-Muslim' (Rauf, 2011, p. 62). Moreover, what was ignored was the fact that the developers are Sufi Muslims – a strand of Islam which is perhaps less doctrinal than any other and which stresses mysticism and spiritualism and, importantly, non-violence (the pop star Madonna at one time was sympathetic to Sufism). As a consequence, many orthodox Sunnis and Shia are uncomfortable with it, whilst others are implacably opposed; for

---

[44] This may also lead to alienation from the majority society as well as from other religious-ethnic minorities – a phenomenon I have termed 'psychic detachment' (for a discussion of this, see Hasan, 2010, ch. 3).

example, Sufism is repressed in Iran whilst in Pakistan, Sufi mosques are deemed to be 'places of worship' (and not accorded the status of mosque [or *masjid*]) and have been the targets of sectarian attacks by elements of the Sunni majority. Ironically, the 9/11 Al Qaeda hijackers – most of whom were Saudi wahhabis – would, in all likelihood, have opposed the building of Sufi mosques.[45] Such a nuanced understanding might have offered a different light on the Park 51 development but, alas, this was of no consequence to the opponents.

In fact, it was a progressive Jewish website ('Mandoweiss') which drew attention to the reality with an article poignantly headed 'Pro-Israel extremists have campaigned against an Islamic cultural center before'. The first two paragraphs of the article by Jeff Klein highlight the Zionist politics of the key players:

> Haven't we seen this movie before? Yes, in Boston, and with nearly the same cast of characters. The fight against the Roxbury Mosque and Cultural Center planned by the Islamic Society of Boston (ISB) was framed as a battle against "Muslim extremists" and "terror supporters." In reality (as court documents showed) the campaign was organized by activists with the far-right pro-Israel David Project and CAMERA, spearheaded by founder Charles Jacobs, who now heads a front group with the Orwellian name "Americans for Peace and Tolerance". Later, the story was picked up and promoted by the Murdoch-owned Boston Herald and the local Fox TV affiliate. When the ISB eventually sued its attackers for defamation, the defendants were represented by an attorney who was also a leader of New England AIPAC (American-Israel Public Affairs Committee).
>
> Likewise, the New York Islamic Community Center project in lower Manhattan was uncontroversial until it began to be labeled falsely as "the Ground Zero Mosque" and was vilified by right-wing bloggers with a pro-Israel agenda. Although the media has reported on the way the Right has used anti-Muslim bigotry to stir up racist outrage against the Islamic Center, *there has been little*

---

[45] Indeed, from evidence provided by Lawrence Wright, Al Qaeda deemed Shia Muslims to be one of the 'enemies of Islam' (Wright, 2007, p. 303).

The Clash in the USA

notice of the Israel connection [emphasis added by RH]. Jihad Watch founder Robert Spencer and Atlas Shrugged blogger Pamela Geller, who led the charge, are active in the same circles as the pro-Israel extremists in Boston. Geller is a regular commentator on the far-right Israeli radio network Arutz Sheva. Together they created a front-group to promote the anti-Muslim crusade called Stop Islamization of America. The campaign of slander against the "Ground Zero Mosque" was first mainstreamed in the Murdoch-owned New York Post and has been trumpeted relentlessly by Fox News, as well as by Neocon operatives like Bill Kristol and Liz Cheney (Klein, 2010).

Klein then provides the true, but hidden motive, of these Zionists:

Why? Because promoting a "culture-clash" between the "West" and Islam is seen as a way to bolster support for Israel and to sustain a permanent US "War on Terror" (*loc. cit.*).

Geller and her fellow campaigners might argue that they have every right to support Israel as, like America, it is also under threat from Islamism. The truth is that in her campaigning against the Islamic Centre, she did not explicitly press her support for Israel. In fact she very cleverly focused on the offence caused to New Yorkers and Americans in general; otherwise her real agenda would be exposed – and then likely to be fiercely opposed. Moreover, she would doubtless argue that as American citizens, she and her allies have genuine concerns about the 'Islamization of America' and are merely exercising their democratic right to protest on an issue of profound importance to fellow Americans. Indeed, this is plausible and may have been the animating factor behind the large numbers who later joined her bandwagon.

One manifestation of the bandwagon is that opposition began also to be expressed to the construction of mosques in other US cities. In Tennessee, in the summer of 2010, three plans for new Islamic Centres in the Nashville area 'provoked controversy and outbursts of ugliness'. In Murfreesboro, a suburb of Nashville, opponents of a mosque project brandished placards with the sign 'Keep Tennessee Terror Free' (Gowen,

2010). Interestingly, the key campaigner against this mosque is an African-American, Kevin Fisher, who asserts that '[s]o many things about Islam are disconcerting ... As they get bigger, there will be concerns about the ideology, what they preach and what they believe'. When told that this was an expression of bigotry against Muslims, he retorts 'it's offensive to me. [My] stepmother was dragged off restaurant stools in the 1960s and has cigarette burns in her arm. That's discrimination' (*loc. cit.*). There was also trenchant opposition to mosque applications in Temecula, about 60 miles north of San Diego, and in Sheboygan, Wisconsin (Goodstein, 2010).

Despite the hue and cry around the Manhattan Islamic Centre, the clamour abated and the project duly proceeded: the first phase opened in September 2011 without attracting any controversy. One of the developers, Sharif El-Gamal, clearly bruised by the hostility to the centre, acknowledged '[w]e made incredible mistakes. The biggest mistake we made was not to include 9/11 families. We didn't understand that we had a responsibility to discuss our private project with family members that lost loved ones ... [we] never really connected with community leaders and activists' (quoted in Hartman, 2011).

The reason for the lack of protest at the time of opening, we may surmise, is because opponents had done their job thoroughly well, despite having no legal or constitutional basis to their goal of blocking the centre. Knowing that a significant majority of Americans were on their side, a very powerful shot across the bows was sent to Muslims in general and Islamists in particular in the US; to the Zionist instigators, this had the enormous bonus of facilitating the blocking of criticisms from such quarters regarding Israel. Indeed, this controversy was not so much a clash, but a verbal assault and campaigning blitz by Zionists and their supporters against very moderate Muslims whose main motive was to secure a place of worship and community centre on the site of a disused building. The fact that they had also condemned the 9/11 attack – and repeatedly so – was to no avail. Despite her denial, for Pamela Geller and her co- accusers there is, to all intents and purposes, no material distinction between 'Muslim' and 'Islamist': both are presumed to be potential terrorists or sympathetic to terrorism. As such, they are considered irredeemably suspect and, in effect, *persona non grata*. By extension, therefore, for hard line Zionists such as her, Muslims in general fall in the same category.

A profound warning is in order: highly politically-motivated people such as Pamela Geller will doubtless carefully survey the political landscape for opportunities to press 'buttons' that generate such whirlwinds relating to the Muslim and Islamist presence in the US which, in turn, may trigger an Islamist reaction that can reverberate around the world. Needless to say, this does not bode well for community cohesion and social harmony. Those who wish to nurture social cohesion in the US must pay heed to the lessons of the 'Ground Zero Mosque' saga and be alert to the potentially dangerous nature of the conflict between Islamism and Zionism. This is not to deny that people have the right to protest at the construction of mosques, or indeed of other religious and civic buildings, or to suggest that Geller and her associates have resorted to illegality. It is, rather, to highlight how tensions between peoples driven by irreconcilable ideologies can be heightened by resorting to duplicitous methods – and that these have the potential of triggering an unsavoury response, with the danger of a downward spiral of retaliatory acts.

Two years after the furore surrounding the Manhattan Islamic Centre, in September 2012, Geller did precisely press one such 'button'. In her capacity as the executive director of the American Freedom Defense Initiative, she was behind anti-Islam adverts on the New York subway. This was in the context of massive protests by Islamists (especially by Salafists) around the world against a short online anti-Islam film *Innocence of Muslims* that led to many deaths, including the murder of the US ambassador to Libya.[46] In these adverts she openly linked

---

[46] The producer of the film is thought to be one Sam Bacile who professed himself 'an Israeli-born Jewish estate agent who had raised millions of dollars from Jewish donors to make the film' (*BBC News*, September 2012a). But it later transpired that he is an Egyptian Copt though, at the time of writing, firm evidence of this has yet to be provided.

her hatred of Islam with a call for support of Israel: 'In any war between the civilized man and the savage, support the civilized man. Support Israel Defeat Jihad' (*BBC News*, September 2012b).

Contemporaneously with the 'Ground Zero mosque' project, another Islam-related controversy blew up in America. This was the notorious 'Koran burning day' organised by a maverick pastor, Terry Jones, of the small, non-denominational church, the Dove World Outreach Centre, in Gainesville, Florida. In July 2010, Jones announced that he planned to burn 200 copies of the Koran on the 9th anniversary of 9/11. Jones' threat and his clarion call of 'Islam is of the devil', based on the title of his book, inevitably generated much anger and protest in the Muslim world and almost unanimous opposition in the US, including from right wing establishment figures who, as we have seen, almost in their entirety opposed the Manhattan Islamic Centre. Pressure was mounted on Jones to abandon his provocation which he singularly refused to do, despite receiving death threats. But, seeing an opportunity, he explicitly linked his stunt with the Islamic Centre project in Manhattan and offered a quid pro quo: if the Islamic Centre was abandoned, he would cancel the Koran burning. However, despite the developers of the centre – including Feisel Rauf – refusing to do so, Jones finally relented and gave the assurance that he would not proceed with Koran burning on the anniversary of 9/11 (Gerhart and Londoño, 2010). But, a few months later, he presided over a mock trial of the Koran which he found to be 'guilty of crimes against humanity' and then burned a copy in his church in Gainesville on March 20th 2011. After Afghan President Hamid Karzai gave publicity to this, calling for the arrest of Jones, Afghan protestors attacked a UN compound killing 12 civilians (*New York Times*, 2011).

Curiously, though Jones' provocation was widely opposed, the opportunistic hitching of his 'event' with the Islamic Centre did not appear to lessen opposition to the latter. Be that as it may, this was a dangerous moment for the US: if an ayatollah or imam in the Muslim world had issued a fatwa against Jones (as Ayatollah Khomeini had done against Salman Rushdie) and which had been carried out so that Jones was murdered or his church destroyed, then the fall-out would have been incalculable. The likes of Pamela Geller would have surely seized upon the ensuing outcry, doubtless in tandem with cries of hell and damnation from Christian fundamentalists and Christian Zionists. Such a worrying vista is a clear and present danger in the tinderbox atmosphere of the US regarding Muslims and Islam.

In April 2012, Terry Jones once more threatened to burn the Koran: he demanded the release of an Iranian Christian cleric on death row by April 28th. The cleric, Youcef Nadarkhani, had been charged with apostasy and sentenced to death for leaving Islam and converting to Christianity. The Iranian government refused to release Nadarkhani so Jones carried out the Koran burning but, this time, there was no protest; the local Fire Authority, however, fined Jones and his church $271 for violating the city's fire ordinances (El-Shenawi, 2012). Unlike Karzai, the Iranian government – somewhat counter-intuitively – kept a diplomatic silence and refrained from raising objections or inciting protests in Tehran. By so doing, doubtless many lives were saved.

King Hearings on Radicalisation of Muslim Americans

Soon after the Ground Zero mosque and Koran burning controversies of 2010, another Muslim-related controversy arose: this was the announcement in December 2010 by the Republican congressman Peter King that upon his becoming chair of the Homeland Security Committee, he intended to hold hearings on the radicalisation of Muslims in the USA. Given the timing, one might surmise that he was influenced in this decision by the uproar over the Manhattan Islamic Centre. Despite King not being a self-proclaimed Zionist, the purpose of these hearings chimed very well with, as we have seen, the views of extreme Zionists. Be that as it may, his intention aroused anger and opposition not only from Muslim groups such as the Council on American Islamic Relations but also from wide layers of society, including from human rights organisations such as Amnesty International, who wished the hearings to be rescinded. The White House spokesperson Jay

Carney cautioned: '[i]n the United States we don't practise guilt by association ... We believe Muslim Americans are part of the solution' (cited in Goldenberg, 2011). But there was no attempt by the President to block the hearings. King, however, maintained an uncompromising stance, basing his reasoning on the Justice Department's finding that in the previous two years, 50 people had been charged with terrorist offences, all influenced by Islamic radicalism. Accordingly, he insisted on the hearings proceeding (convened as The House Committee on Radicalization of Muslim Americans) under the title 'The Extent of Radicalization in the American Muslim Community and that Community's Response'. The first hearing was duly held on March 10th 2011.

In his opening address, in justification of the hearings, King used remarks made by Denis McDonough, the Deputy National Security Advisor to President Obama, where he (McDonough) cautioned:

> [A]l Qaeda and its adherents have increasingly turned to another troubling tactic: attempting to recruit and radicalize people to terrorism here in the United States. For a long time, many in the U.S. thought that we were immune from this threat. That was false hope, and false comfort. This threat is real, and it is serious. (Al Qaeda does this) for the expressed purpose of trying to convince Muslim Americans to reject their country and attack their fellow Americans (Homeland Security, 2011).

King then invoked Attorney General Eric Holder's remark that 'the growing number of young Americans being radicalized and willing to take up arms against our country "keeps [me] awake at night"' (*loc. cit.*)[47]. He further reasoned '[o]nly al Qaeda and its Islamist affiliates in this country are part of an international threat to our nation. Indeed by the Justice Department's own

---

[47] But King omitted to mention another of Holder's remarks made in December 2010: '[t]he cooperation of Muslim and Arab-American communities has been absolutely essential in identifying, and preventing, terrorist threats. We must never lose sight of this' (cited in Wan, 2011).

record not one terror related case in the last two years involved neo-Nazis, environmental extremists, militias or anti-war groups' (*loc. cit.*).

King, however, attempted to allay fears that the hearings would tarnish the whole Muslim community in America by stating:

> I have repeatedly said the overwhelming majority of Muslim-Americans are outstanding Americans and make enormous contributions to our country. But there are realities we cannot ignore. For instance a Pew Poll said that 15% of Muslim-American men between the age of 18 and 29 could support suicide bombings. This is the segment of the community al Qaeda is attempting to recruit (*loc. cit.*).

Prior to 9/11, Peter King had a record of support for the Muslim community in his Long Island constituency (as well as gaining notoriety for his support for Irish republicanism) including giving speeches at the local Islamic Center, taking on Muslim interns, and for supporting the war against Serbia ostensibly in defence of Kosovar Muslims (Wan, 2011), which, in stark contrast to the wars against Afghanistan and Iraq, Muslims overwhelmingly supported. After 9/11, however, he was angered by conspiracy theories which suggested that Muslims were not behind the attacks, and particularly by a Long Island mosque leader Ghazi Khankan's statement 'who really benefits from such a horrible tragedy that is blamed on Muslims and Arabs? ... It must be the enemy of Muslims and Arabs. An independent investigation must take place' (*loc. cit.*). Such freedom of opinion was intolerable for King who retorted: '[a]t this key moment for our country, the worst attack on us in history, these people who I thought were my friends were talking about Zionists and conspiracies ... They were trying to look the other way while friends of mine were being murdered' (*loc. cit.*). Indeed, this riposte is a classic example, noted above, of a US politician unwilling to countenance exploring the reasons for the 9/11 attacks: *res ipsa loquitur*. Period. King, accordingly, did a *volte face*: from being supportive, he became a ferocious critic, denouncing mosques as hot-beds of terrorism and raising the clarion call of the dangers of Islamic extremism.

But, echoing similarities with the Manhattan Islamic Centre, despite widespread and vociferous opposition, there was considerable national support for the hearings. A Gallup poll published just before the first hearing (on 8th March 2011) found that a majority (52 per cent) of Americans thought the hearings were appropriate: the political split was 69 per cent of Republicans, 40 percent of Democrats, and 51 per cent of Independents in favour of the hearings (Gallup, 2011). This resonates with evidence of considerable unease among Americans regarding Islam and Muslims (in the same poll, 36 per cent thought that Muslims living in the US are 'too extreme in their religious views' – somewhat odd in a country where religiosity, often of an 'extreme' kind, is by far the greatest in the developed world). As such, these views are not those of far right cranks. It further underscores the effectiveness of the attacks used by extreme Zionists against Islamists: paint the whole Muslim community as suspect and you greatly hinder Islamists within it to effectively organise and challenge your hegemony regarding the Israel/Palestine conflict. In this endeavour, King's hearings were indubitably helpful.

If for extreme Zionists, the presence of Muslims in America is unwanted, for some Republican Congressmen – doubtless influenced by the King hearings and/or the campaign against the Manhattan Islamic Centre – a Muslim presence in the US military is unacceptable. This indeed is the view of the State Representative of Tennessee, Rick Womick, who averred in November 2011, on Veteran's Day: 'I don't trust one Muslim in our military because they're commanded to lie to us through the term called aqiyya.[48] And if they truly are a devout Muslim, and

---

[48] This is actually a misrepresentation and shows inexcusable ignorance. The 'command to lie' (or conceal one's religion which the term *taqiyaa* refers to) only applies under threat or duress. Its usage is most common in Shia Islam, which has a long history of persecution by the Sunni majority. This is of no relevance to Muslims serving in the US military where one can openly declare one's religion without persecution (under the protection of the First Amendment). Hence, there is no need to resort to *taqyiaa*. A form of 'political

follow the Quran and the Sunnah, then I feel threatened because they're commanded to kill me'. When asked if Muslims should be forced out of the military, Womick responded bluntly 'absolutely, yeah' (cited in Clifton and Fang, 2011). This is in direct contradiction to the US constitution's First Amendment, but, most revealingly, Rep. Womick was not reprimanded for this discriminatory, unconstitutional outburst.[49]

Christian Zionism

In America, the rise of Christian Zionism – taken to mean Christians who support Zionism and the state of Israel – has added to the cogency of the Israel Lobby which, in turn, has accentuated the hostility towards those supporting Palestinians and opposing Israel. As ever, the prime targets are Islamists. Christians who support Zionism do so, as noted in chapter 2, because they advocate the 'restoration' of Jews to Palestine: the creation of Israel affirms this biblical prophecy. Nur Masalha (2007, p. 86) argues that modern Christian Zionism is based on 'the most primitive and savage elements of Old Testament Hebrew tribalism, of "promised land-chosen people" theology'. Rosemary Ruether summarises the basic tenets of the creed and their interconnectedness:

> i.   God gave the Jews all of the land of Palestine as a promised land in Biblical times, and this divine donation of land gives Jews today a permanent and unconditional right to occupy all of this

---

taqiyaa' applies, of course, to double agents – a common occurrence during the Cold War.

[49] Though he did not refer to it, Womick's brazen disregard for the constitution may have been related to the notorious killings of 13 military personnel by the US Major Nidal Malik Hasan (of Palestinian Muslim origin) at the Fort Hood base in Texas in November 2009 (*BBC News,* November 2009).

land, regardless of people who have been living there historically (i.e. Palestinians);

ii. as preparation for events that will culminate world history, all the Jewish people must return to the land, resettle all of it, rebuild the temple; and

iii. The founding of the State of Israel and Jewish settlements of the land are fulfillments of Biblical prophecy which will usher in the final days of judgment and redemption. This will be completed when the Jews are converted to (evangelical Protestant) Christianity. The battle of Armageddon will then take place, killing the enemies of God (unbelievers, Communists, Muslims). The saints (including the converted Jewish elect) will be raptured to heaven when God cleanses the earth of evil doers. Then those saints will descend to a purified earth and enjoy millennial blessing (cited in Masalha, ibid., p. 87).

Precisely because of this zealous support for Israel, Christian Zionists have not been subjected to lobbying by Jewish Zionist organisations. The power and influence of Christian fundamentalism increased significantly in the 1980s during the Presidency of Ronald Reagan: the focus then was on the Soviet Union but after its collapse and the rise of anti-Western radical Islam, the latter began to attract particular attention and animus. Christian fundamentalism and Christian Zionism are closely allied to the Republican Party – indeed Rammy Haija (2006, p. 75) considers them as constituting the largest voting bloc in the Republican Party. Estimates vary as to the number who adhere to Christian Zionism but it probably runs into tens of millions. An estimate by Grace Halsell in 1999 put it at between 25 and 30 million, led by 80,000 pastors, with their ideas disseminated by 1,000 Christian radio stations and 100 Christian TV stations (cited in Sizer, 2004, pp. 23-24).

The largest Christian Zionist organisation is Christians United for Israel (CUFI) founded by Pastor John Hagee in February 2006 with reputedly over one million members. Apart from the expected and obligatory denunciations of Islam and Muslims, Hagee has made numerous rabid anti-Semitic remarks that seem not to have bothered Israelis and American Jewish

Zionists. For example, in regard to the Holocaust, he offers this choice explanation:

> God then sent the hunters. The hunter is one who pursues his target with force and fear. No one could see the horror of the Holocaust coming, but the force and fear of Hitler's Nazis drove the Jewish people back to the only home God ever intended for the Jews to have -- Israel. I stand amazed at the accuracy of God's Word and its relevance for our time. I am stricken with awe and wonder at His boundless love for Israel and the Jewish people and His divine determination that the promise He gave Abraham, Isaac, and Jacob become reality (cited in Blumenthal, 2007).

The unrelenting support for Israel and opposition to Islam can be gleaned by unambiguous statements made, in the aftermath of 9/11, by two of the other most important Christian Zionist evangelical preachers: Jerry Falwell and Pat Robertson. In an interview in October 2002 on CBS News' *60 Minutes*, Falwell stated his fulsome support for Israel and warned of threats against President Bush should he dilute the US government's support for Israel (CBS, 2002). In the same interview, Falwell also denounced the prophet Mohammad as a 'terrorist' and argued that a clear division now exists: Christians and Jews on one side, Muslims on the other. Pat Robertson issued a similar warning: '[i]f the United States takes a role in ripping half of Jerusalem away from Israel and giving it to Yasser Arafat and a group of terrorists, we are going to see the wrath of God fall on this nation that will make tornados look like a Sunday school picnic' (cited in Sizer, 2004, p. 251). His views of Muslims and Islam also firmly accord with Falwell's. In an interview with the Christian Broadcasting Network's *700 Club* he was asked why, given their contempt for US foreign policy, Muslims wished to live in America. Robertson replied:

> Well, as missionaries possibly to spread the doctrine of Islam ... I have taken issue with our esteemed President in regard to his stand in saying Islam is a peaceful religion. It's just not. And the Koran makes it very clear, if you see an infidel, you are to kill him ... the fact is our immigration policies are so skewed to the Middle East and away from Europe that we have introduced these people into

our midst and undoubtedly there are terrorist cells all over them (cited in Sizer, *ibid.*, pp. 248-249).

Stephen Sizer, a vicar and Chairman of the International Bible Society (UK), explains the mentality behind these hardline beliefs:

The implacable conviction that God has mandated in scripture exclusive and sovereign Jewish rule over Eretz Israel, the entire city of Jerusalem and the Temple Mount, leads Christian Zionist leaders to invoke God's wrath on those opposing them, even fellow evangelicals ... Since Christian Zionists are convinced there will be an apocalyptic war between good and evil in the near future, there is no prospect for lasting peace between Jews and Arabs. Indeed, to advocate that Israel compromise with Islam or coexist with Palestinians is to identify with those destined to oppose God and Israel in the imminent battle of Armageddon (*ibid.,* p. 252).

As the rhetoric by Christian Zionists intensified following the second intifada in 2000 and after 9/11, mainstream Christian organisations began to take a stance against the phenomenon. In August 2006 (after the formation of CUFI), the highest ranking Christian leaders of Jerusalem issued a statement expressing concern at the rising popularity and extreme ideological positions of Christian Zionism:

> The Christian Zionist programme provides a worldview where the Gospel is identified with the ideology of empire, colonialism and militarism. In its extreme form, it places an emphasis on apocalyptic events leading to an end of history rather than living Christ's love and justice today. We categorically reject Christian Zionist doctrines as false teaching that corrupts the biblical message of love, justice and reconciliation (cited in National Council of Churches USA [NCCUSA], nd).

The Interfaith Relations Commission of the National Council of Churches USA drew attention to the adverse affect of Christian Zionism's theological stance, including on justice and peace in the Middle East, on relationships with Jews, 'since Jews are seen as mere pawns in an eschatological scheme', and relationships with Muslims since it ignores the rights of

Muslims (*ibid.*). However, the fact that 'Jews are seen as mere pawns in an eschatological scheme' has not aroused the concern of American Jewish Zionist organisations or indeed of Israeli leaders. Quite the contrary: both have, in fact, wholeheartedly embraced their Christian allies' fanatical support for Israel and value their trenchant hostility to those who demur from this stance. Indeed, Israel allowed the setting up of the International Christian Embassy in Jerusalem in 1980. Matters of theology and eschatology are of little consequence in this powerful ideological and geo-political alliance.

In the clash between Islamism and Zionism in the US, Zionists have overwhelmingly prevailed in numbers supporting their ideology and in all the corridors of power: the government, Congress, myriad institutions in Washington, the media, business and finance and, not least, in campaigning zeal. It is no exaggeration to maintain that they have truly obtained 'full spectrum dominance' over Islamists. Such an imbalance of power and influence, however, and of the sense of injustice, felt by so many Muslims of America not only accentuates their marginalisation but also risks provoking unsavoury responses by Islamists who are not likely to be cowed in perpetuity and to meekly accept the formula of 'might is right': the venting of their frustrations by 'rising up' in the warning given by Omid Safi in the first section of this chapter becomes a clear and present danger.

Chapter 6

The Clash in Western Europe

Background

Whereas in America, the clash between Islamism and Zionism has overwhelmingly been to the advantage of the latter, the situation in Europe[50] is not quite so heavily skewed. Various reasons account for this. There are far more Muslims settled in Western Europe in absolute and percentage terms than in America – and their numbers are far in excess of Jews (17 million Muslims; in comparison there are 1.1 million Jews in Western Europe), and their settlement has been over a longer duration than their co-religionists in the US[51]. Moreover, myriad explicitly Islamist organisations exist and these campaign vigorously for matters that concern them. Furthermore, they tend to be assertive, confident, and are keen and able to project a public profile. In stark contrast, as indicated in the previous chapter, Islamists (and indeed Muslims generally) in America have a much more defensive outlook, and tend to operate – unless provoked – beneath the radar of national public life. Nevertheless, the influence of Islamists in mainstream European society and centres of power is minimal, and a tiny fraction of that of Zionists.

---

[50] For the sake of convenience, in this chapter, 'Europe' is taken to mean 'Western Europe', specifically the region of Europe in which large numbers of Muslims have settled in recent decades.

[51] Pew estimates the total Muslim population of Western Europe at 17 million; estimates of the Muslim population of France, Germany, the Netherlands, and the UK as 5.7, 5.0, 5.5, and 4.6 per cent respectively (Pew Forum, 2010b). The estimate for the Jewish population is from World Jewish Population, 2010, p. 16. France and the UK have the highest Jewish population in Europe at 483, 000 (0.8 per cent of French population) and 292, 000 (0.5 per cent of UK population) respectively (*ibid*, p. 18).

The Clash in Western Europe

As we noted in chapter 1, Jews have long been settled in Europe and have achieved a truly impressive standing in all walks of life, not least in the corridors of power. As in America, European Jewish Zionists are passionate supporters of Israel and work tirelessly to safeguard and extend its interests. Given that Arab and Muslims have long been considered as part of the 'Other', this has aided the Zionist argument that Israel is part of Western civilisation, surrounded by and battling against backward Muslim Arab neighbours; a dichotomy and narrative that have widely been acknowledged in Europe.

Notwithstanding feelings of guilt emanating from the Nazi Holocaust, there has been warm acceptance of Israel into European society writ large: including EU Associate membership, and admittance into an array of European institutions and cultural and sporting bodies and events (such as the Eurovision Song Contest and European football tournaments). To all intents and purposes, Israel has been viewed as a European country since its inception. In its conflicts with the Arab world, we can suggest that prior to the first intifada in 1987, Israel encountered little opposition in Europe where the Zionist narrative had been utterly dominant since its inception in 1948. However, certainly since the second intifada starting in 2000 and post 9/11, vociferous, sustained, opposition and hostility to Israeli policies and to Zionism generally, especially regarding Palestinians, has grown exponentially – most notably from Islamists who, in the main, have adopted European citizenship. As we shall see, just as in America, there are now very serious concerns regarding the influence of Islam and Islamism throughout Europe – and Zionists have utilised this fact most effectively. But less well known is the fact that the reputation of Israel is also very poor. For example, a European Commission opinion poll in 2003 showed that *60% of Europeans see Israel as the greatest threat to world peace*. The poll surveyed 7,500 people in 15 EU countries who said *Israel was a bigger threat to world peace than Iran, North Korea and the US* (McGreal, 2003).

In this chapter, we examine the clash between Islamism and Zionism in three European countries where they are the most significant: Britain, the Netherlands, and France.

Britain

In chapter 1, we drew attention to the support Britain provided to Islamist groups during empire as an act of political expediency to ward off left, secular and nationalist movements fighting for independence and, in the post-colonial, cold war, era, to prevent Communist Parties from coming to power in the former colonies. Prior to the 2000s, we may suggest that though Palestine was important to Muslims and Islamists, it did not warrant particular angst and campaigning zeal. Though by this stage Muslim communities had been well established and some Muslims had entered politics, there was no appreciable importance of the issue of Palestine among Muslims in Britain; indeed, for many Muslims from a Pakistani background, Kashmir was of far greater importance. Matters changed, however, in 2000 with the advent of the second intifada and, soon after, the 'war on terror' as Palestine became a core issue for Islamists and its importance resonated strongly in the anti-war movement that mushroomed after the invasion of Afghanistan in October 2001. There was particular poignancy for Islamist and jihadist groups as Osama bin Laden and Al Qaeda made Palestine a core reason for their jihadist terrorism.

Britain has several Islamist organisations which vary in their ideology and purpose. These vary from community-oriented groups which do not stress political campaigning as their prime concern (such as the British Muslim Forum, Islamic Society of Britain, Sufi Muslim Council, Ahmadiyya Muslim Association UK, and Muslim Educational Trust). In contrast are those organisations which tend to be highly political with a strong campaigning zeal (such as Islamic Forum of Europe, Muslim Public Affairs Committee UK, Islamic Human Right Commission, Muslim Council of Britain, Muslim Association of Britain); and there are those with a jihdist outlook such as Hizb-ut-Tahrir, Al Muhajiroun and its successor organisations (all of whom have been proscribed). There are, of course, individuals and cells of global jihadi terrorist groups, the most notable of which are Al Qaeda and Al Shabaab of Somalia.

As stressed throughout this book, there is, across the globe, complete consensus among Islamist groups over opposition to Western wars in Muslim-majority countries and opposition to Israel and Zionism. Unlike in the US, however, many Islamist groups, particularly since 9/11, have been actively campaigning on these core issues. Necessarily, therefore, they have clashed with strongly pro-Israel Zionist individuals and organisations which have generally supported these wars. It would be a fair generalisation to aver that prior to the 2000s, Muslims in Britain tended to adopt a quietist – albeit resentful – approach in regard to perceived double standards of British foreign policy which sided with Israel's oppression of Palestinians, a quietism and resentment also shown towards Jewish Zionists who openly lobbied for Israel and vigorously defended its actions. Thus, for example, there was no significant or sustained protest by Islamists against Israel's repression of the first Palestinian intifada of 1987. Indeed, the first significant protest by many Muslims *qua* Islamists, where simmering resentment was replaced by fuming anger, was in 1989 not against an unjust foreign policy but against a private citizen and his work: Salman Rushdie and *Satanic Verses*. But, two years later, Islamists rather retreated back into their shell over the UK's involvement in the attack on Iraq in February 1991. Concerns over foreign policy had still not attained the enormous importance they would a decade later.

Nevertheless, this was a period which saw the cementing of 'multiculturalism' – and later, 'multifaithism' – with concomitant diversification of migrants into various religious-ethnic communities and identities, facilitated by the entrenchment of segregated neighbourhoods in many town and cities across the country. One of the largest such was the 'Muslim community' which naturally aided the development of Islamist organisations. By far the most important city was London where the interaction between resident and overseas Islamists, including jihadists, flourished especially in some of the main mosques, notably Finsbury Park and East London mosques. As highlighted in chapter 1, the burgeoning of Islamist groups in London gave rise to the phenomenon of 'Londonistan', a pejorative epithet which, according to BBC security correspondent Gordon Corera (2006, p. xvi) was coined by 'French officials infuriated at the growing presence of Islamist radicals in London and the failure of British authorities to do anything about it'. During the 1990s, the British intelligence services nurtured Islamists as informers, and many were granted asylum and given free rein to operate in London. As Mark Curtis explains, 'a key feature of Londonistan was the operation of a so-called "covenant of security" between radical extremists in London and the security services. Crispin Black, a former Cabinet Office intelligence analyst, described the covenant as "the longstanding British habit of providing refuge and welfare to Islamist extremists on the unspoken assumption that if we give them a safe haven here they will not attack us on these shores"' (Curtis, 2010, p. 257). This cynical realpolitik received a traumatic blow with the 9/11 attacks: though these were on America's shores, the British government feared that there was real danger that London risked receiving similar treatment. Hence a public *volte face*: Islamists became pariahs, their hitherto indulgence curtailed, though not ended as Islamist collaborators were used by security services in the attempt to track down violent jihadists.

It was after 9/11 and the commencement of the 'war on terror' that Islamist organisations became publicly active and gained national prominence – a sea-change from the relatively quietist stance they had hitherto taken. No matter their *raison d'être* or religious sect, they all firmly opposed the war on terror: Muslims in general and Islamists in particular, mobilised against it in great numbers, some such as the Muslim Association of Britain with great vigour. Given that Zionists strongly supported the war on terror – as we saw in the previous chapter, American Zionists were decisive in pushing for the invasion of Iraq – the clash between Islamists and Zionists was an inevitable outcome as the two camps became bitter rivals with little to unite them. Inevitably, also, this has strained community relations to the point, we may aver, where mutual trust has well-nigh evaporated.

A crucial reason for the acute sense of frustration and anger felt by Islamists *vis-à-vis* their Zionist counterparts is that they have little influence in mainstream society – in stark contrast, Zionists are very much part of the establishment, be it in

The Clash in Western Europe

national politics, business and finance, the arts and media, and in academia. Thus, the Zionist narrative has long been internalised as the common sense view, and this implicitly acknowledges the dual identity of Jewish Zionists, that is to say, it has never been thought problematic that a British Jew also has a strong loyalty to Israel, to which he or she could publicly proclaim without reproach; a loyalty that can include serving with the Israel Defence Force[52]. It is hard to imagine such an indulgence being afforded to any other ethnic, religious, or national group. That said, the British state has been cognisant of the possible conflict of such a dual identity as was manifested in the unwritten rule that the UK ambassador to Israel ought not be Jewish (a similar rule has applied to the ambassador to the Vatican not being Catholic). This changed in 2010 with the appointment of Stephen Gould, a fervent Zionist, who became Britain's first Jewish ambassador to Israel. The issue came to prominence in 2011 during the scandal involving Defence Secretary Liam Fox which ultimately led to his resignation. It transpired that Fox, his friend and advisor Adam Werrity, and Stephen Gould had held meetings which it was claimed amounted to 'running a pirate (pro-Israel, or anti-Iranian?) foreign policy' (Brady, 2011). Labour MP Paul Flynn aroused controversy by stating 'Britain's first Jewish ambassador to Israel has divided loyalties because he has "proclaimed himself to be a Zionist"' (cited in Bright, 2011). However, Flynn's remarks were, unsurprisingly, condemned by several Labour and Conservative members of parliament. (*loc cit.*)[53]

---

[52] An example of this was the recently deceased renowned hairdresser Vidal Sassoon who, in 1948, at the age of 20, fought for the Haganah before returning home to London. He described this as the 'best year of my life' (Iley, 2011).

[53] Doubtless stung by this disclosure and after a suitably calming time period, in August 2012, Gould issued a robust statement to counter the insinuation that he was no more than a Zionist propagandist: '[t]he centre ground, the majority, the British public may not be expert, but they are not stupid and they see a stream of announcements about new building in settlements, they read stories about what's going on in the West Bank, they read about restrictions in

In stark contrast, Islamists are relative newcomers and deemed to be outsiders, having far less media exposure and political representation. That said it is, however, true that the mainstream media has, particularly since 9/11, offered an outlet for the views of both 'moderate' and 'extreme' Islamists (for example, Islamists have regularly been invited to partake in debates and discussions on television and radio, and documentaries by Islamist thinkers such as Tariq Ramadan and Ziauddin Sardar have been aired by the BBC and Channel 4). Furthermore, the liberal press in particular has provided an outlet for Islamists, including pandering to the existence and dangers of 'Islamophobia'.[54]

Student Islamists have been particularly active in colleges and universities where they have clashed with Jewish student groups, notably with the Union of Jewish students (UJS) which is a stridently Zionist body strongly supportive of Israel. Unlike Islamist groups, the UJS is long-established, well-funded, with very significant influence in the National Union of Students. However, Islamist student societies do have a large Muslim student body to target their ideology and activities – at the core of which are foreign policy issues relating to the Muslim world, not least the Israel-Palestine conflict. Although no extensive research is available on the nature and extent of the tensions between Islamists and Zionists on college campuses, anecdotal evidence suggests that this is an issue of genuine concern. In the context of the post-2000 intifada and the war on terror, and with rising Islamist activism and assertiveness, there is good reason to think that tensions between them over the Israel/Palestine conflict have intensified since 2000. Indeed, as far back as 2000, the National Union of Students banned the jihadist group

---

Gaza. The substance of what's going wrong is really what's driving this ... Israel is now seen as the Goliath and it's the Palestinians who are seen as the David (cited in Sherwood, August 2012).

[54] On my critique of 'Islamophobia', see Hasan, 2010, ch. 4

The Clash in Western Europe

Al Muhajiroun for 'distributing literature of an anti-Western, and sometimes anti-semitic and anti-Sikh nature, describing the west as "infidels", Jews as "terrorists"' (Major, 2001). The group was subsequently proscribed by the government under the Terrorism Act.

Also, tensions and animosities at SOAS (School of Oriental and African Studies) in London have long been at high levels. The SOAS student union has a policy of equating Zionism as a form of racism – in accordance with a UN resolution of 1976 and so, in line with their policy on racism, disallows all forms of Zionism on campus. Unsurprisingly, Zionist groups have attacked this as a manifestation of anti-Semitism – which led to the SOAS authorities to overturn the ban on the grounds that it breached the college's commitment to freedom of speech after the student union had refused to allow an Israeli embassy official to speak on campus (P. Curtis, 2005).

The Muslim Public Affairs Committee UK (MPACUK) – the name is obviously inspired by AIPAC in the US – is an Islamist organisation, one of whose core principles is opposition to Zionism:

> MPACUK oppose the racist political ideology of Zionism and aim to counter the influence of the Zionist lobby. Openly available evidence demonstrates a Zionist agenda to dominate the Middle East and push a 'clash of civilisations' between Islam and 'The West'. We therefore believe that anti-Zionism is a strategic priority to counter the greatest and most urgent threat facing the Ummah (MPACUK website).

Accordingly, MPAC campaigns against pro-Israel politicians and has taken credit for unseating the pro-Israel Labour MP Lorna Fitzsimons from her Rochdale constituency, which has a large Muslim population, in the 2005 general election. Fitzsimons subsequently became Chief Executive Officer of the pro-Israel lobbying group BICOM (British Israel Communications and Research Centre). In the 2010 general election, MPAC campaigned against – and took credit for the ousting of – Labour MPs Phil Woolas in Oldham (Kemp, 2010) and Andrew Dismore in Hendon (Hayes, 2010) on the grounds of their pro-Israel and pro-Iraq war position.

Another source of tension has been the Holocaust Memorial Day: Muslim groups have expressed unease, thinking it too narrowly focused on Jewish suffering and ignoring the suffering of other peoples, not least the Palestinians. For this reason, many Islamist organisations, including the Muslim Council of Britain (MCB) have boycotted the event advocating instead a 'Genocide Memorial Day'. But the MCB reversed its stance in December 2007 – a decision that was fiercely attacked by many Islamists, including within the MCB. Thus, Anas Altikriti of the Muslim Association of Britain made the following charge:

> Why did the MCB apparently give in to the pressure and vilification of the pro-Zionist lobby ...? [I]t is striking that ... all those who have spoken for the change in policy have failed to give even a passing mention of the party whose suffering is paramount in this whole scenario, namely the Palestinians. The whole issue with the HMD [Holocaust Memorial Day] event is that rather than a mere remembrance of victims of one of the most heinous crimes in history, it has become a political event. It glorifies the state of Israel, turning a collective blind eye to the immeasurable suffering of Palestinians at the hands of Israelis every single day (Altikriti, 2007).

Concurring with this view, the Islamic Human Right Commission has, since 2010, indeed commemorated a 'Genocide Memorial Day'. Unsurprisingly, however, Zionist organisations are delighted by the official imprimatur accorded to the HMD, which is commemorated throughout the country. Nevertheless, an event that ought to bring different peoples and 'communities' together to remember a genocidal crime against humanity has, instead, brought discord and resentment amongst significant numbers from one 'faith community'.

Since the creation of Israel, Zionists have used a most effective tactic to ward off any criticism, opposition, and hostility to Israel and Zionism by the sleight of hand of equating anti-Zionism with anti-Semitism so that Jewish identity is felt to be so entwined with Zionism that any perceived slight to the latter is tantamount to an affront to the former. Given Europe's feelings of guilt and remorse over the destruction of much of its Jewish population, this device has long been effective in inducing widespread self-censorship in regard to criticism of Israel. But it has not been effective in doing the same to Muslims in general and Islamists in particular, for whom similar feelings of guilt are entirely absent – on the contrary, and unlike in the US, they tend to have few qualms about aiming fire directly on Jewish and non-Jewish Zionists whom they hold responsible for the persecution of, and the theft of land, of their co-religionists in Palestine.

Indeed, in their hatred of Israel and Zionism, some Islamists have resorted to naked anti-Semitism. A typical example is provided by the ex-Jihadi Ed Husain who, in his autobiography *The Islamist,* makes reference to being convinced that the principal of his college, as well as members of its management, were 'Zionist agents'. 'Without question we despised Jews and perceived a Jewish conspiracy against our nascent Islamic Society' (Husain, 2007, p. 54). The Islamist organisation which Husain had been a member of, Hizb-ut-Tahrir, published a leaflet (entitled 'Muslim ummah will never submit to the Jews') which included the following diatribe:

> The American people do not like the Jews nor do the Europeans, because the Jews by their very nature do not like anyone else. Rather they look at other people as wild animals which have to be tamed to serve them. So, how can we imagine it being possible for any Arab or Muslim to like the Jews whose character is such'? (Hizb-ut-Tahrir, (nd)).

In Channel 4's documentary *Undercover Mosque*, an imam is seen proclaiming 'you have to bomb the Indian businesses, and as for the Jews you kill them physically (Channel 4, 2007).

In response, Zionists have deemed such views as a manifestation of a 'new anti-Semitism' for which supposed phenomenon they have attempted to obtain formal recognition. One important manoeuvre utilised was to request that the European Monitoring Centre on Racism and Xenophobia (EUMC) – subsequently replaced by the EU's Agency for Fundamental Rights (FRA) – adopt a definition of anti-Semitism that encompasses anti-Zionism. This it duly did as a 'working definition'. As Anthony Lerman points out, a report completed in 2002 by the EUMC on anti-Semitism was never published; a suppression that led to much controversy. Lerman explains that:

> Some members of the [EUMC] Board were unhappy that hostility to Israel was included and that the report laid the blame for much of the post-2000 upsurge in antisemitic incidents in Europe on young Muslims and pro-Palestinian perpetrators. Jewish members of the Board linked to the European Jewish Congress based in Paris were angry and leaked the report to the press, complaining that appeasement of Europe's large Muslim population was behind the decision not to publish (Lerman, 2011).

The upshot was pressure on the EUMC by Zionist groups such as the American Jewish Congress and the Centre Européean Juif d'Information (a Brussels-based body linked to the American Anti-Defamation League) that led to the drafting of the 'working definition' which conflated anti-Semitism with anti-Zionism; indeed those not sympathetic to the notion of a 'new anti-Semitism' were simply not invited by the EUMC (*loc. cit.*).

Unsurprisingly, however, the working definition has been vigorously resisted, so much so that the FRA has shelved, if not abandoned, it. But Lerman points out that it is now widely used:

> The US State Department treats it as gospel in its antisemitism reports. The influential All-Party Parliamentary Enquiry into Antisemitism urged the British government to adopt it formally. The Organization for Security and Cooperation in Europe (OSCE) employs the definition. The European Forum on Antisemitism, founded in 2008 with participants from 15 European countries as well as the USA and Israel, but effectively a front organization for the American Jewish Committee, seems to exist primarily to promote use of the working definition. The Anti-Defamation League and the Simon Wiesenthal Centre back it, as does the European Jewish Congress and numerous official national Jewish representative bodies and Jewish communal defence groups [such as the Community Security Trust] (*loc. cit.*).

Knowing full well the effectiveness of the utilisation of the charge of 'anti-Semitism', Islamists have utilised a similar ruse of their own, that is, admonishing those who are critical of Islam or Muslims as being 'Islamophobic' (for a fuller discussion, see Hasan, 2010, ch. 4). A clash of ideologies and identities has enveloped a competition of beggar-my-neighbour sensitivities and victimhood.

Just as all Islamist groups are deeply hostile to Israel and Zionist organisations, so too are Zionists opposed to Islamists and Islamist organisations. The oldest British Jewish organisation, the Board of Deputies of British Jews, founded in 1760, has been staunchly pro-Israel since its formation[55]. As Brian Klug of Independent Jewish Voices has pointed out:

> On its own account, the Board of Deputies of British Jews (which calls itself 'the voice of British Jewry') devotes much of the time and resources of its international division to 'the defence of Israel'. When a 'solidarity rally' was held in London last July [2006] in the midst of the conflict with [Hezbollah in] Lebanon, it was the board that organised it (Klug, 2007).

In the same article, Klug points also to the strength of the Chief Rabbi, Sir Jonathan Sacks' support for Israel when, addressing the aforementioned rally, he proclaimed: 'Israel, you make us proud' (*loc. cit.*). Given the widespread death and destruction unleashed by Israel, such a statement naturally caused outrage not only among Islamists but among many in the general public. Klug provides sober and wise words of advice which, alas, would not likely to have been picked up by Islamists – for whom the July 2006 rally provides ample testimony of organised Jewry in Britain being a bastion of Zionism:

---

[55] It is interesting to note that the Board of Deputies had earlier been *anti-Zionist* as evidenced by a letter written by David Alexander, President of the Board of Deputies of British Jews (with Claude Montefiore, President of the Anglo-Jewish Association) to *The Times* in 1917, shortly before the Balfour Declaration: 'a Jewish nationality in Palestine ... must have the effect throughout the world of stamping the Jews as strangers in their native lands, and of undermining their hard-won position as citizens and nationals of those lands' (cited in Wheatcroft, 2003).

> [T]he board has no business taking a partisan position on the Middle East. Let groups such as the Zionist Federation or perhaps the Israeli embassy organise solidarity rallies. The role of the board is to promote the welfare of British Jews in all their variety, not to defend Israel. Similarly, the chief rabbi is entitled, ex officio, to bring a religious perspective to political matters, but it is not his role to act as political spokesman for his flock (*loc. cit.*).

Apart from Zionist organisations, leading Jewish politicians and commentators invariably have strong Zionist sympathies and have generally supported the wars in Afghanistan and Iraq (see Seymour, 2007). In the eyes of Islamists, this further cements the conflation of British Jewry with Zionism and of being key proponents of the war on terror which they think is a surrogate for a war on Islam.

The three main political parties in Britain have 'Friends of Israel' (FOI) sections which attract to their membership some of the most powerful politicians of the land and, accordingly, have been highly effective in lobbying for Israel. The issue of Friends of Israel came up in the furore concerning funding to the Labour Party in 2007; it transpired that three of the key players in the saga (David Abrahams, John Mendelsohn, and Lord Levy) were members of Labour Friends of Israel. A rare article that highlighted this important yet neglected fact was by Yasmin Alibhai-Brown in *The Independent*. The foreboding she had about writing the piece – hence about the power of the Israel Lobby – was made clear in her first paragraph:

> Pardon me for asking. Perhaps I shouldn't. For an easy life, some things, you learn, are best left unsaid. Nervous, am I? You bet. But these questions will not stand aside or lie down. They have been bothering me since the Labour party donor row broke last week. They are raised here in good faith. I have no wish to bring the wrath of Moses upon me and I can already hear the accusations of anti-Semitism because I dare to raise the question: Can someone explain what exactly is the role of the Labour Friends of Israel (LFI) in our political life? And its twin, the Conservative Friends of Israel (CFI) too. In an open democracy, we are entitled to make such queries indeed, it is a duty (Alibhai-Brown, 2007).

The Clash in Western Europe

A Channel 4 *Dispatches* documentary by Peter Oborne ('Inside Britain's Israel Lobby') put on air in November 2009 duly made further queries – the first such programme on this issue on British television. It claimed that an astonishing 80 per cent of Conservative MPs are members of Conservative Friends of Israel, including the present Prime Minister David Cameron (Oborne, 2009). Education Secretary Michael Gove is also a staunch Zionist and on the board of the Community Security Trust, the Zionist body that seeks to protect Jewish communities. Included in the ranks of Labour Friends of Israel are former Prime Ministers Tony Blair and Gordon Brown.

Newspapers catering for the Jewish population, including the influential *Jewish Chronicle*, also take a strong pro-Israel stance and are relentless in opposing those critical of Israel, not least Islamists. A popular Zionist website *Harry's Place* has made a central plank of its politics the opposition to Islamism. Most importantly, all of the national media has journalists (Jews and non-Jews) sympathetic to Zionism and the editorial line of most of the press tends to be highly supportive of Israel; a corollary of which is their hostility to Islamists who campaign against Israel. In the phone-hacking scandal which has so shaken Rupert Murdoch's News Corporation empire, there has been silence in regard to Murdoch's longstanding and very strong support for Israel – which view his papers have dutifully adopted. Richard Desmond, owner of Express Newspapers, is also strongly pro-Israel, as too, unsurprisingly, are his papers. It is also noteworthy that Murdoch's greatest rival in the 1980s, Robert Maxwell, who owned Mirror Group Newspapers, was a staunch Jewish Zionist – so much so that he was accused of being 'Israel's "superspy"' (see Thomas and Dillon, 2002).

Interestingly, despite the overwhelming media bias in favour of Israel (see research by Greg Philo and Mike Berry [2011] of the Glasgow University Media Group), an opinion poll on the Israel-Palestine conflict in 2002 by ICM Research for *The Guardian* showed, somewhat surprisingly, that in answer to the question: '[i]n the dispute in the Middle East between Israel and the Palestinians, from what you have seen and heard about the conflict, which of the two do you sympathise with more, Israel or the Palestinians'? 14 per cent sympathised with Israel whilst

28 per cent sympathised with the Palestinians (ICM Research, 2002).

Again, as in America, the Israel-Palestine conflict permeates the relationship between Muslims and Jews in Britain, and both Islamists and Zionists apply the maxim 'my enemy's enemy is my friend'. So, on the one hand, Islamist groups – notably the Muslim Association of Britain (MAB) (comprising mainly of Arabs, with links to the Muslim Brotherhood)[56] – have campaigned with non-Muslim organisations on Palestine as well as opposition to the wars in Afghanistan and Iraq. Indeed, MAB's vociferous support for Palestine under the banner of fundamentalist Islam, doubtless contributed to the 'Islamisation of Palestine' highlighted in chapter 2. On the other hand, Zionists tend to welcome support from Christian Zionists – and controversially – some Zionists have allied with right wing anti-Islamist forces, most notably the English Defence League which is discussed below.

The Labour government encouraged dealings with Islamist groups and began to view the Muslim Council of Britain (MCB) as a body representing all Muslims, whom it could utilise for political purposes. An important gesture in this endeavour was the offering of a knighthood to then Secretary General Iqbal Sacranie in 2005. The MCB is an umbrella grouping of many South Asian Muslim organisations and relished this attention and acclamation by the Labour government; the liberal media in particular followed suit by offering indulgence to MCB's leading personnel who became fixtures on television, radio and the press. But this did not last long and what scuppered this unwritten agreement was, unsurprisingly, the issue of Israel and Palestine – especially Israel's assault on Gaza in December 2008/January 2009. In its

---

[56] Alison Pargeter claims that 'most of the senior leadership of the MAB are or were at one stage heavily involved with the Ikhwan [Muslim Brotherhood]'. She points out that the father of Anas Tikiriti (who was the most visible member of MAB in the anti-war movement) was head of the Iraqi branch of the Brotherhood (Pargeter, 2010, p. 158).

aftermath, a declaration by various Islamists was issued in February 2009 in Istanbul at a Global Anti-aggression conference – a signatory to which was Daud Abdullah, Deputy Secretary General of the MCB. What particularly upset the government was the declaration's call to attack foreign navies (including the Royal Navy) in the vicinity of Gaza. As Jamie Doward explains:

> But, according to the Istanbul declaration, there is an obligation for 'the Islamic Nation to regard the sending of foreign warships into Muslim waters, claiming to control the borders and prevent the smuggling of arms to Gaza, as a declaration of war, a new occupation, sinful aggression, and a clear violation of the sovereignty of the Nation ... This must be rejected and fought by all means and ways'. (Doward, 2009).

The government, as represented by Hazel Blears, at the time Communities Secretary, called for Abdullah to resign and proceeded to tone down its dealings with the MCB. Yet, we may surmise this is not what the Labour government would have wished for given its nurturing of the MCB (and indeed of supposedly 'moderate' Islamists in general) as part of a counter-terrorism strategy whose aim was to utilise religious leaders such as Abdullah in the hope of luring away young Muslim radicals from violent Jihadism towards something more benign: otherwise their beliefs, no matter how pernicious and reactionary, were of no concern. Thus, a Mosques and Imams National Advisory Board was set up to train 'moderate' English-speaking imams, which had within its ranks, leading MCB members. Indeed, this is a logical outcome of the pursuit by the previous government's 'faith agenda' whereby importance and legitimacy are accorded to various 'faith communities' in a 'multi-faith society'. It has also been persisted with by the successor Coalition government. Unsurprisingly, such a policy stance accentuates the existence of faith identities, not least a Muslim identity among those from an Islamic background in Britain. It is a short ideological step from this to an espousal of explicitly Islamist politics – a moment's reflection tells us that, contrary to expectations, the 'faith agenda' actually militates against the government's goals of reducing Islamist radicalism and increasing social cohesion.

A worrying clash has, in recent years, manifested itself largely at the street level: that between the relatively new English Defence League (EDL) and Islamists and their leftist supporters. A striking aspect of the EDL's street marches has been the presence of Israeli flags; moreover, EDL supporters have frequented rallies organised by Zionist groups which has led to suspicions among some Islamists as to whether the EDL is, in fact, a Zionist front organisation which should be viewed as the 'Israeli Defence League'. Thus, in September 2010, MPACUK put an article on its website with the heading 'Exposed! The EDL and its Zionist connection'. This is, *prima facie,* odd given that many consider the EDL a fascist organisation; but a defining characteristic of British fascism has been anti-Semitism, yet the EDL, which has a 'Jewish Division', is positively philo-Semitic.[57]

In regard to its strong support for Israel, the EDL provides the reasons on its website:

> We support Israel's right to exist, and we support Israel's right to defend itself. But there is no reason why we cannot continue to support Israel whilst still being fully committed to halting the advance of radical Islam in our own country ... In many ways there are parallels to be drawn between the radicalisation that has infected the Palestinians and their supporters and the radicalisation that continues to breed in British Mosques. In this way at least, the people of England and the people of Israel have a great deal in common ... The war against radical Islam has no borders, even if Israel is the front line of the battle. It is an international problem, and it would be foolish of us not to ally ourselves with like-minded

---

[57] However, the *Jewish Chronicle* points out that 'The Board of Deputies, CST [Community Security Trust] and other communal groups have repeatedly warned British Jews against supporting the EDL' (Dysch, 2011).

individuals and organisations across the world (EDL, 2011).[58]

It is clear that EDL's support for Israel stems from the latter's hostility to radical Islam – and as we have stressed throughout this book, it is the Islamists who are the most determined opponents of Israel and Zionism. Hence, the EDL adopts the principle of 'my enemy's enemy is my friend', thus obviating the need to trouble itself with history and the unfolding of events in the Middle East. Indeed, the organisation's website displays wilful ignorance of the Israeli-Palestine conflict and no understanding for the rise of Islamism in Palestine – which, as we saw in chapter 2, Israel helped to nurture in the 1970s and 1980s. A Zionist front organisation is hardly likely to show such crude simplicity and risible lack of knowledge and understanding. That said, the EDL can be considered a de facto Zionist organisation despite the fact that most of its supporters are non-Jewish.

The most detailed study of the EDL has been conducted by Jamie Bartlett and Mark Littler of the Demos think-tank; their findings, published in November 2011, reject the notion of the EDL being a fascist organisation. Instead, it is deemed to be a populist movement with some 'illiberal and intolerant elements ... [but] many members are in an important sense democrats' (Bartlett and Littler, 2011, p. 7).[59] Nonetheless, the report of the findings points to significant far-right sympathy as evidenced

---

[58] This statement was provided in August 2011 after controversy had arisen in regard to attempts by the leader of the EDL's Jewish Division (Roberta Moore) 'to co-ordinate her efforts with those of the far-right American Jewish Task Force, whose leader Victor Vancier has been imprisoned for terrorism offences. The move, in February [2011], was heavily criticised by the EDL leadership' (Lipman, 2011). Moore, who had been a follower of the outlawed far-right Rabbi Meir Kahane's Kach Party in Israel, subsequently resigned from the EDL.

[59] The authors utilised 'responses from 1,295 sympathisers and supporters, and includes data on their demographics, involvement in EDL activity, political attitudes and social views' (Bartlett and Littler, 2011, p. 3).

by 34 per cent of EDL supporters voting for the BNP (*ibid*, p. 5). However, Bartlett and Littler point out that 'the group does not accept the characterisation of [itself] as a BNP affiliate. It has often gone out of its way to distance itself from fascist groups, burning a swastika flag at one of its first demonstrations and brawling with members of the National Front in Birmingham. Similarly, the BNP has forbidden its members from joining the EDL' (*ibid.*, p. 12).[60]

Another important characteristic which is thoroughly at odds with the history of British fascism is that the EDL welcomes not only Jews but members of non-white ethnic minorities; indeed, for a while, one of its spokespersons was an Asian (Guramit Singh). However, if not in content, the *form* of EDL protests is certainly akin to fascist parties such as the National Front and BNP of yesteryear. It is a rare sight to see non-whites at its protests – in fact, the vast majority of those who attend are young white men behaving in a menacing demeanour, sometimes to the point of violence; hence the fascist appellation. True, those who attend protests might not provide an accurate reflection of the organisation's membership but the leadership appears to have made little attempt to curb this ugly image.

What is beyond dispute is that the EDL is a novel organisation in that its *raison d'être* is explicitly to oppose militant Islam. The group's origins are in Luton with a significant Muslim population (Casciani, 2009). The founder of the EDL, a young man and former BNP member called Stephen Yaxley-Lennon who uses the *nom de plume* Tommy Robinson, has stated (in an interview given to the BBC's *Newsnight* programme on 1st February, 2011) that the EDL is a 'symptom' of the failure of UK governments to tackle Muslim extremism. Interestingly, a Muslim member of the EDL, Abdul Salaam

---

[60] The Demos report does suffer from an egregious weakness: the authors did not ask EDL supporters about the organisation's strong, highly visible, support for Israel and why this should relate to the rise of Islamism in England.

from Glasgow, has also made the same point (*BBC News*, September 2011). Yaxley-Lennon states that he formed the group because of a protest organised by Islamists in Luton directed against British Army soldiers returning from Iraq, where slogans such as 'Butchers of Baghdad' were shouted against them. He had also been concerned by the campaigning of Al Muhajiroun and its successor group Islam4UK and by their demands for Sharia law to be implemented in Britain; and by the fact they were not being opposed. He was also outraged by a 'road show' which the jihadist Anjem Chaudhury (whose group Ahlus Sunnah Wal Jama'ah is another splinter group of Al Muhajiroun) took to towns and cities with a view to convert people to Islam. Though it drew Yaxley-Lennon's ire, this is actually quite legal. But what he found particularly inflammatory was a public ceremony (in June 2009) in which an eleven year old white boy was shown converting to Islam. These acts were the catalyst for Yaxley-Lennon to start his group – which he duly did by targeting football fans ('casuals' and 'firms') in particular (Casciani, *op. cit.*).

Very quickly, the EDL was mobilising hundreds of supporters and organised protests in several towns and cities in England – and began to attract support from other parts of the UK and Europe. The Demos report estimates that by early 2011, that is, some 18 months after its formation, it had organised over 50 demonstrations and that the total size of its active membership is between 25,000-35,000 people (Bartlett and Littler, 2011, p. 4); an astonishing growth rate for a grassroots organisation that is so universally reviled. The EDL targets Islamist events such as the counter-protest against Muslims Against Crusades' (subsequently proscribed) protest outside the US Embassy on 11th September 2011 that marked a remembrance service in honour of the British victims of 9/11; it also targets 'radical' mosques, and has helped establish the European Freedom Initiative, an umbrella of anti-Islamic groups in Europe. It has also developed links with the US Tea Party and Stop the Islamification of America (*ibid.* pp. 10-11); and sent members to the protest against the 'Ground Zero Mosque' discussed in the previous chapter (Booth, 2010). In line with its pro-Israel stance, it has organised events in support of Israel: for example, in October 2010, it invited a notorious Rabbi from America, Nachum Shifren (also known as the 'Surfing Rabbi'), associated with the Tea Party, to speak at a rally outside the Israeli Embassy in London to 'oppose Islamic fascism'. The Rabbi provided the choice words: 'Muslims eat each other alive, like the dogs that they are ... We shall prevail, we will not let them take over our countries. We will never surrender to the sword of Islam' (Elgot and Lipman, 2010).

Though its rise can be considered an extreme response to militant Islam and threats of terrorism by Jihadist groups, evidence suggests that the gap between the EDL's ideology and large sections of mainstream society on Islam is not so large. This is attested by the British Social Attitudes survey of 2010 which highlighted the fact that of all the major religions in Britain, only Islam generated an overall negative response (Voas and Ling, 2010, p. 78). The authors of the chapter detailing this finding provide the following conclusion: '[s]ome degree of generalised xenophobia is always likely to exist. Conceivably, there is a spill-over effect, so that people who are worried about Muslims come to feel negatively about 'others' in general. In any case, the adverse reaction to Muslims deserves to be the focus of policy on social cohesion, because no other group elicits so much disquiet' (*ibid.*, pp. 80-81).

Further evidence is provided in a Populus opinion poll conducted in January 2011, considered the largest survey into identity and extremism in the UK: 52 per cent of respondents agreed with the proposition that 'Muslims create problems in the UK'; in stark contrast, only 6 per cent agreed with the proposition that 'Muslims create no problems in the UK' (Populus, 2011, table 96)[61]. An online survey of over 2,000 UK adults in June 2010 showed that 58% of people associate Islam with extremism, that 50% associate the world religion with

---

[61] In fact, 32 per cent agree think that 'Muslims create a lot of problems for the UK'. The percentages agreeing with 'create problems in the UK' for other religions are as follows: Jews 7 per cent; Christians 14 per cent; Hindus 15 per cent; Sikhs 15 per cent (Populus, *op. cit.*).

terrorism, and 69% believe Islam encourages the repression of women (cited in Linden [for PA], 2010).

So, as in America, and indeed throughout Western Europe, there is considerable 'disquiet' among a significant proportion – perhaps majority – of the population regarding the role of Islam in society so it would not do to assume that this is solely confined to far right cranks.

But it is important to stress that the supposed danger of Islamism *to Israel*, which the EDL is so keen to highlight, is not what concerns ordinary people in Britain; indeed even before Israel's assaults on Lebanon in 2006, on Gaza in 2008/09, and on the Turkish flotilla in 2010, Israel's standing among ordinary Britons was extremely low. For example, in a survey conducted by YouGov for the *The Telegraph* in December 2004,

Israel comes top of the list of countries where people would least like to live and would least like to take a holiday. It is also the country thought least deserving of international respect ... it is also thought to be among the world's 'least democratic countries'. Of the 12 criteria set out in YouGov's check-list, Israel comes out bottom in four cases and among the bottom five in a total of eight. Only Russia has a worse overall score (King, 2005).

Such popular antipathy towards Israel has not deterred many Zionists; on the contrary, they have opportunistically availed themselves of the widespread negative attitudes to Islam and Islamism to push their pro-Israel agenda. Indeed, the first head of the EDL's Jewish Division, Roberta Moore, admitted so much in an interview with the Israeli paper *Haaretz* by stating '[t]hey [British Jewish organisations] think the league is exploiting us, while it is really we who initiated the Jewish division. If anything, we are exploiting them' (Adar, 2010).

Given its lack of sophistication, being 'exploited' by Jewish Zionists is not likely to be of much concern to the EDL; rather, it will continue to find militant Zionism appealing precisely because they both share an irreconcilable conflict with Islamism, regardless of being given a wide berth by official Zionist organisations. Conversely, those sympathetic to the cause of Palestinians find Islamism's vigorous hostility towards Israel likewise appealing and so tend to remain silent about, or treat with kid gloves, its reactionary aspects. Accordingly, the clash between Islamism and Zionism is not likely to abate in Britain: indeed an Israeli attack on Iran, for example, will inevitably greatly intensify it.

The Netherlands

The Netherlands, which has long had a reputation for being one of Europe's most liberal, tolerant, countries has, in recent years, witnessed a clash between Islamism and Zionism that has centred on two non-Jewish politicians whose ideas have had a profound effect on the Dutch polity and society, and with international repercussions. Though discussions of these two politicians have not been formulated in the terms of such an ideological clash, the underlying motives in both cases are precisely this.

A frontal assault on Islam, Islamic fundamentalism, and the Muslim presence in the Netherlands was launched in the Netherlands by an academic turned politician in the 1990s which led to the publication of a book (in Dutch) by the title *Against the Islamisation of Our Culture* in 1997: the author was Pim Fortuyn who, in a very short space of time, was to shake Dutch society like no other politician had done in the post-World War 2 era. In August 2001, that is, a month before 9/11, Fortuyn stated 'I am also in favour of a cold war with Islam. I see Islam as an extraordinary threat' (Fortuyn, 2001).

A few weeks before the elections in May 2002, Fortuyn was expelled by the Leefbar (Liveable) Party for advocating an end to Muslim immigration; undeterred, he set up his own party, the Pim Fortuyn List (PFL). But, a few days before the general election, he was assassinated by an animal rights activist angry with his anti-Islam tirades. In the elections, however, the PFL won 26 out of 150 seats (17 per cent of the vote), a remarkable result for a party barely 3 months old. Doubtless, the PFL benefited from a significant 'sympathy vote' – which only confirms that Fortuyn's views on Islam were resonating with wide layers of the Dutch population. Even though the PFL proceeded to suffer a rapid decline and was subsequently dissolved, Fortuyn's legacy remained strong – indeed, in 2004, he was voted the greatest figure in Dutch history (Buruma, 2006, p. 42). Fortuyn's views on Muslim immigrants and Islam had truly become mainstream and, as we shall see, were soon propelled by another politician and his new party.

In his acclaimed book on the Netherlands and its Muslim population, *Murder in Amsterdam,* Ian Buruma posits the following explanation for the sudden rise of Pim Fortuyn:

> Fortuyn's venom is drawn more from the fact that he, and millions of others, not just in the Netherlands, but all over Europe, had painfully wrested themselves free from the strictures of their own religions. And here were these newcomers injecting society with religion once again (Buruma, 2006, p. 69).

There is doubtless truth in this explanation – almost certainly so for those who voted for Fortuyn's party in large numbers – but Buruma neglects to mention that Fortuyn was also an ardent supporter of Israel (Simpson, 2002) and had published a book (in Dutch) in 1998 with the revealing title *50 Years Israel, but for How Long? Against the Tolerance of Fundamentalism.* Clearly, for Fortuyn, Israel was deemed a bastion of Western liberal democracy in the Middle East, and the first defence against Islamic fundamentalism which the book's title was referring to. Hence, for him (as for the EDL) Zionism and anti-Islamism were like salt and pepper.

This coupling also applies to the second Dutch politician in this clash, who has most vigorously propagated the views of Pim Fortuyn, one Geert Wilders. At first, Wilders had another ally in Parliament, the Somali-born Ayaan Hirsi-Ali (who had come to the Netherlands as a refugee) who had also made waves in her sustained criticisms of Islam and especially its oppression of women. But, amid much controversy, Hirsi-Ali was forced to stand down in 2006 after it was revealed that she had provided false information on her asylum claim. Though apparently isolated (after being expelled by the VVD party in 2004, Wilders proceeded to set up his own 'Party of Freedom'), he was soon to capitalise on the path forged by Fortuyn.

Wilders stance had initially been at odds with Fortuyn's as he had criticised the latter's 'cold war' remark: '[a] terrible remark because it tars all Muslims with the same brush. I have nothing against Islam. I respect it as a faith' (clip shown in documentary by Joost van der Valk, 2011). Soon, however, he began to launch a blistering attack on Islam and Islamism à la Fortuyn and Hirsi-Ali. He campaigned on stopping the 'Islamisation of the Netherlands', including putting a halt to Muslim immigration, and (unlike Fortuyn) advocated the banning of the Koran, deeming it be akin to *Mein Kampf* because it urges Muslims to kill unbelievers (Waterfield, 2007). He was a star speaker at a rally against the 'Ground Zero Mosque' organised by Pamela Geller in September 11 2010.

In a speech to Parliament in September 2007 on Islamic activism in the Netherlands, Wilders provided perhaps his most influential assault on Islam and Muslim culture:

> Madam Speaker, the Islamic incursion must be stopped. Islam is the Trojan Horse in Europe … Where is our Prime Minister in all this? In reply to my questions in the House he said, without batting an eyelid, that there is no question of our country being Islamified. Now, this reply constituted a historical error as soon as it was uttered. Very many Dutch citizens, Madam Speaker, experience the presence of Islam around them. And I can report that they have had enough of burkas, headscarves, the ritual slaughter of animals, so-called honor revenge, blaring minarets, female circumcision, hymen restoration operations, abuse of homosexuals, Turkish and Arabic on the buses and trains as well as on town hall leaflets, halal meat at grocery shops and department stores, Sharia exams, the Finance Minister's Sharia mortgages, and the enormous overrepresentation of Muslims in the area of crime, including Moroccan street terrorists (Wilders, 2007).

Like Fortuyn, his uncompromising message was clearly getting through to large numbers of the Dutch population. In 2006, his PVV party (Partij voor de Vrijheid) had won a respectable 9 seats in the Dutch parliament for a party just two years old, but in the 2010 general election it saw a sharp increase in support winning 24 seats with 16 per cent of the vote, almost identical to the PFL's count in 2002. The PVV was now the third largest party in parliament, it had become a real power broker whose ideas had to be taken seriously; moreover, its leader was one of the most popular public figures in the Netherlands.

It is important to recognise that, as in Britain (and indeed in Europe generally), there is significant unease regarding Islam in the Netherlands – and it is this which was tapped into first by Pim Fortuyn and, later, by Geert Wilders. For example, a survey conducted by Paul Sniderman and Louk Hagendoorn in 1998, that is (like Fortuyn's books) *before* 9/11 and the war on terror, showed that approximately half the Dutch population thought that 'Western European and Muslim ways of life are *irreconcilable*' (Sniderman and Hagendoorn, 2007, p. 22; emphasis added)[62]. In a similar vein, Anouk Smeekes, Maykel Verkuyten, and Edwin Poppe (2011, p. 268) argue that 'we live in a world of nations where most citizens care about their country's national identity and culture, although not on a continuous basis and not necessarily in the form of patriotic and nationalistic sentiments ... Hence, most members of the national community should be willing to respond to circumstances that are defined as undermining the historical continuity of the nation'. In regard to the Netherlands, they suggest that 'Islamic schools, mosques, veiled women, Islamic public holidays, and other visible signs of Islam are typically presented as being incompatible with a traditional Christian identity'. Given this stark reality, the well for PVV's politics is indeed very deep.

In 2010-2011, Wilders was put on trial for criminally insulting, inciting hatred and discriminating against Muslims, because of their religion. However, he was cleared of all charges in June 2011; the judge ruled that his remarks were 'acceptable within the context of public debate' ... although the bench found remarks by Mr Wilders 'gross and denigrating', they had not given rise to hatred (*BBC News,* June 2011). Wilders' response was unsurprising:

---

[62] Some of the reasons for this irreconcilability include 'nine out of every ten agree that Muslim men in the Netherlands dominate their women ... Three out of every four Dutch agree that Muslims in the Netherlands raise their children in an authoritarian way' (Sniderman and Hagendoorn, 2007, p. 23).

> It's not only an acquittal for me, but a victory for freedom of expression in the Netherlands ...Now the good news is that it's also legal to be critical about Islam, to speak publicly in a critical way about Islam and this is something that we need because the Islamisation of our societies is a major problem and a threat to our freedom and I'm allowed to say so (*ibid.*).

If hostility to Islam is one side of the ideological coin for Wilders, ultra-Zionism is the other. With a Jewish grandmother and a Hungarian-Jewish wife, he spent time working in Israel as a youth and has visited the country many times. Unsurprisingly, he has many admirers in Israel and access to some of its leading politicians (van der Valk, *op. cit*). The main foreign policy concern of his party centres on Israel: he believes that if Jerusalem falls to Islam, Athens and Rome will be next. At the 'Facing Jihad conference' in Jerusalem on 14th December 2008 (at which Pamela Geller was also an attendee), organised by hardline Zionists, he spoke of a 'creeping Islamisation, stealth jihad, every Islamic neighbourhood is regarded by many Muslims as building blocks of ... domination' (*ibid.*). He has support from the likes of Chaim Ben Pesach of the Jewish Task Force, who was convicted and imprisoned for 5 years for terrorism charges in the USA. A corollary of his passion for Israel is his contempt for Palestinians: the solution he advocates for their plight is to have them transferred to Jordan (*ibid.*), a policy which places him in the most fanatical ranks of Zionism, alongside the likes of Israel's Foreign Minister Avigdor Lieberman.

Wilders has forged links and gained financial backing from American ultra-Zionists such as Daniel Pipes, Director of the Philadelphia-based pro-Israel think-tank Middle East Forum (MEF). The MEF's Legal Project has helped Wilders with legal fees to the tune of six figures (Scott-Smith, 2010; van der Valk, *op. cit.,*). Another important donor is David Horowitz of the online *FrontPage Magazine* and the David Horowitz Freedom Center which finances *Jihad Watch*. Zionists helped fund his controversial film *Fitna* (which was used as evidence against him in his trial) and their donations are used to cover campaigning and travel costs (*ibid.*).

Despite the Netherlands' historically supportive stance towards Israel, Wilders' ultra-Zionism has aroused concern in official circles as well as in the media. Thus, an article in the *Vrij Nederlands* newspaper in 2007 had the heading 'Is Geert Wilders a spy?' (Fallaux, 2007). A high-ranking official in the Foreign Affairs department who became so concerned about Wilders constantly asking very detailed questions about the Netherlands' relations with Israel, concluded that 'even though we couldn't prove it, it was obvious that Wilders was being informed by the Israeli embassy' (van der Valk, *op. cit.*). In regard to the allegation that he is an Israeli spy, this has not been discussed in Parliament though Wilders acknowledged that he was visiting the Israeli embassy at least once a month in his capacity as the Middle East specialist for his then party the VVD.[63] One suspects that visits to the embassies of other Middle East countries were much rarer or non-existent.

Curiously, Islamist groups in Netherlands have been silent regarding Wilders; instead they have tended to join protests organised by left groups.[64] This is in contrast to Britain where, as we have seen, there are several Islamist groups who demonstrate vocally against the EDL and on other issues of concern to them. There is, of course, a decisive difference: Wilders does not organise street marches and rallies à la the EDL – instead he (as Pim Fortuyn had done before him) has always used the media and parliament to propound is views. On this terrain, Islamists have always been very weak as they are trapped within dogmatic thinking which makes it most difficult to effectively counter arguments that so robustly challenge their world view, and which so resonate in Dutch society. Moreover, as the leader of the third largest political party in the Netherlands, they cannot traduce his legitimacy. Where they are more likely to embarrass Wilders is on his fanatical support for another country and espousal of its ideology (Zionism) that is

---

[63] Information provided to author by Joost van der Valk.

[64] Same source as in note 14.

not germane to the Dutch people but, again, Islamists have largely remained silent on the issue.

But it must not be forgotten that, apart from Germany, the Netherlands has perhaps had the most consistently pro-Israel stance since 1948 which is obviously derivative of the destruction of much of Dutch Jewry in World War 2. Atonement and remembrance for the lost Jews – Ann Frank's tragic life, for example, has long been a central feature of Dutch education – has translated into unerring governmental support for the Jewish state. So, despite the population of Jews (43,000)[65] in the Netherlands being a small fraction of Muslims (914,000)[66], there is good reason to think that the former induce far greater empathy and solidarity. But this does not imply unyielding support on the part of the mass of the population to Zionist ideology, state of Israel, and its oppression of Palestinians. Indeed, this is evident from an ICM survey (conducted in January 2011) of the opinion of European citizens regarding the Israel-Palestine conflict. This found that 32 per cent of Dutch people think 'Israel is not a democracy, where there is oppression of and domination by one religious group over another'; whilst 33 per cent of Dutch people think 'Israel is a democracy, but where there is oppression of and domination by one religious groups over another' (ICM, 2011, table 2). Furthermore, only 9 per cent think that Europe should support the Israelis rather than the Palestinians which, of course, is the position of Wilders (*ibid.*, table 30).

In his attacks on Islam in the Netherlands Wilders has, however, tended to refrain from invoking the importance of Israel to his beliefs. That said, unless he tempers his aggressive Zionism – as ostentatiously displayed in visits to America or Israel – there is the real possibility of the allegation that he is an 'Israeli spy' might stick – which Dutch Islamists might try and utilise – with the inevitable haemorrhaging of support of

---

[65] World Jewish Population (2010), p. 49

[66] Pew, 2010

ordinary Dutch voters.[67]

France

France has the greatest numbers of Jews (half a million)[68] and the largest or second largest numbers of Muslims (3.6 million)[69] in Europe. As in other West European countries, Jews have long been citizens; by comparison Muslims settled in France in the post-colonial era, mostly from the former colonies, especially from North Africa. However, despite long being citizens of France, most French Jews have supported the state of Israel (Safran, 2007, p. 443); unsurprisingly, therefore, the faultline between Jews and Muslims in general and Zionists and Islamists in particular is, as ever, the Israel-Palestinian conflict. In comparison with Britain, however, militant Muslims are not so public and vociferous, nor do they appear to have quite the same campaigning zeal. For example, Olivier Roy (2004 [2002], p. 45) notes that 'an informal survey of young *beurs* (French of North African descent) who claimed to protest Israeli policy by targeting French Jews showed that none was able to name a Palestinian town or to even map Palestine; and none of them was linked to any Islamic organisation or even a mosque'.

A key reason for the relative inactivity of French Islamist groups is that France refused to join up with the American assault on Iraq in 2003. One crucial difference between France

---

[67] In the Dutch general election held in September 2012, Wilders' party did indeed haemorrhage support as it lost nine of its 24 seats. But this was due to its anti-European stance: Wilders had called for the Netherlands to leave the EU. The biggest winners were the pro-EU parties (*BBC News,* 13 September 2012).

[68] World Jewish Population (2010), p. 47. Germany is estimated to have 4.1 million – some estimates, however, give France as having the highest Muslim population in Europe.

[69] Pew, 2010

and Britain is that France has a long tradition of anti-clerical secularism which has also permeated sections of the Muslim Arab segment of the population; by contrast, principled secularism is virtually absent among Muslims in Britain. One might also tentatively suggest – hard evidence is not available – that the passion felt by French Muslims regarding Palestine is somewhat of lesser intensity than their British counterparts. Accordingly, the conflict between Islamists and Zionists over Israel-Palestine has not been so severe but, of course, this is not to suggest that it is of negligible importance. Indeed, beneath the more tranquil surface lurk the same eddies of resentment, frustration, and anger: the enormity of the issue means it cannot be ignored.

As elsewhere in the West, tensions came powerfully to the fore after the second intifada in 2000 and – albeit less so in France – after 9/11 and the ensuing war on terror. Attacks on Jews by Muslims increased markedly: in the autumn of 2000, 'half a dozen synagogues were attacked' (Roy, *op. cit.* p. 146). In 2002, the Commission nationale consultative des droits de l'homme (National Consultative Commission on Human Rights) reported six times more anti-Semitic incidents than in 2001 (193 incidents in 2002). The commission's statistics showed that anti-Semitic acts constituted 62% of all racist acts in the country, compared to 45% in 2001, but less than an astonishing 80% in 2000) (Zappi, 2003). The Parti des Musulmans de France (PDMF) (Muslim Party of France), formed in Strasbourg in 1997, has promoted radical Islamism, taken part in demonstrations against Israel, and organised boycotts of Israeli or Jewish products. In 2000 the Ligue Internationale Contre Le Racisme et L'Antisemiitisme (International League against racism and Anti-Semitism) took legal action against the PDMF for inciting racial hatred (Safran, 2004, pp. 435, 437).

Between 2000 and the elections of 2002, Jewish student groups and Conseil Répresentatif des Institutions Juives de France [CRIF] (Representative Council of Jewish Institutions in France) organised many mass rallies in Paris against anti-Semitic attacks, and to counter pro-Palestinian rallies organised by Arab Muslim and left groups, and supported by some prominent politicians. 'The rallies sometimes degenerated into attacks on Jews, and in turn provoked counter-demonstrations by extremist Jewish groups' (*ibid.*, p. 441). Among leading politicians who empathised with the pro-Palestinian protests was Foreign Minister Hubert Védrine who 'expressed understanding for the solidarity of young French Muslims with the Palestinians'. Pascal Boniface, the director of the Institut des Relations Internationales et Stratégiques (Institute of International and Strategic Relations) and member of the Executive of the Socialist Party opined in 2001 'it is the CRIF, not the Beur [Arab] community, that has been importing the Arab-Israeli conflict into France'; for which statement he was dismissed (*ibid.*, p. 439).

An article in the *New York Times* reported in 2006 that even though 'the number of reported incidents has fallen since peaking in 2004, anti-Semitism is now entrenched in many of the country's working-class housing projects. The Arab communities of North Africa had no postwar sense of Holocaust guilt. If anything, distress over the creation of Israel in 1948 reinforced anger at Jews ...' (Smith, 2006).

As was discussed above in regard to this supposed 'new anti-Semitism', attacks by French Arabs and Muslims on Jews are motivated by the perceived allegiance of Jews to Israel; a very different phenomenon to the anti-Semitism that had so virulently prevailed in Europe before World War 2.

It is this very perception that was graphically exposed in a short article written in 2003 by the Islamist academic Tariq Ramadan (after the commencement of the US-UK invasion of Iraq) which caused much debate and consternation in France. The author is, in fact, a Swiss national of Egyptian parentage (his grandfather, Hassan el Banna, was the founder of the Muslim Brotherhood). The piece was refused by the leading French papers including *Le Monde, Liberation, and Le Figaro*, so was put on an Islamist website, *Oumma.Com*.[70] Rather than being quietly ignored, it was widely read and quickly gained

---

[70] It is most revealing that the article is no longer on both the *Oumma.Com* and Tariq Ramadan's websites.

notoriety because Ramadan made an explosive allegation: 'over several years (even before the second intifada) French Jewish intellectuals who until then had been considered as universal thinkers, began both nationally and internationally to develop analyses more and more directed by community concerns that aspire to relativise the defence of universal principles of equality and justice ...' (Ramadan, 2003).[71] He proceeded to name names: Pierre-André Taguieff, Alexandre Adler, Alain Finkielkraut, André Glucksman, Bernard Kouchner, and Bernard-Henri Lévy. Alain Finkielkraut is accused of becoming a 'community intellectual' who is 'not troubled by supporting [then Israeli Prime Minister Ariel] Sharon' and following up with the inflammatory 'Jews or Zionists (those who make a difference are anti-Semites) can never be victims or oppressors like others' (*ibid.*). Ramadan then makes his key inference and charge:

> Intellectuals as different as Bernard Kouchner, André Glucksman or Bernard-Henri Lévy ... have curiously supported the American-British intervention in Iraq ... we know that Israel supported the intervention ... We also know that the architect of the operation in the Bush administration is Paul Wolfowitz, a notorious Zionist who has never hidden that the overthrow of Saddam Hussein would guarantee better security for Israel ... Bernard-Henri Lévy, selective defender of great causes, hardly ever criticises Israel to whom he never stops proclaiming his "solidarity as a Jew and as a Frenchman" (*ibid.*).

Ramadan then concludes his assault thus:

> If we demand from intellectuals and other Arabs and Muslims that they condemn, in the name of the law and universal, commonly

---

[71] Curiously, Ramadan's charge is reminiscent of a similar one famously made by the French Jewish intellectual Julien Benda in his 1927 book *The Treason of the Intellectuals* (*La Trahison des Clercs*). Benda's fury was inspired by many of France's leading intellectuals siding with the state during the Dreyfus affair (see Niess, ch. Vii, 1956).

held values, terrorism, violence, anti-Semitism and the dictatorial Muslim states from Saudi Arabia to Pakistan, shouldn't we at least expect from Jewish intellectuals that they denounce, in a clear manner the repressive policies of the state of Israel and that they are in the first rank in the fight against the discrimination their Muslim co-citizens are subjected to (*ibid.*).

The Economist (2004) pointed out '[i]n the code of the Paris intelligentsia, this was a deadly punch ... Bernard-Henri Lévy called the cyber-attack a "nauseating" case of anti-Semitism'. Elsewhere, Lévy asserted: 'I will let pass the infamy of these claims which, under the guise of a principled defense of communal spirit, only resuscitates the good old theme of Jewish conspiracy: Lévy and Adler as secret ambassadors of Sharon . . . the "Protocol of the Elders of Zion" is not far behind' (Lévy, 2004). Alain Finkielkraut (2003) also denounced Ramadan's article arguing that 'contemporary anti-Semitism was expressed in the language of anti-racism'; however he did admit to being a Zionist albeit not a supporter of Sharon as Ramadan had charged.

Though Lévy's response was typically overblown, nonetheless, Ramadan's piece was undoubtedly crude and clumsy, from which an inference of anti-Semitism could be made. The inclusion of Pierre-André Taguieff who, in fact, is not Jewish merely attests to this – a blunder compounded by the fact that Ramadan later acknowledged that he was aware of this fact. But he is clearly not anti-Semitic and has argued against the hatred of Jews among Muslims of France.[72] That is to say, he has been careful to make a distinction between Jews and Zionism. Indeed, he concluded his short article by doing precisely this: '[w]e note with respect of those Jews ... who have decided to

---

[72] For example, in an article in *Le Monde*, he wrote: 'We have heard the cries of "down with the Jews!" shouted during protest demonstrations, and reports of synagogues being vandalized in various French cities. One also hears ambiguous statements about Jews, their secret power, their insidious role within the media, and their nefarious plans. ... Too rarely do we hear Muslim voices that set themselves apart from this kind of discourse and attitude' (cited in Buruma, 2007).

rebel against all injustice and notably those injustices committed by Jews (Ramadan, *op. cit.*). This rather contradicts his thesis about 'Jewish intellectuals'' support of the Iraq war and Israel because of 'communitarian' interests.

A crucial reason why Ramadan's assault hit a raw nerve is surely because of the nature of the French Republic which is ostensibly based on the ideals of the enlightenment and the French Revolution in which the secular state and civic culture unify all citizens and so trump an individual's culture and religion which are confined to the private sphere. This understood, we can see that Ramadan's indictment not only highlighted the contradiction between universalism (in this case, of principles of equality and justice) and 'communitarian interests' but also the conflict between the foundational principles of the Republic and the foreign policy stance of 'Jewish intellectuals': sectarian interests which should be private have taken priority over Republican interests. Moreover, the official foreign policy stance against the invasion of Iraq had forcefully been settled by President Jacques Chirac: he threatened to invoke the French veto at the UN Security Council. As a result, no UN vote authorising the war on Iraq was passed, giving Chirac – and France – great prestige not only in the Muslim world but well beyond. At the same time, it was an open secret (as highlighted in the previous chapter) that the push for the war in Washington came from Neocons, and many of the leading Neocons were Jewish Zionists including Paul Wolfowitz.

Had Ramadan levelled his charge against French Zionists or French Jewish Zionists (in which case leaving out Taguieff) supporting the Iraq war, that would have been factually accurate. Indeed, it would have hardly aroused controversy as the intellectuals on his list openly supported the Iraq war and proclaimed their sympathy for Israel and Zionism. The ensuing debate could then have been productive: an exploration of the reasons why some leading French intellectuals supported an invasion that was so strongly opposed by the French government and the majority of the population and which had no legal basis whatsoever.

But, in the hue and cry of anti-Semitism, what was ignored

was Ramadan's own 'communitarian interest' given that he has based his career on advocating separate 'communitarian' rights for Muslims in the liberal democratic states of Europe. The fact that he is not a French citizen does not preclude him from commenting on developments in France – on this there was unanimity. Indeed, because his ideas were being taken seriously by many Muslims in France meant that he had to be taken seriously by the rest of society, including the powers-that-be. This is evident by his being invited to debate, soon after the acrimony surrounding his article in 2003, with then Interior Minister Nicolas Sarkozy on French television's *100 Minutes to Make Your Case* (which was watched by 6 million people). Sarkozy bluntly told Ramadan 'your article was not just a blunder; it was a moral failure'. Ramadan responded by stating: '[t]hey call me a Muslim intellectual; I wrote about Jewish intellectuals. I don't see any harm in that'. Sarkozy then proceeded to attack his brother in a telling exchange: 'your brother Hani published a piece in which he justified the stoning to death of adulterous women. It's monstrous'. Rather than agreeing that this was indeed monstrous and to be universally condemned, Ramadan stated: 'I'm in favour of a moratorium so that they stopped applying these sorts of punishments in the Muslim world' (cited in Fourest, 2008 [2004], pp. 82-83). If anything, this stance achieved more notoriety in France than the article in *Oummah.Com*.

Ramadan's jurisprudence was made crystal clear in a recorded speech in which he proclaims 'I will abide by the laws, but only so insofar as the laws don't force me to do anything against my religion' (cited by Buruma, 2007). In other words, he disparages the universalism of the law that is a foundational principle of liberal democracies, not least the French Republic; as such, his critique of others who apparently also reject universalism is hardly convincing: indeed it smacks of hypocrisy.[73]

---

[73] This is indeed why Ramadan is often accused of 'doublespeak' by critics and is the essence of the charge made by Caroline Fourest in her book *Brother Tariq: The Doublespeak of Tariq Ramadan* (2008).

Dangerous Liaisons

What is undeniable is that leaving aside the allegations of anti-Semitism, the manifest tensions on the ground in France between Muslims and Jews suddenly erupted into the public sphere by the catalyst of a short article written by a foreigner on an obscure website. At its core, however, this altercation was not only a clash between Islamism and Zionism but also the direction the French polity would take on this vexed issue. The result, typically of such a clash, is to accentuate differences between not just the purveyors of the two ideologies but also between fellow citizens of two religious-ethnic communities.

In March 2012, the dark shadow of the Israel-Palestine conflict appeared seemingly out of the blue in the city of Toulouse when a young man (23 year old Mohammed Merah) shot and killed 3 children outside a Jewish school. This shooting had followed the murder of three French soldiers – one near Toulouse airport, the other two in Moutauban – from an ethnic minority background (one was Caribbean, the other two North African) . Before being shot dead by the police, Merah proclaimed that he would 'bring France to its knees' for its involvement in the war in Afghanistan. His reason for the shooting of the Jewish children was to avenge Israel's treatment of Palestinians. Mohammed Merah had made two visits to Afghanistan and plainly become radicalized by the experience (Lichfield, 2012). But his wanton murder spree was clearly that of a madman – and so makes it difficult to meaningfully generalise from such behaviour. Indeed, because France did not partake in the Iraq imbroglio, it has largely escaped the threat of terrorism from jihadists that have periodically occurred in Britain and America. Be that as it may, the Merah killings will inevitably not only accentuate the hostility between Islamists and Zionists in France but exacerbate tensions between Muslims and Jews – and the fact that the bodies of the three Jewish children were immediate transported to Israel for burial further militates against a unifying French republican identity.

The French Muslim organisation UOFI [The Union of Islamic Organizations of France] argued that the Israel-Palestine conflict must not be imported into France. This is likely to be wishful thinking: as the divisions run so deep, any 'truce' on this pivotal issue is likely to be superficial. In the aftermath of the killings, the French government deported and refused entry to a number of imams whom it deemed not to be conducive to the public good, including the influential Qatar-based theologian, Youssef al Qaradawi. The UOFI (2012) issued a statement on this decision condemning the Merah killings and to reject the importation of the Israel-Palestine conflict into France. This is likely to be wishful thinking. As the divisions run so deep, any 'truce' between Islamists and Zionists is likely to be superficial. Both camps will, and of course have the right to, campaign politically on this issue which so animates them – with the proviso of course that there is no recourse to violence, or threat of violence.

A brief coda to this chapter concerns a country in which there is a tiny Jewish population but in which over the past two decades significant numbers of Muslims have claimed asylum and settled, that is, Norway. During Israel's assault on Gaza in December 2008- January 2009, riots erupted outside the Israeli embassy and the Norwegian parliament (Storting) in the capital Oslo as pro-Israel and pro-Palestinian supporters (doubtless including many Islamists) fiercely clashed (*Ynetnews.com* [from AP]). This quite unique occurrence shows graphically that the Israeli-Palestinian conflict had seeped into a hitherto peaceful part of northern Europe.

In the same country, some two and a half years later, a horrific act occurred: the cold-blooded murder of nearly 100 people (mostly youths) by a young Norwegian man by the name of Anders Behring Breivik. Initially, psychiatrists had deemed him to be insane – which seemed sensible in view of the unprecedented and apparently wanton, nature of his crime. Yet, it soon transpired that Breivik had developed a very firm world view which he explicated in a 1500 page 'manifesto' that he uploaded before his killing rampage. In the manifesto, he expressed very strong anti-Muslim and pro-Israeli views – the 'salt and pepper' coupling we have elaborated upon in this chapter. Here is a small sample:

> Western Journalists again and again systematically ignore serious Muslim attacks and rather focus on the Jews ... Jews that support multi-culturalism today are as much of a threat to Israel and

Zionism as they are to us ... So let us fight together with Israel, with our Zionist brothers against all anti-Zionists, against all cultural Marxists/multicultural-ists ... If one acknowledges that Islam has always oppressed the Jews, one accepts that Israel was a necessary refuge for the Jews fleeing not only the European, but also the Islamic variety of anti-Judaism. [He expressed his disgust at the Norwegian government's awarding of] the Nobel peace prize to an Islamic terrorist [Arafat] and appeasers of Islam (cited in Hartman, 2011).

Of course, it would not be appropriate to generalise from the murderous acts of madmen such as Mohammed Merah and Anders Breivik – but a responsible politics requires us to be cognisant of the corrosive, divisive, impact of the Israel-Palestine conflict and the related clash between Islamism and Zionism even in countries and societies that historically have had nothing to do with these issues and ideologies.

It is, however, important to note that when it comes to matters of religion, Muslims and Jews – and by implication, Islamist and Zionist organisations generally – have vigorously united over some key societal issues against secular laws and institutions and against guidelines based on scientific evidence. This was the case in France when they opposed the law on the prohibition of religious symbols and attire (including the *hijab* and skullcap) in French state schools in 2004; in Britain, they strongly advocate 'faith schools'; everywhere they vigorously lobby for the right to conduct religious slaughter of animals (which animal welfare organisations have long recommended against); and as highlighted by a court ruling in Germany in the summer of 2012, they strongly demand the right to male circumcision. But this unity pales into insignificance when the question of Israel and Palestine is raised. In the next, concluding, chapter we attempt to provide a way out of this troubling morass.

Chapter 7

Concluding Remarks

Mutually reinforcing ideologies

Here is a Jewish joke that attempts to shine a humorous light on Israel's predicament:

> On the sixth day, God turned to the Angels and said: 'Today I am going to create a land called Israel. It will be a land of mountains full of snow, sparkly lakes, forests full of all kinds of trees, and high cliffs overlooking sandy beaches with an abundance of sea life'. God continued, 'I shall make the land rich so as to make the inhabitants prosper, I shall call these inhabitants Israelis, and they shall be known to most people on earth'.
> 'But Lord', asked the Angels, 'don't you think you are being too generous to these Israelis?' 'Not really', God replied, 'just wait and see the neighbours I'm going to give them' (cited in Minkoff, 2010, p. 196).

Amusing as it is, the joke rather masks reality. Of course the neighbours have been, to put it euphemistically, none too happy with Israel's presence in their midst – the Jewish state was not a gift from God but had to be fought over in a most bitter struggle which has never abated. As we have seen in the first two chapters, the founding fathers of Zionism were very clear-sighted about the nature of their project: Herzl acknowledged that it was a colonial enterprise; Nahum Syrkim accepted that it would necessitate the expulsion of the indigenous Arab population; and Ben Gurion truthfully admitted that 'we have stolen their country'. Whilst it is undoubtedly true that a very large majority of Jews in the world have (in the absence of hard data) positive feelings towards the state formed in their name, the majority have chosen *not* to exercise their supposed 'right to return'. As we have also seen, increasing numbers of Israelis have sought and obtained dual nationalities thus allowing one foot to be firmly placed in another land; furthermore, many

Jewish Israelis are following this up by undertaking a 'reverse aliyah', that is, have chosen to emigrate *from* Israel to either America or Europe. Islamists, Palestinians, and Arabs of all persuasions doubtless welcome this phenomenon and indeed would desire that all the Zionist colonisers and their offspring would return to the lands from whence they came. But this is a pipe dream.

What is surely beyond dispute is that the partition of Palestine in 1948 and subsequent expulsion of Palestinians from their homeland was monumentally unjust and is the core cause of the Arab/Palestine-Israeli conflict and which has also propelled the clash between Islamism and Zionism that we have elaborated upon in preceding chapters. The latter clash has, however, arisen from two illegitimate claims based on religious justification for the 'holy land': the 'promised land' for Zionists and a 'waqf' (endowment) for Islamists. There is a long history of the explosive mix of religion and politics of which Islam/Islamism and Judaism/Zionism is a particularly pernicious instance.

It ought to be clear that the normative stance of the present author is that these two ideologies are dangerous, reactionary, and have long destabilised the world. That said, both have proved resilient and highly successful. Taking Zionism first, until the 1930s it was supported only by a small minority of Jews in Europe but the single-mindedness and relentless drive of the movement's leaders kept the flame burning despite enormous and myriad obstacles. The rise of the Nazis and the Holocaust provided the tragic catalyst that thrust the ideology to the first rank among Europe's broken Jewry so that its ultimate success owed much to this cataclysmic defeat. Nonetheless, even after the Second World War, the majority of the displaced Jews of Europe did not wish to settle in Palestine: the preferred destiny was invariably America. It is a stark fact that had the US government accepted mass Jewish immigration during and after the war, the push for the Jewish state might have been

Concluding Remarks

considerably weaker.[74] This is, however, not to suggest that the project would have failed; again, the fierce determination and diplomatic skills of the leading Zionists must never be underestimated. But the US severely limited immigration and President Truman supported the partition of Palestine that was, by November 1947, agreed upon by the victorious allies, including the USSR: 14th May 1948 was the crowning and staggering achievement of Zionism. The new state quickly built its military might with considerable support from the Americans and Europeans as the Soviet Union was perfunctorily by-passed. After the 1956 Suez debacle, a further glittering success was the enormous impact that Israel began to exercise on the policies of the strongest superpower regarding the Middle East. It is no exaggeration to think that from the October 1973 war onwards, Israel has become de facto a domestic policy issue for the US government, no matter its political hue; the one issue on which there has long been overwhelming consensus on Capitol Hill. This unique success is the result of the work of the Israel Lobby which has performed an invaluable role in pushing Israel's interests and shielding it from criticisms and attacks in the US – as well as in Western Europe.

For very different reasons, Islamism has also been a very successful ideology. In that the role of Islam in Muslim-majority countries has always been very strong – a consequence of the absence of an enlightenment in the Islamic world – and the fact that Islam encompasses every aspect of life from birth till death, it is inevitable that Islamic beliefs will permeate deeply into the body-fabric, especially the political landscape, of these countries and societies. Like Zionists, however,

---

[74] This was how the Labour MP Richard Crossman bluntly summed up America's view of the partition of Palestine: 'half the people in America don't care two hoots ... while the other half, either for Zionist reasons or because they don't want any more Jews, back the Jewish case ... By shouting for a Jewish state, they are diverting attention from the fact that their own immigration laws are the basic cause of the problem' (cited in Keay, 2003, p. 354).

Islamist leaders were relentless and messianic in pushing their agenda. But, under colonial rule, political power was beyond their reach; moreover, as we highlighted in chapter 1, Islamists were used by the colonial powers to suppress nationalists and leftists but this did not prevent the ascendancy of Arab nationalism (the Communist Parties had been thoroughly discredited because of the Soviet Union's decisive role in the partitioning of Palestine) – above all in Egypt under Nasser – the corollary of which was that the political reach of Islamists was minimal.

Yet, before too long, the nationalists of all Arab countries were blundering, faltering, and resorting to dictatorial methods, hence increasingly becoming discredited. Politics abhors vacuums so into the breach stepped Islamists. Reactionary and anti-modernist they may be, nonetheless, they all had a fine record of diligently and honestly working 'on the ground', providing all manner of welfare and charitable facilities which were not provided by the nationalist governments. Alongside such material resources, however, came a very strong dose of systematic Islamic indoctrination – especially of the mass of the poorly educated or illiterate population. A very clear manifestation of this was in Palestine in the post-Oslo (1993) period. The nationalists of the PLO – led by Fatah – became mired in corruption (both political and societal) so that in the elections to the Palestinian Authority in 2006, they were soundly beaten by Hamas, the Muslim Brotherhood's organisation in the occupied territories which had for years provided corruption-free welfare to so many of its people, especially in Gaza. Presently, the full fruits of the Islamists' labours have been visible in the Arab Spring as they have taken pole position in all countries that have held free and fair elections.

Naturally, secular progressives who have provided the dynamo for the Arab uprisings have been left stunned. In the Arab world, concerns about Islamism had in fact been forcefully made well-before the Arab Spring. Almost completely ignored by mainstream politicians and commentators in the West, such concerns no less equated Islamism with fascism. Thus, in 2007, the Algerian dissident

Concluding Remarks

Mohamed Sifaoui, who gained political asylum in France in 1999, claimed that he was 'one of the first Muslims to consider Islamism to be fascism. This is not a subjective decision but rather a serious, academic argument' (Sifaoui, 2008, p. 14). The Lebanese-Palestinian journalist, Samir Kassir (prior to being murdered in 2005) also bluntly averred that Islamism is a deeply reactionary movement and its coming to power would be a grave setback to the Arab world. He provided a gloomy warning that is indubitably likely to demoralise progressive modernists:

> [O]nce the religious veil is removed the societal attitudes of the Islamist movements reveal many similarities with fascist dictatorships. If one is to admit political Islam's claim to be a force of change, therefore, one must accept that the democratic deficit is permanent and that the Arab world will never make its appointment with modernity (Kassir, 2006, p. 29).

Was Kassir correct to make this harsh judgement? When looking at the programme of the Salafists, derived from Saudi-style Wahabbism, there is little doubt that these are indeed akin to 'fascist dictatorships'. That said, critics of a progressive bent, albeit with Islamist sympathies, might nevertheless argue that Kassir's is an unduly pessimistic judgement which cannot truthfully be said of the non-Salafist Islamists – in the main the Muslim Brotherhood – and point to the example of the Tunisian Ennhadha Party which has forsaken a constitution based on Sharia law. Perhaps, also, the Muslim Brotherhood's Freedom and Justice Party, which gained the largest share of the vote in the Egyptian parliamentary elections of 2011-12, will follow suit and resist unduly reactionary demands of the Salafists of the Al Nour Party. Similarly, even if Islamists dominate the new democratically-elected Libyan parliament, they may also opt for a Tunisian-style constitution. This would run counter to the blatantly undemocratic proclamation made by the National Transition Council Chairman Mustafa Abdul Jalil who, in a speech on 23 October 2011 declaring Libya's 'liberation' from the Gaddafi regime, stated that Islamic Sharia law would be 'the basic source of legislation, and so any law which contradicts

Islamic principles is void' (cited in Madi, 2011)[75].

It is too soon to predict with any certainty the political trajectory of Islamist-dominated parliaments but we can argue with some legitimacy that attempts will doubtless be made to ensure that laws emanating from such legislatures will indeed be moulded to comply with the Sharia. That said, there is no denying that the Salafists are the worst nightmare for progressives and secularists, representing precisely the fascistic face of Islamism. However, the Free Democratic Party in Egypt, which is liberal and secular warned, in May 2012, about the dangers of the Muslim Brotherhood's attempts to force 'a new form of fascism in the name of divine rule' (*Egypt Independent*, 2012).

The same fears are echoed by the Egyptian writer Alaa Al Aswany who uncompromisingly uses the epithet Islamic 'religious fascism' to highlight its threat to the Egyptian revolution:

> Even if we differ ideologically with groups advocating political Islam, don't they have a right to seek power through democratic means? Of course the answer is yes, but here we have to distinguish between democratic groups advocating political Islam and groups of religious fascists. Many supporters of political Islam believe that they alone represent Islam, consider anyone who disagrees with them as hostile to Islam, and are fully prepared to impose their ideas on others by force. Some of them have a long history of attacking churches and tombs, setting fire to video shops, robbing Christian shops, and murdering people such as President Anwar Sadat, foreign tourists, and innocent Egyptians. One only has to see how these fascists deal with Copts and liberals, how they hate and despise them, how they heap insults and accusations on them, and how these fascists talk about what they would do to Egypt if they came to power. There would be no music, no theater, no cinema, and no political parties for those who

---

[75] Jalil went on to provide two examples: first, 'the legislation putting restrictions on polygamy is contradictory to Islamic legislation and so is annulled'; second that interest on some bank loans - regarded as usury in Islam - would not be allowed (*loc. cit.*).

Concluding Remarks

disagree with them. There would be no tourism and ancient Egyptian monuments would be covered up out of sight. There would be no great literature, because one leading religious fascist said that Naguib Mahfouz, one of the greatest novelists in the world, was responsible for the moral decadence of Egyptians through his indecent writings. Religious fascism threatens to plunge Egypt into total darkness, exploiting the religious sentiments of Egyptians to gain power. If you are an ordinary candidate for office, you try to convince your constituents of your electoral program, but the religious fascists do not offer a program: they tell people, more or less, "If you are Muslims, we are Islam, and if you don't vote for us, you are secularists and infidels." (Al Aswany, 2011).

Al Aswany points to the large amounts of money being channelled by Saudi Arabia to Salafist/Wahabi groups, some of which they use to distribute food at heavily discounted prices – the sort of welfare provision noted above. But here's the rub: though they might renounce secularism and fear many aspects of modernity, Islamists' support for Palestinians and hostility to Israel – at least at the level of principle – gives them added kudos among large swathes of the Arab masses which has translated into votes in the ballot boxes.

In his book *Israel's Fateful Hour*, published in 1986, Yehoshafat Harkabi, who had been Head of Israel's Military Intelligence Directorate, gave this stark warning:

> Israel is the criterion according to which all Jews will tend to be judged. Israel as a Jewish state is an example of the Jewish character, which finds free and concentrated expression within it. Anti-Semitism has deep and historical roots. Nevertheless, any flaw in Israeli conduct, which initially is cited as anti-Israelism, is likely to be transformed into empirical proof of the validity of anti-Semitism. For this reason discrimination against Christians living in Israel threatens not only Israel but Jews throughout the world. These actions weaken the Jews' ability to defend themselves against anti-Semitism. It would be a tragic irony if the Jewish state, which was intended to solve the problem of anti-Semitism, was to become a factor in the rise of anti-Semitism. Israelis must be aware that the price of their misconduct is paid not only by them but also Jews throughout the world (Harkabi, 1988 [1986],

pp. 219-220).

Leaving aside his concern about 'discrimination against Christians living in Israel' (but not Muslims who are far greater in number), Harkabi's sober caution nevertheless holds much validity. We have seen how Islamists have frequently conflated 'anti-Israelism', and anti-Zionism generally with an overt hatred for Jews *qua* Jews. In the Arab and wider Islamic world, we can aver that this conflation is highly prevalent and close to being universal. In the West, where large and increasing numbers of Muslims have settled, and where Islamism has taken root, this conflation appears to be reaching worrying proportions (alas, doubtless because of the sensitivity of the issue, data based on large scale surveys of this phenomenon are not available). Matters in this regard are not helped by the enormous power of the Israel Lobby which has a long history of defending Israel's actions uncritically and which instills self-censorship among critics of Israel (be they Jewish or not) by the wounding charge that they are motivated by anti-Semitism. Such a charge, however, does not have the same self-censoring affect on Islamists – hence their continual conflation of Jewry with Israel. But it would not be altogether surprising if non-Islamists also make this conflation in greater numbers, precisely what Harkabi feared, because of the widespread, uncritical support Israel receives from the global Israel Lobby.

Defusing the clash

As we have seen in chapters 5 and 6, many Western anti-Islamists support Zionism on the grounds that Israel represents a bulwark against Islamism in Islam's heartlands. But no evidence is provided for this hypothesis, presumably because none such exists. In fact, the reality is quite the contrary: as we have highlighted in this book, Zionism has fuelled Islamism not only in Muslim-majority countries but also in the West. A question that anti-Islamist Zionists will need to grapple with is that of their stance on the Arab uprisings. Take Egypt for example: it is already clear that the forces which were central to the revolution, had dominated Tahrir square in Cairo, were the

Concluding Remarks

progressive secularists. But, as we saw in chapter 4, it was the Islamists which overwhelmingly came out on top in the parliamentary elections which were by-and-large free and fair; furthermore the Brotherhood's Mohammed Morsi won the presidential elections in June 2012.

If and when military rule is truly broken, the struggle in a democratic Egypt will inevitably centre on these two forces (though sectarian tensions, particularly between Sunnis and Copts, will remain acute). Now, will the trumpeted liberalism of the Western anti-Islamists side with the progressive secularists who are at the cutting edge of the battle against the Islamism they so fear and despise, bearing in mind that they (the Arab progressives) are united with their Islamist adversaries in their opposition to Israel and support Palestinians? If they do not, then such blind fealty to Zionism will aid Islamism. And what of their stance on the religious Orthodox Jews in Israel who are breeding at a rate akin to Muslims in Europe which also fills them with dread? If the fear of Islamisation of the West is legitimate, is the fear of the Orthodox Judaisation of Israel not equally so? After all, the anti-Islamists support for Israel is not because it is a state based on Jewish laws (indeed it is not a theocracy, despite the presence of religious parties in the Knesset) but because it is supposedly a democracy with secular laws (in fact, rather than being a Jewish state, it is more accurate to think of Israel as a state for global Jewry).

Perhaps such contradictions will not be of much concern nor have significant impact on political campaigning in the West if the reality is that a robust anti-Islamist politics is a vote-winner. As evidence provided in this book highlights, there are indeed genuine, legitimate, concerns about the influence of Islam and Islamism in Western societies which provides traction for such a political stance. But if these contradictions are simply set aside, then this is an abandonment of principle, hence a manifestation of patent hypocrisy.

Whilst Zionism has fuelled Islamism, Islamism has also served Zionism well which is precisely why Israel supported Islamists in the occupied territories prior to the first intifada. This was compounded by the failure of nationalists and the continued depredations of Palestinians. Whist the main beneficiaries of this – Hamas and, to a much lesser extent, Islamic Jihad in Gaza – have been little more than a thorn in Israel's side, the rise of Islamists in the Arab Spring throughout the Arab world potentially presents an altogether different proposition. As we have repeatedly stressed, Palestine lies at the core of their politics and it is the one issue that can galvanise Sunni and Shia Islamists into forging an alliance against Israel. Therefore, if Israel is foolish enough (with or without overt American support) to launch an attack on Iran, and Iran (possibly with Hezbollah's assistance) retaliates by launching missile attacks on Israel, the consequences will inevitably spill into Arab countries. Whilst the old dictators would clamp down hard on the 'Arab street', the new democratic regimes, led by Islamists, will doubtless be pushed into taking at least some meaningful action; potentially escalating into a regional war in which the Americans, albeit reluctantly, intervene on Israel's side. It is this scenario that is so perilous not only to the Middle East but also to the wider world. It is not hard to imagine the ugly reaction by Islamists in the West, poisoning yet more the already fractious relations between not only Islamists and Zionists but also between Muslims and Jews generally. Those concerned by the profound dangers and reactionary nature of the Islamist movement and its strong appetite for power must come to terms with this reality.

Can such a gloomy prognosis be avoided? Yes, but it requires resolution to the Israel-Palestine conflict, a *sine qua non* for which is justice for the Palestinians – within Israel, in the occupied territories, in refugee camps, and in the diaspora. Justice minimally necessitates the recognition and redressing of their dispossession since 1948 – anything less, such as the utterly failed 'two state solution' advocated by the Oslo accords of 1993, will not even begin to address the deep sense of injustice and anger – one crucial consequence of which has been the massive resurgence of Islamist politics. Whilst Iran's nuclear programme provides the most likely catalyst (or pretext) for a conflagration between Israel and Islamism, other causal factors in the post-Arab Spring – such as clashes on the Israel-Egypt border – can also do the same in the prevailing tinderbox climate. The outrage felt by Israel's decades' long humiliation

Concluding Remarks

of Palestinians and the wider Arab world is of astonishing intensity; which is rooted in the very nature of Israel and the unyielding support it receives from Western powers despite it being in breach of myriad UN conventions and international laws.

Indeed, there is now mounting and incontrovertible evidence to show that Israel is in breach of the crime of apartheid: this was precisely the finding of the third session of the *Russell Tribunal on Palestine* (held in Cape Town, South Africa) in November 2011 to deal with the question 'Are Israeli practices against the Palestinian people in breach of the prohibition on apartheid under international law?' The first summary paragraph is unambiguous:

> The Tribunal finds that Israel subjects the Palestinian people to an institutionalised regime of domination amounting to apartheid as defined under international law. This discriminatory regime manifests in varying intensity and forms against different categories of Palestinians depending on their location. The Palestinians living under colonial military rule in the Occupied Palestinian Territory are subject to a particularly aggravated form of apartheid. Palestinian citizens of Israel, while entitled to vote, are not part of the Jewish nation as defined by Israeli law and are therefore excluded from the benefits of Jewish nationality and subject to systematic discrimination across the broad spectrum of recognised human rights. Irrespective of such differences, the Tribunal concludes that Israel's rule over the Palestinian people, wherever they reside, collectively amounts to a single integrated regime of apartheid (RTOP, 2011).[76]

---

[76] The panel comprises an array of eminent persons: Stéphane Hessel, Ambassador of France, a participant in the drafting of the Universal Declaration of Human Rights; Mairead Corrigan Maguire, Nobel Peace laureate 1976, Northern Ireland; John Dugard, Professor of international law, former United Nations Special Rapporteur on Human Rights in the Occupied Palestinian Territories; Lord Anthony Gifford, senior barrister and hereditary peer; Gisèle Halimi, lawyer, former Ambassador to UNESCO, France; Ronald Kasrils, writer and activist, former Minister, South Africa; Michael Mansfield, barrister, President of the Haldane Society of Socialist Lawyers; José Antonio Martín Pallín, Emeritus Judge, Chamber II, Supreme Court, Spain; Cynthia

In a similar vein, the 80th session of the UN Committee on the Elimination of Racial Discrimination, held in February-March 2012, also found Israel in violation of the crime of apartheid in the treatment of its Palestinian citizens inside Israel by determining that many state policies within Israel violate the prohibition on apartheid as enshrined in Article 3 of the International Convention on the Elimination of all Forms of Racial Discrimination (CERD, 2012, p. 2)[77].

In 2009, the Human Sciences Research Council of South Africa (HSRC) released a study indicating that Israel is practicing both colonialism and apartheid in the Occupied Palestinian Territories (OPT). The Report found that Israeli practices in the OPT exhibit the same three 'pillars' of apartheid as were practised in South Africa:

> The first pillar 'derives from Israeli laws and policies that establish Jewish identity for purposes of law and afford a preferential legal status and material benefits to Jews over non-Jews'.

> The second pillar is reflected in 'Israel's "grand" policy to fragment the OPT [and] ensure that Palestinians remain confined to the reserves designated for them while Israeli Jews are prohibited from entering those reserves but enjoy freedom of

---

McKinney, former Member of the US Congress and 2008 presidential candidate, Green Party, USA; Alberto San Juan, actor, Spain; Yasmin Sooka, Executive Director of the Foundation for Human Rights, South Africa; Aminata Traoré, author and former Minister of Culture of Mali; Alice Walker, poet and writer, USA.

[77] Point 11 makes this clear: 'The Committee notes with increased concern that Israeli society maintains Jewish and non-Jewish sectors, which raises issues under article 3 of the Convention. Clarifications provided by the delegation confirmed the Committee's concerns in relation to the existence of two systems of education, one in Hebrew and one in Arabic, which except in rare circumstances remain impermeable and inaccessible to the other community, as well as separate municipalities: Jewish municipalities and the so-called "municipalities of the minorities" (CERD, 2012, p. 2).

Concluding Remarks

movement throughout the rest of the Palestinian territory. This policy is evidenced by Israel's extensive appropriation of Palestinian land, which continues to shrink the territorial space available to Palestinians; the hermetic closure and isolation of the Gaza Strip from the rest of the OPT; the deliberate severing of East Jerusalem from the rest of the West Bank ...'

The third pillar is 'Israel's invocation of 'security' to validate sweeping restrictions on Palestinian freedom of opinion, expression, assembly, association and movement [to] mask a true underlying intent to suppress dissent to its system of domination and thereby maintain control over Palestinians as a group' (HSRC, 2009).

Indeed, the description of Israel as an apartheid state is nothing new – as far back as 1961, none other than Hendrik Verwoerd, the South African prime minister and architect of 'grand apartheid', famously remarked: '[t]he Jews took Israel from the Arabs after the Arabs lived there for a 1000 years. In this I agree with them. Israel like South Africa is an apartheid- state' (cited in McGreal, 2006).

Another recent phenomenon has graphically exposed Israel's desire to remain an exclusively Jewish apartheid society. Because of its developed status and relatively high living standards, Israel has increasingly become a magnet for Africa asylum seekers – who invariably enter via Egypt (a much poorer, so less desirable country for prospective settlement). An article in *Haaretz* in June 2012, under the astonishing heading 'Israel's five-year war on African migrants', points out that this influx is simply intolerable for many leading Israeli politicians as well as for large numbers of Israelis who have resorted to violent protests in Tel Aviv against these migrants: '[f]rom building a new border fence [along the border with Egypt] to setting up the world's largest detention facility for asylum seekers, Israel's government has tried a number of different strategies designed to keep African migrants out (Weiler-Polak and Cohen, 2012). In an attempt to quell the protests, Prime Minister Benjamin Netanyahu stated '[t]he problem of the infiltrators [*sic*] must be solved and we will solve it' – keeping his word by authorising swift deportation. Interior Minister Eli

Yishai, of the ultra-Orthodox Shas party, unapologetically resorted to naked racism: '[t]he infiltrators along with the Palestinians will quickly bring us to the end of the Zionist dream ... Most of those people arriving here are Muslims who think the country doesn't belong to us, the white man' (cited in Fisher Ilan, 2012). Bizarrely, Yishai dismissed accusations of racism: 'I sound like a racist, a benighted man, or a xenophobe, but I'm motivated by love for my country and the knowledge that I don't have another country' (cited in Sherwood, May 2012). One wonders what his response would be to those Americans and West Europeans who provided a similar defence to keep Jews out during and after the Second World War.

Daughter of a retired Israeli general, Nurit Peled-Elhanan of Hebrew University not only denounces Israel's racism and apartheid system but warns of its lurch to 'fascism':

> 'One question that bothers many people is how do you explain the cruel behaviour of Israeli soldiers towards Palestinians, an indifference to human suffering, the inflicting of suffering. People ask how can these nice Jewish boys and girls become monsters once they put on a uniform. I think the major reason for that is education' ... In 'hundreds and hundreds' of books, she claims she did not find one photograph that depicted an Arab as a 'normal person' ... 'I only see the path to fascism. You have 5.5 million Palestinians controlled by Israel who live in a horrible apartheid with no civil and no human rights' (cited in Sherwood, 2011).

Curiously, it was the former Israeli Prime Minister, Ehud Olmert, who unwittingly provided the path for all those seeking justice to take, that is, to end occupation, racism, and apartheid. At the Annapolis Conference in the US in November 2007, which discussed the move towards a two state solution, Olmert provided a warning to Israelis and their supporters if this was not achieved:

> "If the day comes when the two-state solution collapses, and we face a South African-style struggle for equal voting rights (also for the Palestinians in the territories), then, as soon as that happens, the State of Israel is finished," Prime Minister Ehud Olmert told *Haaretz* Wednesday, the day the Annapolis conference ended in an

Concluding Remarks

agreement to try to reach a Mideast peace settlement by the end of 2008. "The Jewish organizations, which were our power base in America, will be the first to come out against us," Olmert said, "because they will say they cannot support a state that does not support democracy and equal voting rights for all its residents (*Haaretz*, 2007).

Whether Jewish organisations in America – who well know that Israel has never afforded democracy and voting rights to Palestinians – will 'come out against' Israel should 'a South African-style struggle for equal voting rights' ensue in Israel-Palestine is very much open to doubt. Indeed, American Jewish Zionist organisations have been characterised by their steadfast support for *any* action taken by Israel – they represent the bedrock of the Israel Lobby and its 'Israel First' stance. But a sustained non-violent struggle for equality and civil rights by Palestinians holds the prospect of the flowering of a mass anti-apartheid movement of the type seen in 1970s and 1980s that played a pivotal role in the downfall of the South African apartheid regime. At a certain juncture, the influence of the Lobby on the one hand, and historic fealty to the Jewish state on the other, will be significantly weakened and, for the first time since its formation, Israel will face real pressure from US and European powers to implement far-reaching democratic reforms.

Those not convinced by such a scenario ought to consider the likely outcome if the Israelis act in the manner of the Assad regime in Syria in response to unrelenting mass, peaceful, protests. We can then surely imagine a forceful response from Israel's allies and the ebbing away of support by at least some Zionist organisations for a state and ideology that has been their raison d'être. As the power of Zionism wanes, so too will a core *casus belli* of the Islamists, thereby ensuring that the clash between Islamism and Zionism becomes less menacing and, over time, is defused. Moreover, such a vista holds the prospect of avowedly secular Palestinians attracting to their ranks progressive, anti-Zionist Jews, desirous of breaking free from the Zionist straitjacket. This would be a monumental advance equivalent in importance to that of white South Africans who forged an alliance with blacks in South Africa against the apartheid regime.

But how realistic is a mass civil rights movement in Israel-Palestine? It has never occurred before – and a 'Palestinian Spring' has been conspicuous by its absence. There were demonstrations in solidarity with the Egyptian revolution in both Gaza and West Bank in March 2011, but were quickly put down by Hamas and the Palestinian Authority respectively (see, for example, Rakhu, 2012). Throughout Israel's history there have, in fact, been very few mass protests by its Palestinian residents – contrast this with the enormous rallies, doubtless and ironically inspired by the Arab uprisings (including an astonishing 300,000 in Tel Aviv) by Israeli Jews in September 2011 demanding 'social justice' (which, sadly, did not include demanding equal rights for Palestinians) (see Sherwood, 2011). In the occupied territories there have, of course, been mass uprisings in the form of the two intifadas – but these were against the occupation and savage repression.

There were, however, small stirrings of a Palestinian Spring just *before* the start of the Arab Spring. On 14th December 2010 (that is, three days before Mohammad Bouazizi set himself on fire in Tunisia), a manifesto was released under the heading 'Gaza Youth Breaks Out movement' – key extracts are provided below. No detailed information was provided as to the nature of this grouping but its contents are remarkable given the locality from which they emanate. In that the manifesto is uncompromisingly hostile to both the Zionist regime of Israel and the Islamists of Hamas, it chimes in well with the sentiments of this book:

> Fuck Hamas. Fuck Israel. Fuck Fatah. Fuck UN. Fuck UNWRA. Fuck USA! We, the youth in Gaza, are so fed up with Israel, Hamas, the occupation, the violations of human rights and the indifference of the international community! We want to scream and break this wall of silence, injustice and indifference like the Israeli F16's breaking the wall of sound; scream with all the power in our souls in order to release this immense frustration that consumes us because of this fucking situation we live in; we are like lice between two nails living a nightmare inside a nightmare, no room for hope, no space for freedom. We are sick of being

Concluding Remarks

caught in this political struggle; sick of coal (*sic*) dark nights with airplanes circling above our homes; sick of innocent farmers getting shot in the buffer zone because they are taking care of their lands; sick of bearded guys walking around with their guns abusing their power, beating up or incarcerating young people demonstrating for what they believe in; sick of the wall of shame that separates us from the rest of our country and keeps us imprisoned in a stamp-sized piece of land; sick of being portrayed as terrorists, homemade fanatics with explosives in our pockets and evil in our eyes; sick of the indifference we meet from the international community, the so-called experts in expressing concerns and drafting resolutions but cowards in enforcing anything they agree on; we are sick and tired of living a shitty life, being kept in jail by Israel, beaten up by Hamas and completely ignored by the rest of the world.

There is a revolution growing inside of us, an immense dissatisfaction and frustration that will destroy us unless we find a way of canalizing this energy into something that can challenge the status quo and give us some kind of hope. The final drop that made our hearts tremble with frustration and hopelessness happened 30rd November, when Hamas' officers came to Sharek Youth Forum, a leading youth organization (www.sharek.ps) with their guns, lies and aggressiveness, throwing everybody outside, incarcerating some and prohibiting Sharek from working. A few days later, demonstrators in front of Sharek were beaten and some incarcerated. We are really living a nightmare inside a nightmare. It is difficult to find words for the pressure we are under. We barely survived the Operation Cast Lead, where Israel very effectively bombed the shit out of us, destroying thousands of homes and even more lives and dreams. They did not get rid of Hamas, as they intended, but they sure scared us forever and distributed post traumatic stress syndrome to everybody, as there was nowhere to run.

We are youth with heavy hearts. We carry in ourselves a heaviness so immense that it makes it difficult [for] us to enjoy the sunset ... During the war we got the unmistakable feeling that Israel wanted to erase us from the face of the earth. During the last years Hamas has been doing all they can to control our thoughts, behaviour and aspirations. We are a generation of young people used to face missiles, carrying what seems to be an impossible mission of living a normal and healthy life, and only barely tolerated by a massive organization that has spread in our society as a malicious cancer disease, causing mayhem and effectively

killing all living cells, thoughts and dreams on its way as well as paralyzing people with its terror regime. Not to mention the prison we live in, a prison sustained by a so-called democratic country ...
We want to be free, we want to live, we want peace.
FREE GAZA YOUTH! (Gaza Youth Breaks Out, 2010).

Alas, the revolutionary stirrings of this manifesto did not translate into a 'Gazan Spring' – perhaps the numbers involved were too small and, moreover, in a deeply conservative tract of land long dominated by Islamists, its searing indictment of Hamas did not gain much purchase. But the sense of despair, rage, and yearning for a better world free of the oppression and repression by both Zionists and Islamists has great validity for all Palestinian youth.

It is an important fact that major Palestinian organisations do not use the term 'apartheid' to define their existence, nor have they ever campaigned against Israeli apartheid; rather, the apartheid epithet has increasingly been used by outsiders, including by South Africans.[78] Indeed, to all intents and purposes, the PLO and its constituent organisations have been *complicit* in cementing apartheid by their acceptance of the two-state solution since Oslo; moreover by focusing solely on removing the occupation and the creation of a Bantustan-style statelet, they have shown no concern for the apartheid-like discrimination of Palestinians in Israel. If after Oslo the Israelis had retreated to the 1967 borders, that would have sufficed for the PLO and perhaps some kind of uneasy truce might have obtained – but the Israelis have been typically greedy. What seems clear is that if a mass civil rights movement were to

---

[78] In needs pointing out that another, little remarked upon, form of apartheid increasingly exists in Gaza, that is, gender apartheid. For example, in July 2011, as the Arab spring was raging, the Hamas administration decided to enforce a ban on male hairdressers cutting women's hair, a law that had been passed the previous year. This followed the outlawing of women from smoking waterpipes in public places and the barring of men from teaching in girls' schools (Stewart, 2011). An 'industrial strength' form of Islam has taken root in the shattered, blockaded, strip.

Concluding Remarks

mushroom in Palestine, it will do so against the teeth of Fatah and the quisling Palestine Authority.

As for the Islamists, they have a simple desire: to 'return' Palestine to the status of an Islamic *waqf*. Such a state would be an Islamic equivalent of a Zionist state as Islamists do not wish to have Jews living in their midst as equal citizens, that is to say, an Islamic apartheid state under Sharia law is their ultimate goal. This is, of course, quite intolerable and to be fiercely resisted: if a Jewish state is deemed to be undemocratic and unjust, the same applies to an Islamic state. The just solution does not attach any mystery to it, in fact, is plainly evident: a secular, democratic state for those living in the land of historic Palestine which does not confer privileges to any group. This is the minimum requirement for any state with democratic pretensions – for example, the European Union disallows from its membership any aspirant country that is in breach of this fundamental constitutional principle.

Such a 'one state solution' will end the crime of apartheid and begin to address the decades' long injustice to Palestinians. The decisive first step towards this salutary goal lies with the Palestinians themselves. This was alluded to by Palestinian academic and activist Rashid Khalidi in an interview in December 2011 with the Israeli paper *Haaretz*: 'I think that if the Palestinians cannot get their act together, they have no hope of resolving their problems. Palestinian problems are caused, in the first instance, by Palestinians. You can blame Israel, or the United States or the Arabs – and they have their share' (Khalidi, 2011). One crucial element of 'getting their act together' requires, in the present author's view, secular, progressive, Palestinians to come together with Israeli Jews (however few at first) of the same bent – in the manner that blacks in apartheid South Africa did with many whites. This will mark a significant symbolic advance towards a just resolution to this bitter, century-long struggle and mark a blow against both Islamism and Zionism. By so doing, it will inevitably begin to defuse the dangerous clash between these ideologies as highlighted in this book: a prize that surely cannot be overestimated.

Bibliography

Abu-Amr Z (1993) 'Hamas: A historical and political background', *Journal of Palestine Studies,* vol. xxii, no. 4, pp. 5-19

Adar S (2010) 'What are Israeli flags and Jewish activists doing at demonstrations sponsored by the English Defence League?', *Haaretz,* 13 August, http://www.haaretz.com/weekend/magazine/what-are-israeli-flags-and-jewish-activists-doing-at-demonstrations-sponsored-by-the-english-defence-league-1.307803

Adas J (2010) 'Robert Pastor on the U.S., Hamas, and Middle East Peace', *Washington Report on Middle East Affairs,* May-June, http://www.wrmea.com/component/content/article/351-2010-may-june/9051-mazin-qumsiyeh-on-the-history-and-practice-of-nonviolent-palestinian-resistance-.html

Ahmad E (2000) *Confronting Empire: Interviews with David Barsamian,* London: Pluto Press

Al Aswany A (2011) 'Did the Egyptian revolution go wrong?', *Aid Netherlands,* 7 July, http://www.nl-aid.org/continent/northern-africa/did-the-egyptian-revolution-go-wrong/

Al Aswany A (2011) 'Egypt must confront religious fascism', *World Affairs,* 25 October, http://www.worldaffairsjournal.org/blog/alaa-al-aswany/egypt-must-confront-religious-fascism

Al Wafd (2012) 'Leader calls for the liberation of Jerusalem' (in Arabic), 5 July, http://www.alwafd.org

Alibhai-Brown Y (2007) 'The shadowy role of Labour Friends of Israel', *The Independent,* 3 December, http://www.independent.co.uk/opinion/commentators/yasmin-alibhai-brown/yasmin-alibhaibrown-the-shadowy-role-of-labour-friends-of-israel-761363.html?origin=internalSearch

al-Tabaei H (2012) 'Egypt's Muslim Brotherhood reiterates refusal to engage Israel', *Asharq Al-Awsat,* 25 January, http://asharq-e.com/news.asp?section=1&id=28233

Altikriti A (2007) 'Forgetting to remember', *The Guardian,* 4 December, http://www.guardian.co.uk/commentisfree/2007/dec/04/forgettingtoremember

Antonius G (2000 [1938]) *The Arab Awakening: The Story of the National Arab Movement,* London: Kegan Paul

Arendt H (2007 [1948]) 'To save the Jewish homeland', in *The Jewish Writings,* Kohn J and Feldman R (eds.), New York: Schocken Book

Bibliography

Aslan R and Hahn Tapper A (eds.) (2011) *Muslims and Jews in America: Commonalities, Contentions and Complexities*, New York: Palgrave McMillan

Badie M (2012) 'Letter from Mohammed Badi - General Guide of the Muslim Brotherhood' *Ikhwanonline* (in Arabic), 14 June, http://www.ikhwanonline.com/new/Article.aspx?SecID=213&ArtID=111457

Barnard A and Feuer A (2010) 'Pamela Geller: in her own words', *New York Times,* October 8, http://www.nytimes.com/2010/10/10/nyregion/10gellerb.html?pagewanted=1

Bartlett J and Littler M (2011) *Inside the EDL: Populist Politics in a Digital Age*, London: Demos

Bates A (2011) 'The Muslim Brotherhood: A Democratizing Influence?', *Mother Jones,* http://motherjones.com/mojo/2011/02/muslim-brotherhood-democratizing-influence

BBC News (2004) '9/11 probe clears Saudi Arabia', 17 June, http://news.bbc.co.uk/1/hi/world/middle_east/3815179.stm

BBC News (2008) 'Al-Qaeda accuses Iran of 9/11 lie', 22 April, http://news.bbc.co.uk/1/hi/world/middle_east/7361414.stm

BBC News (2009) 'Profile: Major Nidal Malik Hasan', November 12, http://news.bbc.co.uk/1/hi/8345944.stm

BBC News (2011) 'Geert Wilders cleared of hate charges by Dutch court', 23 June, http://www.bbc.co.uk/news/world-europe-13883331

BBC News (2011) 'Muslims boycott Mayor Bloomberg's interfaith breakfast', December 30, http://www.bbc.co.uk/news/world-us-canada-16366971

BBC News (2006) 'Israel to boost troop numbers', July 27, http://news.bbc.co.uk/1/hi/world/middle_east/5221384.stm

BBC News (2011) 'Egyptian protesters break into Israeli embassy building', 10 September, http://www.bbc.co.uk/news/world-middle-east-14862159

BBC News (2011) 'Iran IAEA nuclear report deepens concerns', 8 November, http://www.bbc.co.uk/news/world-middle-east-15642021

BBC News (2011) 'Islamist PJD party wins Morocco poll', 27 November, http://www.bbc.co.uk/news/world-africa-15902703

BBC News (2011) 'Muslim member of the English Defence League on demo', 5 February, http://www.bbc.co.uk/news/uk-politics-12374835

BBC News (2012) 'Egypt President Mursi's first speech: Key quotes', 25 June, http://www.bbc.co.uk/news/world-middle-east-18577334

BBC News (2012) 'UN nuclear chief "positive" over Iran talks', 21 May, http://www.bbc.co.uk/news/world-middle-east-18140539

BBC News (2012a) 'Innocence of Muslims: Mystery of film-maker "Sam Bacile"', 13 September, http://www.bbc.co.uk/news/world-africa-19572912

BBC News (2012b) 'Pro-Israel 'Defeat Jihad' ads to hit New York subway', 20 September, http://www.bbc.co.uk/news/world-us-canada-19665225

BBC News (2012c) 'Dutch election: Pro-Europe VVD and Labour parties win', 13 September, http://www.bbc.co.uk/news/world-europe-19566165

BBC World Service Country Rating Poll (2011) http://news.bbc.co.uk/1/shared/bsp/hi/pdfs/05_03_11_bbcws_country_poll.pdf

Ben Meir Y (2009) 'Operation Cast Lead: political dimensions and public opinion' *Strategic Assessment*, Volume 11, No. 4, February 2009, Institute for National Security Studies, Tel Aviv University, http://www.inss.org.il/publications.php?cat=21&incat=&read=2634

Ben-Gurion D (1970) *Recollections*, edited by Thomas Bransten, London: MacDonald Unit 75

Ben-Gurion D (1973 [1967]) *My Talks with Arab Leaders*, New York: The Third Press

Ben-Meir A (2012) 'Israel and the Muslim Brotherhood: Facing the bittersweet reality', *The Daily News Egypt.Com,* 20 March, http://thedailynewsegypt.com/global-views/israel-and-the-muslim-brotherhood-facing-the-bittersweet-reality.html

Bennett J (2001) A DAY OF TERROR: THE ISRAELIS; Spilled Blood Is Seen as Bond That Draws 2 Nations Closer, 12 September, http://www.nytimes.com/2001/09/12/us/day-terror-israelis-spilled-blood-seen-bond-that-draws-2-nations-closer.html

Bin Laden O (2002) 'Letter to America' [translated from Arabic], *The Observer,* 24 November, http://www.guardian.co.uk/world/2002/nov/24/theobserver

Bin Laden O, Zawahiri A *et al.* (1998) 'Al Qaida's fatwa', Published in *Al-Quds al-'Arabi*, February 23, 1998, available at http://www.pbs.org/newshour/terrorism/international/fatwa_1998.html

Birch D (2012) 'US: Iran has not yet decided to build nuclear bomb', *AP,* reported in *Yahoo News,* 8 January, http://news.yahoo.com/us-iran-not-yet-decided-build-nuclear-bomb-140132073.html

Bishara M (2012) *Empire: A second republic?,* broadcast on *Al Jazeera English,* 12 July

Bishara M (2012) *The Invisible Arab,* New York: Nation Books

Blandford N (2007) 'Introduction' in Noe (ed.) *Voice of Hezbollah: Statements of Sayyed Hassan Nasrallah*, London and New York: Verso

Blumenthal M (2007) 'AIPAC cheers an anti-Semitic Holocaust revisionist (and Abe Foxman approves)' *Huffington Post,* 14 March,

Bibliography

http://www.huffingtonpost.com/max-blumenthal/aipac-cheers-an-antisemit_b_43377.html?

Blumenthal R and Mowjood S (2009) 'Muslims prayers and renewal near Ground Zero, *New York Times*, December 9, http://www.nytimes.com/2009/12/09/nyregion/09mosque.html

Booth R (2010) 'English Defence League members attend New York mosque protest', *The Observer,* 12 September, http://www.guardian.co.uk/uk/2010/sep/12/english-defence-league-mosque-protest

Borger J (2011) 'Unanswered questions over the alleged Iranian assassination plot', *The Guardian,* October 13, http://www.guardian.co.uk/world/2011/oct/12/unanswered-questions-iranian-assassination-plot?INTCMP=SRCH

Boston Globe (2007) 'Army is worn too thin, says general', September 27, http://www.boston.com/news/nation/washington/articles/2007/09/27/army_is_worn_too_thin_says_general/

Brady B (2011) 'Liam Fox, Adam Werritty, and the curious case of Our Man in Tel Aviv', *The Independent,* 27 November, http://www.independent.co.uk/news/uk/politics/liam-fox-adam-werritty-and-the-curious-case-of-our-man-in-tel-aviv-6268640.html

Bright M (2011) 'Jewish envoy not loyal to UK, says Labour MP', *The Jewish Chronicle,* 1 December, http://www.thejc.com/news/uk-news/59300/jewish-envoy-not-loyal-uk-says-labour-mp

Buruma I (2007) 'Tariq Ramadan has an identity issue', *New York Times,* 4 February, http://www.nytimes.com/2007/02/04/magazine/04ramadan.t.html?pagewanted=1&_r=1&th&emc=th

Carré O (1995) 'Hasan al Banna' in *The Oxford Encyclopaedia of the Modern Muslim World*, New York and Oxford: Oxford University Press, pp. 195-199

Casciani D (2009) 'Who are the English Defence League?', *BBC Magazine*, 11 September, http://news.bbc.co.uk/1/hi/magazine/8250017.stm

CBS News (2002) 'Falwell on Islam, Mohammed', 6 October, http://www.cbsnews.com/video/watch/?id=2808715n&tag=mncol;lst;8

CBS News (2002) 'Falwell, Friend of Israel', 6 October, http://www.cbsnews.com/video/watch/?id=2809679n&tag=mncol;lst;7

CBS News (2010) 'Muslim Scholar: Don't Build Islamic Center', September 13, http://www.cbsnews.com/stories/2010/09/11/earlyshow/saturday/main

6855993.shtml?tag=mncol;lst;1

Channel 4 (2007) *Undercover Mosque*, broadcast on 18 January

Chehab Z (2007) *Inside Hamas: The Untold Story of Militants, Martyrs, and Spies*, London: IB Taurus

CIA World Fact Book, 'Israel', https://www.cia.gov/library/publications/the-world-factbook/geos/is.html

CIA World Fact Book, 'West Bank', https://www.cia.gov/library/publications/the-world-factbook/geos/we.html

Clifton E and Fang L (2011) 'On Veterans Day, State Rep Womick (R-TN) calls for purging Muslims from the military', November 11, http://thinkprogress.org/security/2011/11/11/367055/on-veterans-day-state-rep-rick-womick-r-tn-calls-for-purging-muslims-from-the-military/

CNN (2010) 'Overwhelming majority oppose mosque near Ground Zero', August 11, http://politicalticker.blogs.cnn.com/2010/08/11/overwhelming-majority-oppose-mosque-near-ground-zero/

CNN (2010) 'US Muslims underestimate 9/11 effect, Muslim thinker warns, August 5, http://religion.blogs.cnn.com/2010/08/05/u-s-muslims-underestimate-911-effect-muslim-thinker-warns/

CNN Transcripts (2010) 'Anderson Cooper 360 degrees', August 17, http://transcripts.cnn.com/TRANSCRIPTS/1008/17/acd.01.html

Cockburn P (2011) 'Al Qaeda and the myth behind the war on terrorism', *The Independent,* 11 September

Committee on the Elimination of Racial Discrimination [CERD] (2012) *Concluding observations of the Committee on the Elimination of Racial Discrimination: Israel*, 80th Session, 13 February – 9 March, http://www2.ohchr.org/english/bodies/cerd/docs/CERD.C.ISR.CO.14-16.pdf

Corera G (2006) 'Introduction' in Omar Nasiri, *Inside the Jihad: My Life with Al Qaeda, A Spy's Story*, New York: Basic Books

Curtis M (2010) *Secret Affairs: Britain's Collusion with Radical Islam*, London: Serpent's Tail

Curtis P (2005) 'College tells students to reverse Israeli ban, 5 February, *The Guardian,* http://www.guardian.co.uk/uk/2005/feb/05/highereducation.internationaleducationnews?INTCMP=SRCH

Davidson L (2011) 'Are Israeli Jews voting with their feet? Israel's changing demographics', *Counterpunch*, June 15, http://www.counterpunch.org/2011/06/15/israel-s-changing-

Bibliography

demographics/

Dehghan S (2012) 'This covert war on Iran is illegal and dangerous', *The Guardian,* 11 January, http://www.guardian.co.uk/commentisfree/2012/jan/11/covert-war-iran-illegal-dangerous?INTCMP=SRCH

Deutscher I (1967) 'On the Israeli-Arab War', *New Left Review*, I-44, July-August, pp. 30-45

Dombey D and Ward A (2007) 'Bush under attack over Iran', *Financial Times,* December 4, http://www.ft.com/cms/s/0/e9e67502-a430-11dc-a28d-0000779fd2ac.html?nclick_check=1

Doward J (2009) 'British Muslim leader urged to quit over Gaza', *The Observer,* 8 March, http://www.guardian.co.uk/world/2009/mar/08/daud-abdullah-gaza-middle-east

Dreyfuss R (2005) *Devil's Game: How the United States Helped Unleash Fundamentalist Islam*, New York: Holt Paperbacks

Dysch M (2011) 'EDL picks new Jewish division leader', *The Jewish Chronicle,* 8 September, http://www.thejc.com/news/uk-news/54328/edl-picks-new-jewish-division-leader

EDL (2011) 'The English Defence League – Standing Firm', 6 August, http://englishdefenceleague.org/the-english-defence-league-standing-firm/

Egremont M (1980) *A Life of Arthur James Balfour*, Glasgow: William Collins

Egypt Independent (2012) 'Free Egyptians Party warns against "new fascist rule"', 29 May, http://www.egyptindependent.com/news/free-egyptians-party-warns-against-new-fascist-rule

Egypt Independent (2012) 'Sabbahi says he would tear up Israel peace treaty', 6 May, http://www.egyptindependent.com/news/hamdeen-sabbahi-if-it-were-me-i-would-tear-peace-treaty-n1

Eilberg A (2011) 'Children of Abraham in Dialogue', in Aslan R and Hahn Tapper A (eds.), *Muslims and Jews in America: Commonalities, Contentions and Complexities*, pp. 33-44, New York: Palgrave McMillan

El Din G (2012) 'Egypt's post-Mubarak legislative life begins amid tension and divisions', *AhramOnline,* 23 January, http://english.ahram.org.eg/NewsContent/33/100/32384/Elections-/News/Egypts-postMubarak-legislative-life-begins-amid-te.aspx

Elgot J and Lipman J (2010) 'Surfing rabbi tells EDL demo "We shall prevail"', *The Jewish Chronicle, 25* October, http://www.thejc.com/arts/film/40156/surfing-rabbi-tells-edl-demo-we-shall-prevail

Elliott J (2010) 'How the "ground zero mosque" fear mongering began', *Salon.com,* August 16, http://www.salon.com/2010/08/16/ground_zero_mosque_origins/

El-Shenawai E (2012),'U.S. pastor burns Quran, Prophet image; gets fine for "book burning hazard"' *Al Arabiya News,* 29 April, http://english.alarabiya.net/articles/2012/04/29/211022.html

Fallaux E (2007) 'Is Geert Wilders een spion?' ['Is Geert Wilders a spy?'], *Vrij Nederland,* 19 May, http://www.vn.nl/Dossiers/Meer-dossiers/Wilders-en-de-PVV/Artikel-Wilders/Is-Geert-Wilders-een-spion.htm

Farouk K (2012) 'Egypt to boycott "pro-Israel" Adidas kit manufacturer', *Al Ahram,* 19 April, http://english.ahram.org.eg/NewsContent/6/52/39674/Sports/National-Teams/Egypt-to-boycott-proIsrael-Adidas-kit-manufacturer.asp

Finkielkraut A, (2003) 'Le temps des antisémites sympas' ['Time for anti-Semitic cool'] *Le Figaro Magazine,* 30 October, available at http://www.denistouret.net/textes/Ramadan.html#Finkielkraut

Fisher-Ilan A (2012) 'Israel to jail illegal migrants for up to three years', *Reuters,* 3 June, http://uk.reuters.com/article/2012/06/03/uk-israel-immigrants-idUKBRE8520DX20120603?feedType=RSS&feedName=everything&virtualBrandChannel=11708

Fisk R (1990) *Pity the Nation,* London: André Deutsch

Fisk R (1993) Documentary *From Beirut to Bosnia: Muslims and the West. Part 1 The Martyrs Smile,* shown on Channel 4

Fisk R (2006) *The Great War for Civilisation,* London: Harper Perennial

Fisk R (2010) 'Israel feels under siege. Like a victim. An underdog' *The Independent,* 2 February, http://www.independent.co.uk/opinion/commentators/fisk/robert-fisk-israel-feels-under-siege-like-a-victim-an-underdog-1886332.html

Fisk R (2012) 'After the Arab Spring, an Islamic Awakening?', *The Independent,* 27 April, http://www.independent.co.uk/opinion/commentators/fisk/robert-fisk-after-the-arab-spring-an-islamic-awakening-7685143.html

Fontevecchia A (2012) 'Attacking Iran would push the US back into recession' *Forbes,* 24 February, http://www.forbes.com/sites/afontevecchia/2012/02/24/attacking-iran-will-push-the-u-s-back-into-recession/

Fortuyn P (1997) *Tegen de islamisering van onze cultuur: Nederlandse identiteit als fundament* [Against the Islamisation of Our Culture: Dutch Identity as Foundation], Bruna: Netherlands

Bibliography

Fortuyn P (1998) *50 jaar Israel, hoe lang nog?: Tegen het tolereren van fundamentalisme* [50 Years Israel, but for How Long? Against the Tolerance of Fundamentalism], Bruna: Netherlands

Fortuyn P (2001) Quote on 'cold war with Islam', http://www.lpf-leeuwarden.nl/pimfortuyn.htm

Fourest C (2008 [2004]) *Brother Tariq: The Doublespeak of Tariq Ramadan*, trans. into English by I Wieder and J Atherton, New York and London: Encounter Books

Freedom and Justice Party (2012) 'Freedom and Justice Party statement on Israeli aggression against Gaza', 13 March, http://www.ikhwanweb.com/article.php?id=29775

Friedman T (2011) 'Newt, Mitt, Bibi, and Vladimir', *New York Times,* 13 December, http://www.nytimes.com/2011/12/14/opinion/friedman-newt-mitt-bibi-and-vladimir.html?_r=1&ref=thomaslfriedman

Gallup (2011) 'Republicans and Democrats disagree on Muslim Hearings', March 9, http://www.gallup.com/poll/146540/Republicans-Democrats-Disagree-Muslim-Hearings.aspx

Gallup.com (2010) 'In US religious prejudice stronger against Muslims', January 21, http://www.gallup.com/poll/125312/Religious-Prejudice-Stronger-Against-Muslims.aspx

Gaza Youth Breaks Out (2010) 'The manifesto', December, http://www.facebook.com/pages/Gaza-Youth-Breaks-Out-GYBO/118914244840679?v=info

Gedhalyahu T-V (2012) 'Israel praises Muslim Brotherhood', *Israel National News,* 29 January, http://www.israelnationalnews.com/News/News.aspx/152206

Geller P (2008) *Arutz Sheva 7* (Israel National News.com) 'Op-Ed: Indomitable Israel' May 11, http://www.israelnationalnews.com/Articles/Article.aspx/7968

Geller P (2010a) 'Monster Mosque Pushes Ahead in Shadow of World Trade Center Islamic Death and Destruction' *Atlas Shrugs*, May 6, http://atlasshrugs2000.typepad.com/atlas_shrugs/2010/05/monster-mosque-pushes-ahead-in-shadow-of-world-trade-center-islamic-death-and-destruction.html

Geller P (2010b) 'Pamela Geller, American Thinker: Genocide in South Africa', April 16, http://atlasshrugs2000.typepad.com/atlas_shrugs/2010/04/pamela-geller-american-thinker--1.html

Gerhart A and Londoño E (2010) 'Pastor Terry Jones's Koran-burning threat started with a tweet', *Washington Post*, September 10, http://www.washingtonpost.com/wp-dyn/content/article/2010/09/10/AR2010091007428.html

Gladwell M (2000) *The Tipping Point: How Little Things Can Make a Big Difference*, London: Abacus

Goldenberg S (2011) 'Muslim hearings in US Congress dismissed as "equivalent of reality TV"', *The Guardian,* March 10

Goldmann N (1978 [1976]) *The Jewish Paradox*, translated by Steven Cox, London: Weidenfeld and Nicolson

Goldstone Report [Report of the United Nations Fact Finding Mission on the Gaza Conflict] (2009), *Human Rights Council,* 15 September, http://www2.ohchr.org/english/bodies/hrcouncil/specialsession/9/docs/UNFFMGC_Report.pdf

Goodstein L (2010) 'Across nation, mosque projects meet opposition', *New York Times,* August 7, http://www.nytimes.com/2010/08/08/us/08mosque.html

Gowen A (2010b) 'Far from Ground Zero, other plans for mosques run into vehement opposition', *Washington Post*, August 23, http://www.washingtonpost.com/wp-dyn/content/article/2010/08/22/AR2010082202895.html?sid=ST2010082202944

Green L (2010) 'Plan to build mosque near Ground Zero riles families of 9/11 victims, *FoxNews.Com,* May 14, http://www.foxnews.com/us/2010/05/14/plan-build-mosque-near-ground-zero-riles-families-victims/

Greenstein T (2010) 'Review article: myths, politics, and scholarship in Israel', *Holy Land Studies,* vol. 9, no. 1, pp. 99-106

Gunaratna R (2003) *Inside Al Qaeda: Global Network of Terror,* New York: Berkley Books

Haaretz (2007) 'Olmert to Haaretz: Two-state solution, or Israel is done for', 29 November, http://www.haaretz.com/news/olmert-to-haaretz-two-state-solution-or-israel-is-done-for-1.234201

Haaretz (2010) 'Ahmadinejad: Israel has nukes while Iran banned from nuclear energy', 17 April, http://www.haaretz.com/news/ahmadinejad-israel-has-nukes-while-iran-banned-from-nuclear-energy-1.284439

Haaretz (2012) 'IDF chief to Haaretz: I do not believe Iran will decide to develop nuclear weapons', 25 April, http://www.haaretz.com/news/diplomacy-defense/idf-chief-to-haaretz-i-do-not-believe-iran-will-decide-to-develop-nuclear-weapons-1.426389

Hahn Tapper A (2011) 'The war of words: Jews, Muslims, and the Israeli-Palestinian conflict on America university campuses', in Aslan R and Hahn Tapper A (eds.), *Muslims and Jews in America:*

Bibliography

Commonalities, Contentions and Complexities, pp. 71-92, New York: Palgrave McMillan

Haija, R (2006) 'The Armageddon Lobby: dispensationalist Christian Zionism and the shaping of US policy towards Israel-Palestine', *Holy Land Studies,* vol. 5, no.1, May, pp. 75-95

Hamas Covenant [Charter] (1988) *The Covenant of the Islamic Resistance Movement (Hamas),* available at http://www.mideastweb.org/hamas.htm

Hammami R (1999) 'The transformation of gendered/religion identities in the Gaza Strip: literacy and the demise of saints', paper presented at the International Symposium The Palestinian Refugees and UNRWA in Jordan, the West Bank and Gaza, 1949-19, Centre d'Etudes et de Recherches sur le Moyen-Orient Contemporain, Jordan, repository.forcedmigration.org/pdf/?pid=fmo:1946

Hamzeh M (2001) *Refugees in Our Own Land,* London: Pluto Press

Harik J (2005) *Hezbollah: The Changing Face of Terrorism,* London and New York: IB Taurus

Harkabi Y (1988 [1986]) *Israel's Fateful Hour,* translated by Lenn Schramm, New York: Harper and Row Publishers

Hartman B (2011) 'Norway attack suspect had anti-Muslim, pro-Israel views', *Jerusalem Post,* 24 July, http://www.jpost.com/International/Article.aspx?id=230762

Hartman K (2011) 'Ground Zero' mosque opens without much controversy', September 22, *Digital Journal,* http://digitaljournal.com/article/311848

Hasan R (2010) *Multiculturalism: Some inconvenient Truths,* London: Politicos

Hauslohner A (2012) 'Has Egypt's Muslim Brotherhood staged a coup against the military?' *Time World,* 12 August, http://world.time.com/2012/08/12/has-egypts-muslim-brotherhood-staged-a-coup-against-the-military/?iid=gs-main-mostpop1

Hayes A (2010) 'MPACUK claims responsibility for defeat of Andrew Dismore in Hendon', *The Times,* 8 May, http://www.times-series.co.uk/news/8153929.Muslim_group_claiming_responsibility_for_Dismore_defeat/

Hedges C (1992) 'Cairo Journal; After the earthquake, a rumbling of discontent', *New York Times,* 21 October, http://www.nytimes.com/1992/10/21/world/cairo-journal-after-the-earthquake-a-rumbling-of-discontent.html

Hendawi H (2012) 'Egypt's parliament wants Israel's ambassador out', *News Times* [from AP], 12 March, http://www.newstimes.com/news/article/Egypt-s-parliament-wants-

Israel-s-ambassador-out-3399943.php

Herzl T (1960) Letter to Cecil Rhodes, January 11 1902, *The Complete Diaries of Theodor Herzl, Vol. III*, edited by Raphael Patai, London and New York: Herzl Press and Thomas Yoseloff

Herzl T (1960) *The Complete Diaries of Theodor Herzl, Vol. 1*, edited by Raphael Patai, London and New York: Herzl Press and Thomas Yoseloff

Herzl T (1993 [1896]) *The Jewish State: An Attempt at a Modern Solution of the Jewish Question*, 7th edn., London: Henry Pordes

Hezbollah (1985) 'Open letter to the Downtrodden in Lebanon and in the world', available at http://www.standwithus.com/pdfs/flyers/hezbollah_program.pdf

Higgins A (2009) 'How Israel helped to spawn Hamas', *Wall Street Journal*, January 24, http://online.wsj.com/article/NA_WSJ_PUB:SB123275572295011847.html

Hizb-ut-Tahrir (nd) Leaflet entitled 'The Muslim ummah will never submit to the Jews', http://web.archive.org/web/20010305125154/hizb-ut-Tahrir.org/english/leaflets/palestine31199.htm

Homeland Security (2011) 'The Extent of Radicalization in the American Muslim Community and that Community's Response', Hearing Contents, March 10, http://www.hsdl.org/?view&did=4530

Hroub K (2010 [2006]) *Hamas: A Beginner's Guide*, 2nd edn., London: Pluto Press

Human Sciences Research Council of South Africa (HSRC) 'SA academic study finds that Israel is practicing apartheid and colonialism in the Occupied Palestinian Territories', Media Briefs 2009, http://www.hsrc.ac.za/Media_Release-378.phtml

Huntington S (1997) *The Clash of Civilizations and the Remaking of World Order*, London: Simon and Schuster

Huntington S (2005) *Who Are We? The Challenge to America's National Identity*, New York: Simon and Schuster Paperbacks

Husain E (2007) *The Islamist*, London: Penguin Books

ICM Research (2002) 'April 2002 Poll' [on Israel-Palestine conflict], http://www.icmresearch.com/pdfs/2002_april_guardian_april_poll.pdf

ICM Research (2011) 'European Public Perceptions of the Israel – Palestine Conflict', survey prepared for the Middle East Monitor, http://www.icmresearch.com/pdfs/2011_march_memo_israelpalestine_poll.pdf

Ikhwanweb (2007) 'MB Executive Bureau criticizes Bin Laden's latest Audio Release', 30 December,

Bibliography

http://www.ikhwanweb.com/article.php?id=15033&ref=search.php

Iley C (2011) 'Vidal Sassoon interview', *The Telegraph*, 16 May, http://fashion.telegraph.co.uk/news-features/TMG8480525/Vidal-Sassoon-interview.html

Jadaliyya (2011) 'Al-Nour Party', 24 November, http://www.jadaliyya.com/pages/index/3171/al-nour-party

JPost.com (2010) 'Israeli US envoy: Hizbullah has 15,000 rockets on border', *Jerusalem Post*, 9 April, http://www.jpost.com/MiddleEast/Article.aspx?id=187022

Kais R (2011) 'Egypt's Islamists seek changes to Israel peace treaty', *Ynetnews.com*, 24 December, http://www.ynetnews.com/articles/0,7340,L-4166169,00.html

Karmi G (2007) *Married to Another Man: Israel's Dilemma in Palestine*, London: Pluto Press

Kassir S (2006) *Being Arab*, London and New York: Verso

Keay J (2003) *Sowing the Wind: the Mismanagement of the Middle East*, London: John Murray Publishers

Kemp P (2010) 'Phil Woolas defends campaign tactics as appeal fails', *BBC News*, 9 December, http://www.bbc.co.uk/news/uk-politics-11940564

Kepel G (2003) *Jihad: The Trail of Political Islam*, London: IB Tauris

Kepel G (2008) *Beyond Terror and Martyrdom: The Future of the Middle East*, Cambridge Mass. and London: Belknap Press

Kepel G and Milleli J-P (eds.)(2008) *Al Qaeda in its Own Words*, Cambridge MA and London: Belknap Press

Khalidi R (2011) 'Full transcript of interview with Palestinian professor Rashid Khalidi', *Haaretz*, 5 December, http://www.haaretz.com/news/middle-east/full-transcript-of-interview-with-palestinian-professor-rashid-khalidi-1.399632

King A (2005) 'The countries we love and hate', *The Telegraph*, 5 January, http://www.telegraph.co.uk/news/uknews/4194711/The-countries-that-we-love-and-hate.html

Klein J (2010) 'Pro-Israel extremists have campaigned against an Islamic cultural center before', *Mandoweiss*, August 23, http://mondoweiss.net/2010/08/pro-israel-extremists-have-campaigned-against-an-islamic-cultural-center-before.html

Klug B (2007) 'No one has the right to speak for British Jews on Israel and Zionism', *Independent Jewish Voices*, http://jewishvoices.squarespace.com/speaks/

Kolko G (2009) *World in Crisis: The End of the American Century*, London and New York: Pluto Press

Labévière R (1999) *Dollars for Terror: The United States and Islam*, New York: Algora Publishing

Lerman A (2011) 'The farcical attack on the UCU for voting against use of the EUMC 'working definition' of antisemitism', Blog post 2 June, http://antonylerman.com/2011/06/02/the-farcical-attack-on-the-ucu-for-voting-against-use-of-the-eumc-working-definition-of-antisemitism/

Levy B-H (2004) 'The other face of Tariq Ramadan', http://www.mobylives.com/BHL.html

Levy G (2012) 'Israelis should be afraid of their leaders, not Iran', *Haaretz,* 5 February, http://www.haaretz.com/print-edition/opinion/israelis-should-be-afraid-of-their-leaders-not-iran-1.411087

Lichfield J (2012) 'Serial killer reveals why he struck at Toulouse school', *The Independent,* 22 March

Linden M (2010) 'Ad campaign to counter negative views of Islam', *The Independent* [from PA], 7 July, http://www.independent.co.uk/news/uk/home-news/ad-campaign-to-counter-negative-views-of-muslims-1993538.html?origin=internalSearch

Lipman J (2011) 'EDL Jewish division leader Roberta Moore quits', *The Jewish Chronicle,* 29 June, http://www.thejc.com/news/uk-news/50932/edl-jewish-division-leader-roberta-moore-quits

Maclear M (1989 [1981]) *Vietnam: The Ten Thousand Day War,* London: Mandarin

Madi M (2011) 'Libya looks set to chart moderate course on Islam', *BBC News,* 4 November, http://www.bbc.co.uk/news/world-africa-15500682

Major L (2001) 'Extreme Muslim groups step up activity, claim students', *The Guardian,* 5 November, http://www.guardian.co.uk/education/2001/nov/05/students?INTCMP=SRCH

Mandel N (1976) *The Arabs and Zionism Before World War I,* Berkley, Los Angeles, London: University of California Press

Masalha N (2007) *The Bible and Zionism: Invented Traditions, Archaeology, and Post-Colonialism in Israel-Palestine,* London: Zed Books

Masalha N (2012) *The Palestine Nakba: Decolonising History, Narrating the Subaltern, Reclaiming Memory,* London: Zed Books

Mayer T (2002) 'The military force of Islam: the Society of the Muslim Brethren and the Palestine question, 1945-48', in Kedourie E and Haim S, *Zionism and Arabism in Palestine and Israel,* pp. 100-117, London: Frank Cass

McGovern R and Murray E (2011) 'Urging Obama to stop rush to Iran war', *ConsortiumNews.com,* 30 December, http://consortiumnews.com/2011/12/30/urging-obama-to-stop-rush-to-

Bibliography

iran-war/

McGreal C (2003) 'EU poll sees Israel as peace threat', *The Guardian*, 3 November, http://www.guardian.co.uk/world/2003/nov/03/eu.israel?INTCMP=SRCH

McGreal C (2006) 'Worlds apart', *The Guardian*, 6 February, http://www.guardian.co.uk/world/2006/feb/06/southafrica.israel

Mearsheimer J and Walt S (2007) *The Israel Lobby and US Foreign Policy*, London: Allen Lane

Middle East Monitor (2012) 'Al-Ghannouchi tells media that Israel is "ageing" and Palestine is on the top of the Islamists' agenda', 13 March, http://www.middleeastmonitor.org.uk/news/middle-east/3510-al-ghannouchi-tells-media-that-israel-is-qageingq-and-palestine-is-on-the-top-of-the-islamists-agenda

Miller K (2008) *Guardians of Islam: Religious authority and Muslim communities of late Medieval Spain*, New York and Chichester: Columbia University Press

Miller R and Dashefsky A (2010) 'Brandeis v. Cohen et al.: The Distancing from Israel Debate', *Contemporary Jewry*, vol. 30, nos. 2-3, pp. 155-154, http://www.springerlink.com/content/e7l831wh13723423/

Milton-Edwards B (1999 [1996]) *Islamic Politics in Palestine*, London and New York: IB Taurus

Minkoff D (2010 [2005]) *The Ultimate Book of Jewish Jokes*, London: Portico Books

Mitchell R (1993 [1969]) *The Society of the Muslim Brothers*, New York and Oxford: Oxford University Press

Mohammed A and Colvin R (2010) 'Saudi king urged U.S. to attack Iran: WikiLeaks', *Reuters*, 29 November, http://www.reuters.com/article/2010/11/29/us-wikileaks-usa-idUSTRE6AP06Z20101129

Morris B (2008) *1948: A History of the First Arab-Israeli War*, New Haven and London: Yale University Press

Mozgovaya N (2012) 'U.S. military chief: Israeli strike on Iran would not be "prudent"', *Haaretz*, 18 February, http://www.haaretz.com/news/diplomacy-defense/u-s-military-chief-israeli-strike-on-iran-would-not-be-prudent-1.413361

MPACUK (2010) 'Exposed! The EDL and its Zionist connection', 3 September, http://www.mpacuk.org/story/060909/exposed-edl-and-its-zionist-connection.html

MPACUK, MPAC Core Principles, http://www.mpacuk.org/about-mpacuk.html

National Council of Churches USA [NCCUSA] (nd) 'Response to

Christian Zionism',
http://www.ncccusa.org/NCCpolicies/christianzionism.htm
National Post (2012) 'Egypt's new Islamist leader Mohammed Morsi to "reconsider" Israel peace deal, strengthen Iran ties', 25 June, http://news.nationalpost.com/2012/06/25/egypts-new-islamist-leader-mohammed-morsi-to-reconsider-israel-peace-deal-strengthen-iran-ties/
New York Times (2011) 'A selection of the cache from diplomatic cables', June 19,
http://www.nytimes.com/interactive/2010/11/28/world/20101128-cables-viewer.html#report/iran-09TELAVIV1177
New York Times (2011) 'Afghans Avenge Florida Koran Burning, Killing 12', April 1,
http://www.nytimes.com/2011/04/02/world/asia/02afghanistan.html?_r=2&hp
Niess R (1956) *Julien Benda*, Ann Arbor: University of Michigan Press
Noe N (ed.) (2007) *Voice of Hezbollah: Statements of Sayyed Hassan Nasrallah*, translated by Ellen Khouri, London and New York: Verso
Norton A (2009 [2007]) *Hezbollah: A Short History*, Woodstock: Princeton University Press
O'Ballance E (1979) *No Victor, No Vanquished: The Yom Kippur War*, London: Barrie and Jenkins
Oborne P (2009) *Dispatches: Inside Britain's Israel Lobby*, broadcast on *Channel 4*, 16 November
Pappe I (2006) *The Ethnic Cleansing of Palestine*, Oxford: One World Publications
Pargeter A (2010) *The Muslim Brotherhood: The Burden of Tradition,* London: Saqi Books
Parsi T (2007) *Treacherous Alliance: The Secret Dealings of Israel, Iran, and the US*, New Haven and London: Yale University Press
Patai R (1976 [1973]) *The Arab Mind,* New York: Charles Scribner's Sons
Pew Forum on Religion & Public Life (2010) 'U.S. Religious Landscape Survey', http://religions.pewforum.org/affiliations
Pew Forum on Religion and Public Life (2010b) 'Number of Muslims in Western Europe',
http://features.pewforum.org/muslim/number-of-muslims-in-western-europe.html
Philo G and Berry M (2011) *More Bad News from Israel*, London: Pluto Press

Bibliography

Pilger J (2010) *The War You Don't See,* Dartmouth Films

Populus (2011) 'Searchlight Fear and Hope survey', January, http://www.populus.co.uk/uploads/download_pdf-310111-Searchlight-Fear-and-Hope-survey.pdf

Porter G and Lobe J (2012) 'Obama delays U.S.-Israeli war exercise', *Counterpunch,* January 17, http://www.counterpunch.org/2012/01/17/obama-delays-u-s-israeli-war-exercise/

Powell M (2012) 'In shift, police say leader helped with anti-Islam film and now regrets it', *The New York Times,* 24 January, http://www.nytimes.com/2012/01/25/nyregion/police-commissioner-kelly-helped-with-anti-islam-film-and-regrets-it.html?_r=1

Rakha R (2012) 'The Gaza Spring', Interview by Youssef Rakha, *Al Ahram Weekly Online,* 17-23 May, http://weekly.ahram.org.eg/2012/1098/cu11.htm

Ramadan T (2003) 'Critique des (nouveaux) intellectuels communautaires' ['Critique of (new) communitarian intellectuals'], *Oumma.com,* 3 October, available at http://agircontrelaguerre.free.fr/article.php3?id_article=32

Rauf F (2011) 'Evolving from Muslims in America to American Muslims: a shared trajectory with the American Jewish community', in Aslan R and Hahn Tapper A (eds.), *Muslims and Jews in America: Commonalities, Contentions and Complexities,* pp. 57-70, New York: Palgrave McMillan

Reuters (2008) 'No consensus on who was behind Sept 11: global poll', September 10, http://www.reuters.com/article/2008/09/10/us-sept11-qaeda-poll-idUSN1035876620080910

Reynolds J (2012) 'Iran nuclear talks: Stand-off continues' *BBC News,* 24 May, http://www.bbc.co.uk/news/world-middle-east-18200759

Riedel B (2008) *The Search for Al Qaeda: Its Leadership, Ideology, and Future,* Washington: Brookings Institution Press

Rose J (2005) *The Question of Zion,* Princeton and Oxford: Princeton University Press

Roy O (2004 [2002]) *Globalised Islam,* London: Hurst

Roy O (2007) *The Politics of Chaos in the Middle East,* translated from French by Ros Schwartz, London: Hurst Publishers

RT [Russia Today] (2012) 'Israeli ad campaign unsettles US Jews', 1 February, http://rt.com/news/offensive-ad-american-jews-215/

Rucker L (2007) 'Moscow's surprise: the Soviet-Israeli alliance of 1947-1949', Woodrow Wilson International Center for Scholars, Cold War International History Project, Working Paper no. 46, http://www.wilsoncenter.org/sites/default/files/CWIHP_WP_461.pdf

Russell Tribunal on Palestine [RTOP] (2011) 'Are Israeli practices against the Palestinian people in breach of the prohibition on apartheid under international law?', November, http://www.russelltribunalonpalestine.com/en/sessions/south-africa/south-africa-session-%e2%80%94-full-findings/cape-town-session-summary-of-findings

Rutkoff (2010) 'Near Ground Zero, a mosque moves in and meets the neighbors', *The Wall Street journal*, May 5, http://blogs.wsj.com/metropolis/2010/05/05/near-ground-zero-a-mosque-moves-in-and-meets-the-neighbors/

Safi O (2011) 'Who put hate in my Sunday paper? Uncovering the Israeli-Republican-Evangelical networks behind the "Obsession" DVD', in Aslan R and Hahn Tapper A (eds.), *Muslims and Jews in America: Commonalities, Contentions and Complexities*, pp. 21-32, New York: Palgrave McMillan

Safran W (2004) 'Ethnoreligious politics in France: Jews and Muslims', *West European Politics,* vol. 27, no. 3, pp. 423-451

Said E (2001) 'A people in need of leadership', *New Left Review,* vol. 11, pp. 27-33

Said E and Hitchens C (2001 [1988]) *Blaming the Victims: Spurious Scholarship and the Palestinian Question*, London: Verso

Salaita S (2006) *Anti-Arab Racism in the USA*, London: Pluto Press

Sand S (2010 [2009]) *The Invention of the Jewish People*, London: Verso

Sanger D (2012) 'Obama order sped up wave of cyberattacks against Iran', *New York Times,* 1 June, http://www.nytimes.com/2012/06/01/world/middleeast/obama-ordered-wave-of-cyberattacks-against-iran.html?_r=1&pagewanted=all

Scheuer M ["Anonymous"] (2004) *Imperial Hubris: Why the West is Losing the War on Terror,* Dulles: Potomac Books

Scott-Smith G (2010) 'Wilders and the US Israel lobby', *DutchNews.nl,* 16 June, http://www.dutchnews.nl/columns/2010/06/wilders_and_the_us_israel_lobb.php

Seymour R (2008) *The Liberal Defence of Murder,* London and New York: Verso

Shenker J (2012) 'Mohamed ElBaradei warns Egypt it is letting a "new emperor" take over', *The Guardian,* 15 June, http://www.guardian.co.uk/world/2012/jun/15/egypt-mohamed-elbaradei-warning?INTCMP=SRCH

Sherwood H (2011) 'Academic claims Israeli school textbooks

Bibliography

contain bias', *The Guardian,* 7 August, http://www.guardian.co.uk/world/2011/aug/07/israeli-school-racism-claim

Sherwood H (2011) 'Israeli protests: 430,000 take to streets to demand social justice', *The Guardian,* 4 Seprember, http://www.guardian.co.uk/world/2011/sep/04/israel-protests-social-justice

Sherwood, H (2011) 'Binyamin Netanyahu attacks Arab spring uprisings', *The Guardian,* 24 November, http://www.guardian.co.uk/world/2011/nov/24/israel-netanyahu-attacks-arab-spring?INTCMP=SRCH

Sherwood H (2012) 'Israeli government aides attempt to draw sting of former spy chief's attack', *The Guardian,* 29 April, http://www.guardian.co.uk/world/2012/apr/29/israel-yuval-diskin-iran-reaction

Sherwood H (2012) 'Israeli minister inflames racial tensions with attack on "infiltrators"', *The Guardian,* 31 May

Sherwood H (2012) 'Israel losing international support, says British ambassador', *The Guardian,* 3 August, http://www.guardian.co.uk/world/2012/aug/03/israel-losing-international-support-british-ambassador

Shipler D (1987) *Arab and Jew: Wounded Spirits in a Promised Land,* London: Bloomsbury

Shlaim A (2000) *The Iron Wall: Israel and the Arab World,* London: Penguin Books

Sifaoui M (2008) 'I consider Islamism to be fascism', *The Middle East Quarterly,* Spring, pp. 13-17

Simpson J (2002) 'Simpson on Sunday: Holland's anti-Islam dandy is lost for words', *The Telegraph,* 5 May, http://www.telegraph.co.uk/news/worldnews/europe/netherlands/1393260/Simpson-on-Sunday-Hollands-anti-Islam-dandy-is-lost-for-words.html

Sizer S (2004) *Christian Zionism: Roadmap to Armageddon?,* Leicester: Inter-Varsity Press

Smeekes A, Verkuyten M, & Poppe E (2011) 'Mobilising opposition towards Muslim immigrants: National identification and the representation of national history', *British Journal of Social Psychology,* vol. 50, no. 2, 265-280

Smith B (2010) '76 US senators sign on to US letter' *Politico,* 13 April, http://www.politico.com/blogs/bensmith/0410/76_Senators_sign_on_to_Israel_letter.html

Smith C (2006) 'Jews in France feel sting as anti-Semitism surges among children of immigrants', *The New York Times,* 26 March, http://www.nytimes.com/2006/03/26/international/26antisemitism.html?_r=3&pagewanted=1

Sniderman P and Hagendoorn L (2007) *When Ways of Life Collide: Multiculturalism and its Discontents in the Netherlands,* Princeton and Oxford: Princeton University Press

Sobelman D (2004[2003]) *New Rules of the Game,* Tel Aviv: Jaffee Center for Strategic Studies

Stewart C (2011) 'Gaza's male hairdressers cut under Hamas ban', *The Independent,* 7 July, http://www.independent.co.uk/news/world/middle-east/gazas-male-hairdressers-cut-under-hamas-ban-2308120.html

Sylt C (2012) 'Rupert Murdoch's big backer sounds News Corp warning', *The Guardian,* 8 May, http://www.guardian.co.uk/media/2012/may/08/murdoch-big-backer-news-corp

Tadros M (2012) *The Muslim Brotherhood in Contemporary Egypt: Democracy Redefined or Confined?* Abingdon and New York: Routledge

Taraki L (1989) 'The Islamic Resistance Movement in the Palestinian Uprising', *Middle East Report,* no. 156 (Jan-Feb) pp. 30-32

The Economist (2004) 'The provoker: Tariq Ramadan both inspires and infuriates', 4 March, http://www.economist.com/node/2480873

The Economist (2010) 'Mosque building and its discontents', August 19, http://www.economist.com/blogs/democracyinamerica/2010/08/islamic_cultural_centre_sorta_near_ground_zero

Thomas G (2010) 'Radical Islamists try to exploit Islamophobia', *Voice of America,* August 26, http://www.voanews.com/english/news/Radical-Islamists-Try-to-Exploit-Islamophobia-101592048.html

Thomas G and Dillon D (2002) *Robert Maxwell: Israel's Superspy,* New York: Carroll and Graf

Topousis T, 'Panel approves "WTC" mosque', *New York Post,* May 6, http://www.nypost.com/p/news/local/manhattan/panel_approves_wtc_mosque_U46MkTSVJH3ZxqmNuuKmML

Tunisialive.net (2011) 'Final result of Tunisian election announced', 14 November, http://www.tunisia-live.net/2011/11/14/tunisian-election-final-results-tables/

UMD Newsdesk (2012) 'UMD Poll: Israelis Wary of Striking Iran

Bibliography

Nuclear Facilities', 29 February, http://newsdesk.umd.edu/global/release.cfm?ArticleID=2631

UOIF [L'Union des Organisations Islamiques de France] (2012) 'Controverse sur l'affaire Qaradawi', http://www.uoif-online.com/v3/spip.php?article1255

Urquhart C (2007) 'Israel planned for Lebanon war months in advance', *The Guardian*, March 9.

Van Creveld M (2004) 'Sharon on the warpath : Is Israel planning to attack Iran?', *New York Times,* 21 August, http://www.nytimes.com/2004/08/21/opinion/21iht-edcreveld_ed3_.html

Van der Valk J (2011) 'Europe's most dangerous man?', documentary shown on BBC 2

Verkuyten M (2006) *The Social Psychology of Ethnic Identity,* Hove and New York: Psychology Press.

Voas D and Ling R (2010) 'Religion in Britain and the United States', in *British Social Attitudes, 26th Report*, London: National Centre for Social Research, pp. 65-85.

Wan W (2011) 'N.Y. Muslims fear congressman's hearings could inflame Islamophobia', *Washington Post,* January 24, http://www.washingtonpost.com/wp-dyn/content/article/2011/01/23/AR2011012304448.html

Waterfield B (2007) 'Ban Koran like Mein Kampf, says Dutch MP', *The Telegraph,* 9 August, http://www.telegraph.co.uk/news/worldnews/1559877/Ban-Koran-like-Mein-Kampf-says-Dutch-MP.html

Weiler-Polak D and Cohen G (2012) ''Israel's five-year war on African migrants', *Haaretz,* 5 June, http://www.haaretz.com/news/national/israel-s-five-year-war-on-african-migrants.premium-1.434356

Weinstock N (1989 [1969]) *Zionism: False Messiah*, London: Pluto Press

Wheatcroft G (2003) 'The right to voice strong views', *The Guardian*, 14 September, http://observer.guardian.co.uk/comment/story/0,6903,1041577,00.html

Wilders G (2007) 'Mr Wilders' contribution to the Parliamentary debate on Islamic activism', 6 September, http://www.geertwilders.nl/index.php/in-english-mainmenu-98/in-the-press-mainmenu-101/77-in-the-press/1214-mr-wilderss-contribution-to-the-parliamentary-debate-on-islamic-activism

Williams D (2012) 'Israel official "concerned" over future ties with Egypt', *Reuters Africa,* 3 April, http://af.reuters.com/article/commoditiesNews/idAFL6E8F340F20120403

Williams D (2012) 'Israel's former Shin Bet chief warns against "messianic" war on Iran', *Al Arabiya News,* 28 April, http://english.alarabiya.net/articles/2012/04/28/210830.html

World Jewish Population (2010), Mandell L. Berman Institute–North American Jewish Data Bank, http://www.jewishdatabank.org/Reports/World_Jewish_Population_2010.pdf

Wright L (2007) *The Looming Tower: Al Qaeda's Road to 9/11,* London: Allen Lane

YNetNews.Com (2011) 'Barak: I'd want nukes if I were Iranian', 17 November, http://www.ynetnews.com/articles/0,7340,L-4149441,00.html

Ynetnews.com (2012) 'Carter: Egypt's Brotherhood would keep Israel treaty', 26 May, http://www.ynetnews.com/articles/0,7340,L-4234466,00.html

Ynetnews.com [from AP] (2009) '6 injured in violent Gaza protests in Oslo', 9 January, http://www.ynetnews.com/articles/0,7340,L-3653467,00.html

Yoffie E (2011) 'Inaugural address at the Forty-fourth Annual Convention of the Islamic Society of North America', in Aslan R and Hahn Tapper A (eds.), *Muslims and Jews in America: Commonalities, Contentions and Complexities,* pp. 121-126, New York: Palgrave McMillan

Zakaria F (2010) 'The real Ground Zero', *Newsweek,*, vol. 156, issue 7, p. 18, 16 August

Zappi S (2003), '2002 : le racisme progresse en France, les actes antisémites se multiplient' [Racism is progressing in France, anti-Semitic acts are increasing'], *Le Monde,* 28 March, http://www.lemonde.fr/societe/article/2003/03/28/2002-le-racisme-progresse-en-france-les-actes-antisemites-se-multiplient_314637_3224.html

Zionist Organization of America (2010) Press Release, August 10, 'Don't Increase Pain To Families Of 9/11 Victims Of Islamist Terror By Building Mosque Led By Extremist, Anti-U.S., Pro-Hamas Imam', http://www.zoa.org/sitedocuments/pressrelease_view.asp?pressreleaseID=1919

Index

Note: *n* following a page number denotes a footnote

9/11 121–6, 133, 143
see also Ground Zero mosque

Abbas, Mahmood 36, 47, 58
Abdullah, Daud 165
Abu-Amr, Z. 46–7
Afghanistan
    and Bin Laden 94–5
    and Koran burning 140
    Soviet invasion (1979) 26
    US/UK invasion (2001) 28, 126
Ahmad, Eqbal 35
Ahmadinejad, Mahmoud 73, 75
Ahmed, Akbar 131–2
al *see* second syllable of name
Alibhai-Brown, Yasmin 162
Alpher, Yossi 71
Amano, Yukiya 78
anti-Semitism
    definition 159–60
    Dreyfus affair 39, 182*n*
    France 180–81
    and Jewish homeland 40–41
    Russia and Eastern Europe 39
    and students union 157
    Western Europe 15–16
    and Zionism 158–9, 195–6
Antonius, George 62, 104
Arab Spring 99, 104–7, 114, 192, 196–7, 204
Arafat, Yasser 35, 53
Arendt, Hannah 62
Aslan, Reza, *Muslims and Jews in America* 117
Al Aswany, Alaa 106, 194
Azzam, Abdulah 94

Badie, Mohamed 113
Balfour, Arthur 40–41
Balfour Declaration 35
al Banna, Hassan 24, 27, 100, 181
Barak, Ehud 57–8, 79, 102, 110
Bartlett, Jamie, Demos EDL study 167–8, 169
BBC 38, 42–3
Ben-Gurion, David 17, 18, 19, 63, 189
Berry, Mike 42
Bin Laden, Osama 26, 66, 94–7
Bishara, Marwan 105, 112
Black, Crispin 154
Bloomberg, Michael 131
Borger, Julian 76
Breivik, Anders Behring 187–8
Burlingame, Debra 130
Buruma, Ian, *Murder in Amsterdam* 173

Camp David agreement 67, 92, 102, 109, 110
Carter, Jimmy 110
Chechnya 36
Chehab, Zaki 52
Christian Zionism 40–41, 145–9
Churchill, Winston 40
Clash of Civilizations, The (Huntington) 7–8, 125
colonialism 17–18, 24–5, 189
Curtis, Mark, *Secret Affairs* 25, 28–9

Dagan, Meir 79
Dehghan, Saeed 80
Dempsey, Martin 77
Desmond, Richard 163
Deutscher, Isaac 60–62
Diskin, Yuval 79
Dismore, Andrew 157
Disraeli, Benjamin 40
Dreyfus affair 39, 182*n*
Dreyfuss, Robert, *The Devil's Game* 25

Egypt
    Arab Spring 104, 196–7
    Camp David Agreement 67, 92, 102, 109, 110
    elections (2011/12) 104–5
    and Gaza 57–8, 111
    and Iran 113
    and Israel post-2011 107–9,

Index

113
Israeli attacks 111
presidential elections 112
Salafists 105, 108–9
Six Day War (1967) 27, 44, 101–2
Yom Kippur War (1973) 26, 81, 102
see also Muslim Brotherhood
Eilburg, Amy 117
Ellison, Keith 123
English Defence League (EDL) 166–71
Erdogyan, Recep Tayyip 133
European Union
   and Israel 38
   Monitoring Centre on Racism and Xenophobia (EUMC) 159–60

Falwell, Jerry 147
Fatah 35, 57, 58
Finkielkraut, Alain 182, 183
Fisher, Kevin 138
Fisk, Robert 18–19, 61n
Fitzsimons, Lorna 56n, 157
Fortuyn, Pim 172–3
Fox, Liam 155
France 179–87
   anti-Semitic attacks 180–81
   Dreyfus affair 39, 182n
   and Iraq War (2003) 179, 184
   Islamism 180
   Jewish/Muslim population figures 179
   Ramadan's comunitarian article 181–6
   Toulouse shootings 186–7

El Gamal, Sharif 130, 138
Gantz, Benny 79
Gaza
   and Egypt 57–8, 111
   Gaza Youth Breaks Out movement 204–6
   gender apartheid 206n
   and Israel 107, 164–5
   Operation Cast Lead (2008) 55–6, 58
   Turkish flotilla killings 42
Geller, Pamela
   anti-Islam adverts 139–40
   and Ground Zero 128–30, 132–4, 137, 174
Al-Ghannouchi, Rashid 109
Ghazlan, Mahmoud 108
Ghozlan, Mahmud 99
Gilad, Amos 110
Gould, Stephen 155
Ground Zero mosque 126–41
   early support for 127–8
   Geller campaign against 128–30, 132–4, 137, 174
   opening 138
   opposition to other mosques 137–8
   and public opinion 134–5
   Sufi developers 135–6
   Zionist opposition 130, 136–7

Hagee, John 146–7
Hahn Tapper, Aaron, *Muslims and Jews in America* 117, 118
Hamas
   attacks on Israel 54–5, 58–9
   Charter 47–50
   conspiracy theories 48–9
   covert support from Israel 53–4
   election victory (2006) 55, 57
   and Gaza Youth Breaks Out movement 204–6
   and Iran 73
   origins 45
   and Oslo Accords 56–7
   Palestinian problem and religion 48
   and the PLO 49
   viewed as terrorist group 56, 59
   welfare work 46, 192
Hammami, Rema 61
Harik, Judith Palmer 84–5
Harkabi, Yehoshafat, *Israel's*

Fateful Hour 195–6
Herzl, Theodore 15–16, 17–18, 20
Hezbollah 81–90
　and Israel 83–5
　objectives 82–3, 85–6, 87
　rearmament 88
　support for Palestinians 84
US hostages 71
Higgins, Andrew 51
Hirsi-Ali, Ayaan 173
Hizb ut-Tahrir 29, 159
Holder, Eric 75, 142–3
Hooper, Ibrahim 132
Horowitz, David 176
Hroub, Khaled 49–50
Huntington, Samuel 135
　The Clash of Civilizations 7–8, 125
Husain, Ed, *The Islamist* 159

India
　Deobandi Movement 27
　and Kashmir 36
Iran
　and Egypt 113
　foreign relations 65
　and Hamas 73
　Holocaust denial 73
Iran-Iraq war (1980) 66–7, 68–71
Iranian Revolution (1979) 26, 45
　and Iraq 66
　and Israel 65–81
Israeli strike, possible consequences 76–9, 198
　Koran burning and Christian cleric 141
　nuclear programme 73–9
　and Palestinians 26, 65, 67–8, 71–2
　Shia objectives 27–8
　and US 69, 70–71, 72, 73, 80
Iran and Saudi Arabia 91–2
Iran-Iraq war (1980) 66–7, 68–71
Iraq
　First Gulf War (1991) 28
　and Iran 66
　Iran-Iraq war (1980) 66–7, 68–71

Iraq War (2003) 28, 126, 179, 182, 184
　nuclear reactor destruction 70
　weapons of mass destruction 74, 78
Islam
　and 9/11 terrorists 133
　Ground Zero mosque controversy 126–41
　US public opinion 134–5
　UK public opinion 170
　Dutch public opinion 175
Islamic Human Rights Council 29
Islamic Jihad 45, 72*n*
Islamism 23–30
　and anti-Semitism 159
　Arab concerns 192–5
　and Arab Spring 192
　ascendancy 93
　and colonialism 24–5
　Egyptian Salafists 105, 109, 193–4
　France 180
　Netherlands 172–6
　Norway killings 187–8
　objective 23, 207
　and Palestine 36–7
　political activism 26
　Sharia law 185, 193–4
　successful ideology 191–2
　Toulouse shootings 186–7
　UK student activities 156–7
　US 117–21
　and the war on terror 7, 29, 34–5, 123, 126, 154
　welfare work 46, 87, 100, 103, 192, 195
　and the West 25, 36–7
　and Zionism 26, 27, 123–6, 139, 196–8
　see also Muslims
Islamist groups 27
　see also Muslim Brotherhood
Israel
　African migrants 201–2
　apartheid practices 199–202
　and Arab Spring 106–7

Index

Biblical claim to land 17, 145–6, 148
see also Christian Zionism
Camp David agreement 67, 92, 102, 109, 110
creation of 44, 145–6
dual nationalities 8, 189–90
EDL support 166–7
and Egypt 107–9, 111
emigration from 190
and EU 38
first Arab-Israeli War (1948) 18, 62
and Gaza 107, 164–5
Hamas, covert support for 53–4
Hamas attacks on 54–5, 58–9
and Hezbollah 81–90
and indigenous population 59–64
and Iran 65–81, 67, 79–80
Iran-Iraq war (1980) 69–71
Iranian strike, possible consequences 76–9, 198
Iraq's Osirak reactor destruction (1981) 70
and Islamic Jihad 45
Jerusalem 43–4, 148
Lebanese invasions 82, 96n
Lebanese occupation 81–2, 84, 96n
Lebanon War (2006) 10, 81, 87–9, 104
media pro-Israeli bias 42–3, 163
and Muslim Brotherhood 108, 109–110
need for democratic reforms 202–3
negative views of 38, 151, 171
and Netherlands 173, 176–9
nuclear weapons 75
Operation Cast Lead (2008) 55–6, 58
Orthodox Jews 197
Palestinian Arabs 21, 200
Palestinian intifada (1987) 46, 94
and Palestinian Islamists 50–54
right to return 21–2, 189
Six Day War (1967) 27, 44, 101–2
Turkish flotilla killings 42
and UK 155
and US 37–8, 120–21, 191, 203
and US limited post-war migration 190–91
viewed as European 151
Yom Kippur War (1973) 26, 81
Izz ad-Din al-Qassam 44

Jasser, Zuhdi 131
Jerusalem 43–4, 48, 148
Jews
and Arabs 33
dual identity 8–10
France 179
geographical origins 22
Holocaust 190
Holocaust Memorial Day 158
Iran's Holocaust denial 73
Netherlands 178
Orthodox Jews 197
UK organisations 161–3
Union of Jewish Students 156
US 37, 121
in the West 39, 150–51
see also anti-Semitism
Jones, Pastor Terry 140–41
Jordan, Muslim Brotherhood 103

Karmi, Ghada 54*n*
Karoubi, Hassan 70
Karzai, Hamid 140
Kashmir 36
Kassir, Samir 193
Kenya 16, 97
Kepel, Gilles 98
Khalidi, Rashid 207
Khan, Daisy 128, 135
Khomeini, Ayatollah Ruhollah

26, 27, 65, 66, 70
King, Peter 141–5
Klein, Jeff 136–7
Klug, Brian 161
Kohlmann, Evan 132

Lebanon
  Al Qaeda in 99
  Israeli occupation 81–2, 84, 96n
  Israeli war on (2006) 10, 81, 87–9, 104
  suicide bombings 82
  see also Hezbollah
Lerman, Anthony 159–60
Levanon, Yitzhak 108
Lévy, Bernard-Henri 182, 183
Levy, Gideon 89
Libya 193
Lieberman, Avigdor 108
Litani, Yehuda 53
Littler, Mark, Demos EDL study 167–8, 169
Lloyd George, David 40

McDonagh, Denis 142
McGovern, Ray 76
Mandel, Neville 33
Maududi, Maulana Abdul Ala 27
Maxwell, Robert 163
Mayer, Thomas 100
  media
    and Islamists 156
    pro-Israeli bias 42–3, 163
Meir, Golda 81
Menashe, Ari-Ben 70
Merah, Mohammed 186–7
Meshal, Khaled 50
Mirdamadi, Mohsen 72
Moore, Roberta 167n, 171
Morocco, elections (2011) 106
Morsi, Mohamed 112–14
Mubarak, Hosni 57, 58, 92, 105
Al Muhajiroun 34–5, 157, 169
Mujama Al-Islamiya 51, 72n
  multiculturalism 11
  multifaithism 165–6
Murdoch, Rupert 163

Murray, Elizabeth 76
Muslim Brotherhood 100–104
  and Al Qaeda 99–100
  Arab concerns 193–5
  and Camp David agreement 110
  early years 100–101
  election successes 104–5, 106, 192–4
  foundation 24
  and Israel 108, 109–110
  Jordanian branch 103
  Mubarak era 102–3
  Nasser era 101
  objectives 27–8
  Palestine branch 45
  Sadat era 102
  welfare work 100, 103, 195
  and the West 26
  see also Hamas
Muslim Council of Britain (MCB) 29, 158, 164–5
Muslim Public Affairs Committee UK (MPACUK) 29, 157, 166
Muslims
  Arabist tendency 41
  dual identity 10
  Netherlands 178
  Shia 65–6
  in UK 170–71
  in US 121, 123, 141–5
  US conflation with Islamists 138–9
  in US military 144–5
  US radicalisation hearings 141–5
  in the West 28–9, 39–40, 150–51

al Nashashibi, Raghib Bey 34
Nasrallah, Hassan 84, 86
Nasser, Gamal Abdel 44, 101
Netanyahu, Benjamin 37–8n, 79, 123–4, 201
Netherlands 172–9
  anti-Islamism 172–6
  elections 172, 174, 179n
  and Israel 173, 176–9

Index

Jewish/Muslim population
    numbers 178
    public opinion 175, 178
    Second World War 178
    9/11 121–6, 133, 143
    see also Ground Zero mosque
Norway 187–8

Obama, Barack 75, 77
Obsession: Radical Islam's War against the West (DVD 118–19
oil prices 26, 92
Oborne, Peter 163
Olmert, Ehud 202–3
Oren, Michael 88

Pakistan
    Jamaat e Islami 27
    and Kashmir 36
    Sufism 136
Palestinians
    and Al Qaeda 93, 95–9
    and Arab Spring 204
    and Bin Laden 26
    Christian Palestinians 35, 120
    covert support from Israel 50–54
    Egypt on its refugees 112–13
    Gaza Youth Breaks Out movement 204–6
    Hezbollah support 84
    internecine rivalry 43
    intifada (1987) 46, 94
    and Iran 26, 65, 67–8, 71–2
    Islamic Jihad 45
    in Israel 21, 200
    Israel's apartheid practices 199–202
    and Muslim Brotherhood 107, 109
    and Oslo Accords 35–6, 56–7
    and Tunisia 109
    UK campaigns 164
    and Zionism 33–4, 60–64
    and Zionist narrative 59–64
    see also Hamas; PLO
Palmor, Yigal 108

Panetta, Leon 77
Parsi, Trita, *Treacherous Alliance* 67, 69–72, 73
Patai, Raphael 19
Philo, Greg 42
Pilger, John 42
Pipes, Daniel 176
PLO 35, 35–6, 49, 81–2, 192, 206
    public opinion
    on Israel 38, 151, 171
    Netherlands 175, 178
    UK 163–4, 170–71
    US 134–5, 144

Al Qaeda 93–100
    9/11 121–6
    franchises 98
    influences 27
    and Israel-Palestine 93–4, 95–9
    and jihad 29, 66, 95–8, 98–9
    and Lebanon 99
    and Muslim Brotherhood 99–100
    and US 114–17
al Qaradawi, Youssef 187
al-Qurashi, Abu-Ubayd 99
Qutub, Sayyid 27, 101

Rabin, Yitzhak 53, 71
Rahman, Omar Abdur 95
Ramadan, Tariq 181–6
Rauf, Feisal Abdul 127, 135
Reagan, Ronald 120
Red Crescent Society 51
Riedel, Brue 94
Robertson, Pat 147–8
Rose, Jacqueline 20
Rushdie, Salman, *Satanic Verses* 153

Sadat, Anwar 92, 97, 102
Safi, Omid 118–19
Said, Edward 35
al Said, Hafiz Bey 34
Salafists, Egypt 105, 109, 193–4
Sarkozy, Nicolas 185

Saudi Arabia 26, 75–6, 91–2, 91*n*, 96*n*
Scheuer, Michael 93–4, 98–9
Shaftesbury, Lord 40
Sharia law 185, 193–4
Sharon, Ariel 70, 125
Shifren, Nachum 170
Shipler, David 21, 51
Shlaim, Avi 54
Shore, Raphael 119
Shultz, George 120
Sifaoui, Mohamed 193
Sizer, Stephen 148
Sneh, Ephraim 72
Sobelman, Daniel 85
Soffer, Arnon 59
Soviet Union 26, 39
Spain, Muslims in 39
Sufism 135–6
Syria, Yom Kippur War (1973) 81
Syrkin, Nahum 34, 189

Tadros, Mariz 105
Taguieff, Pierre-André 182, 183
Tantawi, Mohamed Hussein 114
Tanzania 97
Taraki, Lisa 52
terrorism
  and Hamas 56, 59
  9/11 121–6, 133, 143
  war on terror 7, 29, 34–5, 123, 126, 154
  WTC attack (1993) 95
  see also Ground Zero mosque
Third Jihad, The (DVD) 119
Tsafrir, Eliezer 71
Tunisia 104, 106, 109, 193

United Kingdom 152–72
  Al Muhajiroun 34–5, 157, 169
  dual identity 155
  English Defence League (EDL) 166–71
  foreign policy 56n
  Friends of Israel 162–3
  Hizb ut-Tahrir 29, 159
  Holocaust Memorial Day 158
  Islamist groups 29, 152–3
  and Israel 155
  Jewish organisations 161–3
  jihadist groups 152
  Londonistan 28–9, 153–4
  media 156, 163
  Mosques and Imams Advisory Board 165
  multiculturalism 153
  multifaithism 165–6
  Muslim Council of Britain (MCB) 29, 158, 164–5
  Muslim Public Affairs Committee UK (MPACUK) 29, 157, 166
  public opinion 163–4, 170–71
  student Islamists 156–7
United Nations, and Israel's Palestinian citizens 200
United States
  and Al Qaeda 95–7
  anti-Islam adverts 139–40
  Christian fundamentalism 146
  Christian Zionism 145–9
  English Defence League (EDL) links 169–70
  ethnic identities 9
  hearings on Muslim radicalisation 141–5
  and Iran 69–70, 72–7, 80, 84
  Iraq (Gulf) War (1991) 28
  Iraq War (2003) 28, 126, 179, 182, 184
  and Islam 134–5
  Islamic Society of Boston 136
  Islamization concerns 137
  Israel lobby 37–8, 120–21, 191, 203
  Israeli strike on Iran, possible consequences 76–9, 198
  Jewish migration limited post-war 190–91
  Jewish population 37, 121
  Jewish/Muslim relations

Index

117–21
Koran burning 140–41
mosque applications,
   opposition 137–8
mosques 127, 129
Muslim population 121, 123
Muslims in the military 144–5
9/11 121–6, 133, 143
public opinion 134–5, 144
Saudi ambassador
   assassination plot 75–6
Sufi Muslims 135–6
Tea Party 169, 170
WTC attack (1993) 95
Yom Kippur War (1973) 26
Zionism 117–21, 128, 130, 133, 136–7, 176
see also Ground Zero mosque
Unsworth, Fran 42

Verwoerd, Hendrik 201

war on terror 7, 29, 34–5, 123, 126, 154
Werrity, Adam 155
Wilders, Geert 173–9
Wolfowitz, Paul 182
Woolas, Phil 157

Yaxlwy-Lennon, Stephen 168–9
Yishai, Eli 202
Yoffie, Eric 117
Yom Kippur (October) War
   (1973) 26, 81, 102
Yousef, Ramzi 95

Zakaria, Fareed 131
Al-Zawahiri, Ayman 66, 96, 97–8, 124*n*
Zionism 15–23
   and anti-Semitism 158–9, 195–6
   and Arab incompetence 18–20
   Christian Zionism 40–41, 145–9
   colonial nature 17–18, 189
   effect on Palestinians 60–64
   and English Defence League
      (EDL) 171–2
   European heritage 29
   and Geert Wilders 176–7, 178–9
   and Islamism 26, 27, 123–6, 139, 196–8
   and non-Jews 40
   objective 20, 33–4
   origins of 15–17, 189
   as racism 157
   right of return 21–2, 189
   successful ideology 190–91
   US 117–21, 128, 130, 133, 136–7, 176
   see also anti-Semitism; Jews
Zippori, Mordechai 69

Dangerous Liaisons

www.ingramcontent.com/pod-product-compliance
Lightning Source LLC
Chambersburg PA
CBHW020836160426
43192CB00007B/672